Mathematical Modelling for Teachers

Resources, Pedagogy and Practice

Ang Keng Cheng

LONDON AND NEW YORK

First published 2019
by Routledge
2 Park Square, Milton Park, Abingdon, Oxon OX14 4RN

and by Routledge
711 Third Avenue, New York, NY 10017

Routledge is an imprint of the Taylor & Francis Group, an informa business

© 2019 Ang Keng Cheng

The right of Ang Keng Cheng to be identified as the authors for his chapters, has been asserted in accordance with sections 77 and 78 of the Copyright, Designs and Patents Act 1988.

All rights reserved. No part of this book may be reprinted or reproduced or utilised in any form or by any electronic, mechanical, or other means, now known or hereafter invented, including photocopying and recording, or in any information storage or retrieval system, without permission in writing from the publishers.

Trademark notice: Product or corporate names may be trademarks or registered trademarks, and are used only for identification and explanation without intent to infringe.

British Library Cataloguing in Publication Data
A catalogue record for this book is available from the British Library

Library of Congress Cataloging in Publication Data
A catalog record for this book has been requested

ISBN: 978-0-815-37088-8 (hbk)
ISBN: 978-0-815-37089-5 (pbk)
ISBN: 978-1-351-24797-9 (ebk)

Typeset in Galliard
by Out of House Publishing

Printed and bound by CPI Group (UK) Ltd, Croydon, CR0 4YY

Mathematical Modelling for Teachers

Mathematical Modelling for Teachers: Resources, Pedagogy and Practice provides everything that teachers and mathematics educators need to design and implement mathematical modelling activities in their classroom. Authored by an expert in Singapore, the global leader in mathematics education, it is written with an international readership in mind.

This book focuses on practical classroom ideas in mathematical modelling suitable to be used by mathematics teachers at the secondary level. As they are interacting with students all the time, teachers generally have good ideas for possible mathematical modelling tasks. However, many have difficulty translating those ideas into concrete modelling activities suitable for a mathematics classroom. In this book, a framework is introduced to assist teachers in designing, planning and implementing mathematical modelling activities, and its use is illustrated through the many examples included. Readers will have access to modelling activities suitable for students from lower secondary levels (Years 7 and 8) onwards, along with the underlying framework, guiding notes for teachers and suggested approaches to solve the problems. The activities are grouped according to the types of models constructed: empirical, deterministic and simulation models. Finally, the book gives the reader suggestions of different ways to assess mathematical modelling competencies in students.

Ang Keng Cheng is an Associate Professor of Mathematics and Mathematics Education, and the Associate Dean for Higher Degrees at the National Institute of Education, Nanyang Technological University, Singapore.

Contents

Preface vii

1 Introducing mathematical modelling 1
Introduction 1
What is mathematical modelling? 1
Approaches to mathematical modelling 2
Modelling skills and competencies 10
A useful modelling tool 12

2 Teaching mathematical modelling 24
Introduction 24
Mathematical modelling classrooms 24
Teacher readiness 26
Levels of learning experience 27
A framework for teaching mathematical modelling 29

3 Empirical modelling 39
Introduction 39
Playing detective 39
In deep water 43
Growing mould 47
Pass it on 51
To cross or not to cross? 55

4 Deterministic modelling 60
Introduction 60
Correct me if I'm wrong 60
Design and park 65
A draining experience 69
Cover up 73
Let's dart 77

5 Simulation modelling 83
Introduction 83
Break it up 83
A walk in the park 88
Pick a door 92
Drop the needle 97
Who do we hire? 102

6 Mathematical modelling projects 110
Introduction 110
A model for queues 110
The SARS epidemic 116
A checksum algorithm 123
Testing Torricelli 127

7 Assessing mathematical modelling 135
Introduction 135
Assessing the process 136
Assessing modelling competencies 138
Assessing modelling projects 145

8 Conclusion 151
Introduction 151
Resources on the Web 151
Advice for teachers 154
Final remarks 156

Appendix A: The Solver tool 157
Appendix B: Sample lesson plan and handouts 161
Index 169

Preface

I was first introduced to mathematical modelling as a student of applied mathematics in my undergraduate days. In particular, I undertook an Honours project on a mathematical study of blood flow through arteries, and that experience set me off in my journey in mathematical modelling. Since then, I have worked on other blood flow problems, studied the modelling of disease epidemics, supervised student projects on topics such as traffic flow, dengue outbreak, tumour growth and water absorption models, and ventured into the teaching of mathematical modelling.

Even though much of what I have experienced in this area was at the university level, either as a postgraduate research student, as an academic or a teacher educator, it remains my firm belief that mathematical modelling is not exclusively for the mathematically-gifted or only for students of higher mathematics. For the past decade, I have been involved in promoting the teaching and learning of mathematical modelling amongst secondary school students and their teachers. I am most fortunate to have been able to work with colleagues in my department at the university, practising teachers and graduate students, from whom I have learnt a lot in this area of work. Therefore, this book, in essence, is a collection of the experiences that I have gained from my interaction with teachers and students in the course of making attempts to place mathematical modelling in the mathematics classroom.

There are many ways in which mathematical modelling and the teaching of mathematical modelling may be introduced to a mathematics teacher. Typically, teachers attend workshops organised by universities, or their local curriculum authorities, and may engage in discussions with fellow teachers on the topic. However, for a teacher who is totally new to the field and who has never experienced mathematical modelling either as a student or a teacher, such one-off workshops may not be very illuminating. In fact, they can sometimes be both intimidating and confusing. This book, therefore, is an attempt to clarify some of the key ideas in mathematical modelling, and provide teachers with sufficient resources to get started.

Rather than introducing modelling task after modelling task and relating them to mathematical topics, I have chosen to introduce mathematical modelling based on the three common approaches, namely, empirical modelling, deterministic modelling and simulation modelling. Consequently, the material in this book is organised along these lines. An introductory first chapter gets the reader acquainted with the essentials of mathematical modelling, emphasising the process and explaining the three approaches with detailed examples. A useful tool often used in the teaching of mathematical modelling and throughout this book, namely the electronic spreadsheet *Excel* by Microsoft, is described at the end of Chapter 1. The chapter is supported by Appendix A, which further explains the use of *Excel*'s tool introduced in the last section.

Chapter 2 expounds on the pedagogical principles and teacher practice in mathematical modelling. This is also where the three levels of learning experience in a mathematical modelling classroom are proposed and explained in detail. For many students, engaging in mathematical modelling for the first time requires getting used to, as well as a more structured process of developing their confidence and competence. This forms the motivation for identifying and categorising modelling activities in terms of different levels of learning experiences based on student preparedness, the level of mathematical knowledge required and the overall demands of the task. A framework for teaching mathematical modelling is introduced and examples of how to use this framework are presented. Chapter 2 ends with remarks on the framework and a reference to Appendix B, which contains a sample lesson plan on mathematical modelling.

The next three chapters contain the modelling tasks and problems. In each chapter, five suggested modelling activities are described: these are classified as empirical modelling, deterministic modelling and simulation modelling tasks, with each category occupying one chapter. Most, if not all, of these tasks have been tried and tested, either in the school classroom, or by in-service teachers, or carried out by the author himself or his students. Naturally, in a book such as this, each task is presented with the teacher in mind, and in addition, each task is accompanied by the framework mentioned in Chapter 2, as a means of supporting the teacher in designing and planning a lesson based on the task. Chapters 3 to 5, therefore, form the main bulk of the resources that teachers may use in starting their own journey in the teaching of mathematical modelling.

In Chapter 6, four modelling activities which are slightly more demanding and which possibly require more sophisticated mathematics are presented. In view of the demands of these activities, they could qualify as projects for students or groups of students. Assessing mathematical modelling, including projects and reports, is a concern often raised by teachers, and this is discussed in some detail in Chapter 7. In this chapter, some suggested rubrics for assessing modelling tasks or projects are presented, along with a brief discussion on assessing modelling competencies from different perspectives and views. The book ends with Chapter 8, in which further sources of information on mathematical modelling are briefly mentioned and some pieces of advice to teachers are given.

It has to be said that some of the tasks may be well known and have been described in other books. Others are relatively new and perhaps refreshing to some teachers. Yet, I believe the inclusion of a framework for teaching mathematical modelling in the description of these tasks would make it interesting and useful for teachers seeking new ideas or teaching resources. Although I had wanted to include a much wider selection of tasks, I have to say that it is not possible given the level of thoroughness that would have been required to describe and deal with each of them. This is one limitation of the book for which I wish to apologise in advance.

In spite of the great care that has gone into preparing the manuscript for this book, there is still a good chance that some errors may have escaped detection. I would certainly appreciate it if these are brought to my attention so that they could be addressed in due course.

In the course of preparing the material and manuscript for this book, I have consulted books, journal articles, various websites, colleagues and, most important of all, practising teachers including my former students. In particular, I wish to thank my former PhD student, Dr Tan Liang Soon for his contributions of some of the tasks, and for sharing his insights into the pedagogical principles involved in teaching mathematical modelling. Dr Tan was also actively involved in the training of a few of the teachers who have conducted lessons

Preface ix

based on some of the tasks described in this book. These are valuable experiences that have gone into the refinement and redesign of some of the modelling activities presented here.

Finally, this book would not have been possible if not for the support provided by the research grant from the National Institute of Education, Singapore (Grant No. RS 1/16 AKC).

1 Introducing mathematical modelling

Introduction

As an activity in the mathematics classroom, mathematical modelling has grown in popularity in the past decades. There have been numerous reports by mathematics educators from all over the world on what has been done and what is possible or can be done to promote mathematical modelling among students, with varying degrees of success. Competitions and contests related to mathematical modelling, such as those organized by the Consortium for Mathematics and Its Applications (COMAP)[1] and the International Mathematical Modelling Challenge (IMMC)[2], have sprouted across different countries at different levels. The importance of mathematical modelling in the cultivation and development of twenty-first century skills among students has also been discussed by mathematics teachers and educators.

In this introductory chapter, the idea of mathematical modelling and the process of mathematical modelling is introduced and described in some detail. The main approaches of mathematical modelling will also be discussed, together with simple but useful examples to illustrate these approaches. The chapter concludes with a discussion on the skills and competencies required of a student who wishes to learn or embark on a mathematical modelling activity.

What is mathematical modelling?

Mathematical modelling is a process of representing or describing real-world problems in mathematical terms in an attempt to find solutions to the problems or to gain a better understanding of the problems. The result of this process is a mathematical model, which can sometimes be considered as a simplification or abstraction of a real-world problem or a system into a mathematical form.

In other words, mathematical modelling begins with a real-world problem whose real-world solution is what we wish to find. However, a direct route from the real-world problem to the real-world solution can sometimes be difficult, if not impossible. This could be because of the complexity of the problem or the need for some analysis of the situation. A first step in mathematical modelling is thus to formulate the problem into a mathematical problem. This is often the most difficult step, yet the most crucial, and involves having to identify the factors or variables in the problem and then formulating a mathematical problem by studying the relationships among these factors.

In the process of formulating the problem, one would normally see if certain assumptions need to be made or stated. Usually, assumptions are made in order to define the boundaries of the problem as well as to simplify the problem. For instance, while identifying the

2   Introducing mathematical modelling

factors that may influence a particular physical situation, it may be decided to first ignore certain variables (or keep them constant) so that a simple, first model can be constructed. Of course, these assumptions need to be reasonable and acceptable, so that the model is sufficiently simple but not simplistic. In a later phase of the modelling process, these assumptions are revisited and may be relaxed or revised. Making assumptions also helps clarify what the model aims to achieve, and is usually a step that precedes the actual construction of the model, which is the next step.

A mathematical model can take various forms; since it is a *mathematical* model, it is naturally a mathematical construct. A mathematical model could be an equation or a formula that relates the various factors involved in the real problem, with a well-defined dependent variable and one or several equally well-defined independent variables. It could also be in the form of a differential equation or an integral equation involving the problem variables. A model could also be a graph (with nodes and edges), an algorithm or set of rules to arrive at a conclusion, a decision tree, or a table with parameter or variable values to be filled. In some cases, a mathematical model could be a computer program or a set of computer codes. Whatever form it takes, a mathematical model is essentially a mathematical construct that assists in solving the mathematical problem formulated to represent a real-world problem.

Given the assumptions for the model, the mathematical problem can then be solved by some suitable method or technique to obtain a mathematical solution. Depending on the type of model and approach adopted in the modelling process, the solution to the model may take different forms.

The solution to the model is then interpreted, in the context of the situation, and translated into or explained as the solution in the real world. It is at this stage of model interpretation that one could assess the "product" and determine if the model is an appropriate, suitable or usable one. If the solution is deemed to be "good enough", which could mean different things to different people, then the model and its solution are accepted, the real-world solution is obtained and the process ends here.

However, if the model solution somehow is thought to be not suitable or not usable, then one may wish to work on the model and improve it, or perhaps develop another one or adopt a different approach. Often, if there is a way to validate or verify the model, it would be useful to do so. Validation could be in the form of comparing the results of the solution with known data, either collected or obtained from other sources, or examining certain variable or parameter values or behaviour in relation to the real situation. Validation could sometimes be a qualitative treatment of the model, performed by considering different scenarios of the real situation.

As a result of this validation process, there may be a need to revisit the assumptions and look for ways to improve or refine the model by modifying or changing the assumptions. If this is possible, then the model may be reconstructed with some improvement, re-solved and the solutions interpreted once more, and possibly validated again. This process of model refinement can go on until one is satisfied or when an acceptable model is obtained. This is also the part of the modelling process that repeats and reiterates, thus giving rise to the commonly used term, "modelling cycle". The stages involved in mathematical modelling can be schematically represented in the form of a cycle depicted in Figure 1.1.

Approaches to mathematical modelling

There are several different approaches to mathematical modelling. Each approach results in a different "type" of model, and possibly utilizes a different set of mathematical techniques in the solution process. Some of the more common classes or types of mathematical models

Introducing mathematical modelling 3

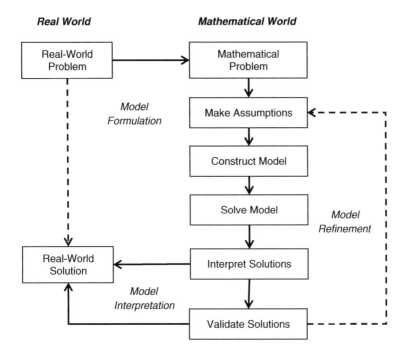

Figure 1.1 A schematic diagram showing the modelling process

include empirical models, simulation models and deterministic and stochastic models. These three approaches are described in this section in detail.

Empirical models

In empirical modelling, the main feature is the use of data. In this approach, some kind of data related to the problem should be available and are used in the construction of the model. The key idea is to construct a relationship, in the form of a formula or equation, which best fits the data.

As an example, consider the data in Table 1.1, which shows the total area of the leaves of a plant recorded at fortnightly intervals in a certain experiment carried out in a laboratory. Figure 1.2 shows a scatter plot of the experimental data.

In this case, one might be interested in finding the relationship between the total area of the leaves and time. That is, how the total area of leaves, which is an important variable in the study of physiology and growth of plants, changes with time. This variable is used in calculating the Leaf Area Index, or LAI, which is the ratio of total projected leaf area per unit ground area. The LAI represents the amount of leaf material in an ecosystem, and is widely used to characterise canopy light conditions. Knowing how the total area of leaves changes with time may help us understand the growth of the plant, or make predictions about its growth over time.

In empirical modelling, we look for a function that may best fit the data. In the present example, we may try a function of the form

$$f(t) = at^2 + bt + c,$$

4 Introducing mathematical modelling

Table 1.1 Total area of leaves recorded at intervals of two weeks

Time (weeks)	Area (nearest sq cm)
0	8
2	37
4	89
6	136
8	189
10	210
12	231
14	238
16	245
18	246

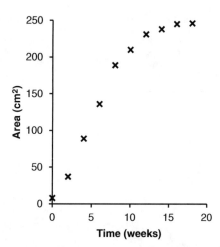

Figure 1.2 Plot of total area of leaves against time

where dependent variable, $f(t)$, represents the total area of leaves and the independent variable is time, represented by t. The parameters, a, b and c, are arbitrary and in this case, physically meaningless. They exist merely because of the form of the function that we have chosen. The functional form, in this case a quadratic function in t, is chosen based on the scatter plot shown in Figure 1.2. That is, by looking at how the points are plotted, we *guess* and *assume* that the relationship could be represented by a quadratic function.

The method of least squares may be used to find estimates for the unknown parameters, a, b and c. In this method, the sum of the squares of the difference between the values of $f(t)$ at each value of t and the data points constitutes the "error" for the function. By minimizing this error, we obtain the estimates of the parameters required. One way to do this is to use the Solver tool in the Microsoft spreadsheet, *Excel*. Details on how to use the Solver tool are found in Appendix A.

Using the Solver tool (as described in Appendix A) for the present example, we obtain $a = -0.8864$, $b = 30.0424$ and $c = 6.4363$. Thus, $f(t) = -0.8664t^2 + 30.0424 - 6.4363$ is a possible empirical model for this problem. The graph of $f(t)$ and the set of data points are plotted in Figure 1.3 (a).

The model obtained earlier was based on the assumption that the relationship between the two variables, the total area of leaves and time, follows a quadratic function. If we use this model, it would appear that a natural assumption is that after some time, the total area of leaves would decrease since the quadratic function $f(t)$ will decrease as t increases, for larger values of t. For very large values of t, $f(t)$ may even be negative, which is absurd! Therefore, this model may not be a suitable one for this particular physical situation.

Another possible way to fit the data points is by assuming that the relationship between the area of leaves and time is given by the function of the form,

$$g(t) = \frac{A}{B + Ce^{-kt}},$$

where $g(t)$ represents the total area of leaves (just like $f(t)$ in the earlier model), t represents time, and the other variables (A, B, C and k) are constant parameters in the model to be

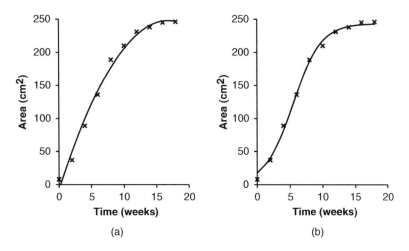

Figure 1.3 Graphs of data points and respective model equations: (a) Graph of data points and $f(t)$ (b) Graph of data points and $g(t)$

determined. The function, $g(t)$ is also known as the logistic growth function. In this case, we note that as t increases and tends towards a large number (that is, after a long time), $g(t)$ tends to a constant. In other words, in this model, the total area of leaves would increase and be limited to a value.

Again, using the same method as before, we can find the values of the parameters, A, B and C, as well as k that best fit the set of data points. In this case, the values are found to be

$$A = 2010.1906, B = 8.2599, C = 106.8787 \text{ and } k = 0.4689.$$

The graph of $g(t)$, together with the data points, is shown in Figure 1.3 (b).

Empirical modelling is a simple approach and can be used readily. However, it is very limited in its application. One major disadvantage is that one cannot be sure whether the model will continue to be valid if the data for the model fall outside the range of the data used in obtaining the parameter values. Therefore, such a model may not be very useful for making predictions.

In addition, the parameters that appear in the model equation (such as a, b and c in $f(t)$, or A, B, C and k in $g(t)$) do not have any specific physical meaning, at least in this present example. In other words, one cannot explain the occurrences of these parameters in the model in terms of the physical problem or their relationships to the independent and dependent variables in the model. They are merely numerical values that arise from the form of equation or formula that have been chosen and from the data set. A different choice of equation will result in a different set of parameters, and a different set of data will result in a different set of parameter values.

Simulation models

Apart from using data in empirical modelling, another modelling approach is simulation modelling. In many modelling situations, the problem that one wishes to investigate cannot be analyzed easily. At times, relevant data are not available or cannot be collected. In such cases, simulation models may be used to model the system.

6 Introducing mathematical modelling

Simulation models often involve the use of a computer program or some technological tool to generate a scenario based on a set of rules. These rules arise from an interpretation of how a certain process or a phenomenon is supposed to evolve or progress. Once the computer program has been written, it can be executed so that one can now examine the outcomes of the interactions of the variables or components in the model.

Typically, computer simulations are used to model a phenomenon or situation when it is either impossible or impractical to construct real physical experiments to model or study it. For instance, one may simulate a certain design for a telecommunication network to find the best design. It would be too expensive to build an actual system to test the design. Using a simulation, one could test how the network performs at different traffic loads, or whether a particular routing algorithm could increase performance levels, and so on.

Simulation models can be models of discrete events or continuous models. In discrete events, the assumption is that the system changes instantaneously in response to changes in certain discrete variables. On the other hand, in continuous simulation models, changes are continuously fed into the system over time and responses are continuously quantified.

As an illustration, consider a game called the "chaos game". In this "game", a triangle is first drawn and the vertices are labelled A, B and C. A starting point P_0 is placed somewhere inside this triangle. The starting point does not need to be inside the triangle; for simplicity, however, we place it inside.

Imagine that we now have a "three-sided dice" which, when rolled, will give only three possible outcomes ("1", "2" or "3") with equal probability. In reality, such a dice does not exist, but the point is that this "dice" will yield outcomes "1", "2" or "3" with equal chance, and we can make use of technology to simulate such a dice. Of course, we can also think of using a fair spinner with three equally probable outcomes.

In the chaos game, the rules for the course of action for each of the possible outcomes are as follows:

- If we roll a "1": find the midpoint between P_0 and vertex A;
- If we roll a "2": find the midpoint between P_0 and vertex B;
- If we roll a "3": find the midpoint between P_0 and vertex C.

Let this midpoint be P_1. The process is repeated for P_1 to get the next point, P_2, and so on. After a large number of repetitions of the same process, what happens?

Doing this by hand would be tedious, and time consuming. This is where a simulation becomes useful. Below are some results of a simulation of the chaos game set up using the electronic spreadsheet, Microsoft *Excel*.

The following results are obtained after about 8 simulated rolls of the dice.

x	y	dice
1.00000	1.00000	2
1.50000	0.50000	3
1.25000	1.25000	3
1.12500	1.62500	1
0.56250	0.81250	3
0.78125	1.40625	2
1.39063	0.70313	1
0.69531	0.35156	2
1.34766	0.17578	

Figure 1.4 After 8 rolls of dice

After about 1500 simulated rolls of the dice, a pattern is slowly forming.

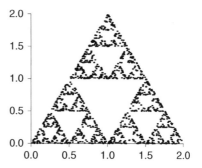

Figure 1.5 After 1500 rolls of dice

With around 3000 repetitions of the chaotic process simulated on the spreadsheet, a clear pattern emerges. This pattern, in fact, is known as the Sierpinski gasket.

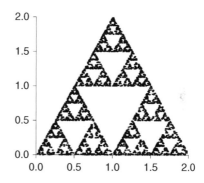

Figure 1.6 After 3000 rolls of dice

This simulation of the chaos game does not actually solve or address any "real-life problem". It is meant to describe and illustrate what a simulation is, and to demonstrate its usefulness. In this case, if we were to do the above by hand, it would take a long time before we can see any pattern forming, and may miss the opportunity to see the final outcome, the Sierpinski gasket.

Deterministic models

A deterministic model involves the use of an equation or a set of equations to describe, represent or model relationships between the various components or parts of a system or problem. The relationships are often known or at least determinable based on some knowledge of the dynamics of the problem.

One simple example of a deterministic model would be Newton's law of motion governing the motion of a particle. For instance, if a ball is tossed vertically upwards, given that certain variables are known, it is possible to determine (at least approximately) where the ball would be at a later time. Of course, some assumptions would have to be made in such models. In this case, it may be assumed that the ball behaves like a particle, that air resistance may be ignored, and so on.

Another example is in the modelling of population growth. For instance, one may wish to obtain an equation relating birth rates and death rates of individuals in a population. These rates may themselves be related to the population size at a given time. Very often,

8 *Introducing mathematical modelling*

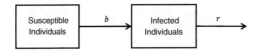

Figure 1.7 Simple model for spread of disease

such models are presented as compartmentalized sub-populations moving from one compartment to another.

Typically, in deterministic modelling, one hopes to investigate how variables in the model may change over time. As such, it is quite common that similar models would involve the use of differential equations. If one were to use discrete time steps, then it is often possible to construct models using *difference equations* instead of having to deal with differential equations.

As an example, consider a simple model for the spread of a disease in a closed community. The population may be thought of as consisting of two sub-populations; the susceptible individuals and the infected individuals. Figure 1.7 shows a schematic of this model.

In this model, the susceptible members become infected with the disease at a rate of b, and the infected members recover (or are removed) at a rate, r. Note that both parameters b and r are positive, and are assumed to be constant.

Suppose $S(t)$ and $I(t)$ represent the number of susceptible and infected members at any time, t respectively. The set of equations that can be used to model the disease spread in this case may be written as

$$\frac{dS}{dt} = -bSI$$

$$\frac{dI}{dt} = bSI - rI$$

This model is also called the "S-I model" for epidemics, for obvious reasons. The first equation describes the rate of change of the susceptible population (or sub-population), S, while the second represents the rate of change of the infected population (or sub-population), I. The S-I model assumes that the susceptible individuals will interact with the infected individuals and get infected, and so the number of susceptible individuals will decrease over time. On the other hand, the number of infected individuals will first increase, and then with recovery, may start to decrease in numbers.

The differential equations above may be approximated if one uses a discrete time step of Δt. This gives the following set of difference equations,

$$S_{n+1} = S_n + \Delta t \left(-b S_n I_n\right)$$

$$I_{n+1} = I_n + \Delta t \left(b S_n I_n - r I_n\right)$$

Consider the application of this model to the spread of influenza. In 1978, the *British Medical Journal* reported an outbreak of influenza at a boarding school in England.[3] In late January to early February of 1978, around 512 boys out of a total of 763 were infected

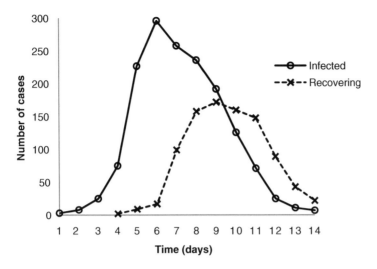

Figure 1.8 The daily total number of boys infected and recovering during the epidemic

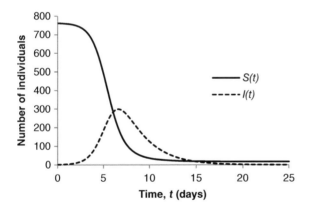

Figure 1.9 Graphical solutions of the model

during the epidemic. Figure 1.8 shows a graph of the number of cases confined to bed or convalescent between 22 January and 4 February.

The epidemic began with just one infected person. Over a period of about three weeks, approximately two-thirds of the population had been infected. The *transmission rate* of the epidemic was estimated to be around $b = 2.18 \times 10^{-3}$ per susceptible per day. The recovery rate was estimated at around 0.44 per day. Using the difference equations given above and by means of a spreadsheet, the graphs for the number of susceptible and infected individuals may be obtained. This is shown in Figure 1.9.

In deterministic modelling, as illustrated in the above example, the dynamics of the process is studied and then a model is built based on the relationships between the variables in the situation. Often, the equations are solved by some means, and then results are either compared and validated with available data or examined qualitatively.

Modelling skills and competencies

Mathematical modelling requires a number of mathematical skills, techniques and tools. While it is impossible to list all the skills which may be needed in mathematical modelling, it is possible to discuss and describe some of the more essential skills that can be directly applied in a modelling situation. Some of these are acquired after years of experience and with much practice, while others are derived from simple reasoning or developed through well-designed exercises.

The more common techniques and skills in mathematical modelling include the following:

- *Identifying factors and variables in a problem*
  In order to cast a real-life problem into a mathematical problem, one needs to be able to identify the factors that are relevant to the problem. Very often, at the initial stage, it is necessary to keep this list of factors short and simple so that the problem remains manageable. As a start, it is good to just list the more important ones, while keeping in mind those which may not be so crucial to the model at this stage.
  Some of these factors may be quantifiable and some may not. When a factor is quantifiable, it may be a mathematical variable that will appear in the model later. It is also useful to note that some of these factors may be constant numbers, while others may be constant parameters.
  Example: Cooling of coffee
  Consider the situation where we wish to find out or predict the time it takes for a hot cup of coffee to cool to a certain temperature. It would be quite natural to immediately think of two variables – the temperature of the coffee and time. But there could be other possible factors to consider, such as the temperature of the surroundings, the type of coffee, the material of the cup used, and whether there is any air movement or wind around the cup, and so on. Just using the two variables, temperature of coffee and time lapsed, may not be enough to construct a reasonable model, but using all the factors mentioned may be too complex.
- *Making assumptions to simplify problem*
  When developing a new model, one should try to keep the model as simple as possible for the start. This may often be achieved by making certain assumptions about the problem. The idea is to begin with something manageable and then slowly build the model as we go along.
  When writing down assumptions, one should also take care not to over-simplify the problem to an extent where the model becomes unreasonable. It is also important to be able to defend or justify the basic assumptions. Listing assumptions is important in mathematical modelling because one may later wish to refine the model by relaxing or re-examining some of these assumptions.
  The following are some possible considerations when making assumptions about the problem or model:
    (a) Excluding certain factors from the model
        Factors which are difficult or impossible to quantify could be omitted at the first instance. For example, in the cooling of coffee example mentioned above, while the type of coffee could have an effect on the cooling rate, it may be difficult to incorporate this directly into the model unless we consider the

Introducing mathematical modelling 11

thermodynamic property, such as the specific heat capacity of different types of coffee.

(b) Type of relationships between variables or factors

In constructing a mathematical model, it is sometimes necessary to look at how one variable or factor may change or vary with another. For instance, we may know that drug concentration in blood decreases with time, but it could decrease linearly, exponentially or perhaps proportionally to some other factor. It is sometimes necessary to make an assumption, which may or may not be based on some known dynamics of the system, in order to construct a reasonably suitable model.

(c) Which modelling approach to use

Depending on the modelling approach that one intends to use, there may be certain assumptions that need to be made in order to facilitate the use of that approach. For instance, suppose we wish to model the movement of a person who is dizzy (or drunk) and walking around in a park randomly. If the simulation model approach is used, we would need to make some assumptions about how or in which direction he would take his next step. We could assume that every possible direction of his next step is equally likely or probable. Alternatively, we could also assume that the next step depends on the previous step in some way. Sometimes, these assumptions are applicable in more than one approach, and sometimes they may not be.

- *Recognising relative impact of terms*

A reasonable model usually would involve a fair number of variables, factors and terms in an equation or a set of equations. Some of these terms may have a larger impact on the model solution than others. It is important to be able to recognise the relative impact or influence of these terms in the overall model. If the impact of a term is not significant compared to another, it may be better to drop that term to simplify the model.

Example: Best correction tape

These days, many students use correction tape as a means of erasing or correcting mistakes made when writing. Suppose we are to decide which brand of correction tape is the "best". When constructing a "decision model" to tackle this problem, one could think of the various factors contributing to the decision on the "best" correction tape. These include the quality of the product (in terms of doing its job of covering or whitening out written errors), the price, the availability, the ergonomics and design, and so on. However, it is not always true that all the factors are equally important, and therefore carries equal weight in the model. For instance, the quality of the product may be twice as important as, say, the price.

- *Knowing units and dimensions of quantities*

Since mathematical modelling deals with problems in the real world, one has to be aware of the units and dimensions of the variables that appear in the model. At times, data collected or obtained from published sources may come in a variety of units or dimensions. It is important to recognise that there may be a need to either "process" the data in order to fit the model, or modify the model to use the data.

Example: Influenza epidemic

In the example on the outbreak of influenza in a boarding school described earlier, the actual data available could be in the form as shown in Table 1.2.

12 *Introducing mathematical modelling*

Table 1.2 Number of students infected during an outbreak of influenza at a boarding school

Date	Infected
22 Jan	3
23 Jan	8
24 Jan	26
25 Jan	76
26 Jan	225
27 Jan	298
28 Jan	258
29 Jan	233
30 Jan	189
31 Jan	128
01 Feb	68
02 Feb	29
03 Feb	14
04 Feb	4

In this case, the data given consist of a list of dates in one column with a corresponding list of numbers in the other. We need to be able to understand what these means, and how to convert the data into something that can be used in a model, and whether there are units that we need to be aware of and to take into consideration.

To use this set of data, it may be necessary to convert the actual dates into "Time". That is, we could set 22 Jan as Day 1, 23 Jan as Day 2, and so on, and thus the left column as a unit of "days". The right column is simply the number of infected individuals and has no units. Hence, the per capita transmission rates or recovery rates will need to be in number per day per individual.

- *Knowing behaviour of relationships*
  In order to describe relationships between variables in mathematical terms, it is essential to know how certain relationships behave. That is, when one variable is varied, how does it affect or influence the behaviour of a related variable? Suppose one such independent variable is time, t, then it is quite useful to consider the following situations:

  - What happens at $t = 0$?
  - What happens when t becomes very large?
  - Are there values of t where the other variable becomes zero?
  - Are there any local maximum and minimum values?
  - Is there an oscillatory behaviour?

  Mathematically, it is convenient and usual to express these relationships in terms of functions and visualize them as graphs.

There has been quite a fair amount of discussion among mathematics educators on what mathematical modelling competencies actually mean or entail. Although not everyone agrees on the definition of the term, most agree that modelling competencies are not only important, they should be what we hope students will develop through modelling tasks. Some of these issues are discussed in Chapter 7. In this chapter, however, we focus on the skills that are useful or required in tackling mathematical modelling tasks.

A useful modelling tool

Besides mathematical skills, other tools that aid computation or problem solving in general are frequently employed in mathematical modelling. These range from simple electronic calculators and data loggers, to very sophisticated special purpose software packages, as well as technical computing systems.

An electronic spreadsheet, such as Microsoft *Excel*, can be a very useful tool in mathematical modelling. It is worth learning how to exploit a tool like *Excel* to perform some of the

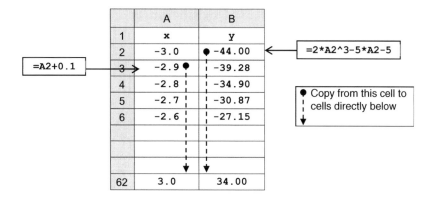

	A	B
1	x	y
2	-3.0	-44.00
3	-2.9	-39.28
4	-2.8	-34.90
5	-2.7	-30.87
6	-2.6	-27.15
62	3.0	34.00

Figure 1.10 Data for a scatter plot

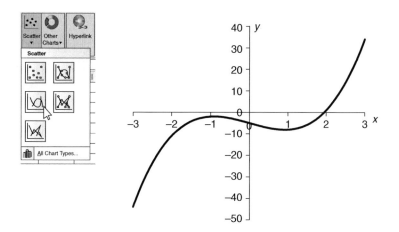

Figure 1.11 Choosing a desired type of scatter plot from the menu buttons to create a plot for the cubic curve, $y = 2x^3 - 5x - 5$

14 Introducing mathematical modelling

tasks involved in modelling. Three basic uses of *Excel* in mathematical modelling are briefly described here.

Plotting of graphs

One of the most useful features in a spreadsheet like *Excel* is its ability to generate **scatter plots**. This can be used to plot a graph of a user-defined function. A table of values can first be created in, say, columns A and B, and then a scatter plot can be inserted. As shown in Figure 1.10, a set of values is generated and then two cells are copied to fill the remaining cells below them.

A scatter plot can then be inserted from the menu, and the plot can be adjusted or modified to the desired display, as seen in Figure 1.11.

Managing data

A spreadsheet is an excellent tool for managing data. One common task in mathematical modelling involves finding functions that can approximately fit a set of data collected. There are sophisticated software tools to do this, but in a spreadsheet like *Excel*, a reasonably good approximating function can be obtained fairly quickly. For some standard forms of functions, the "Add Trendline" feature can be used.

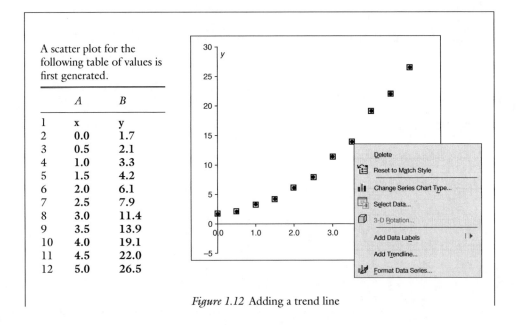

Figure 1.12 Adding a trend line

Using the "Add Trendline" function, and choosing a linear function, a best straight line for this data set is found and plotted.

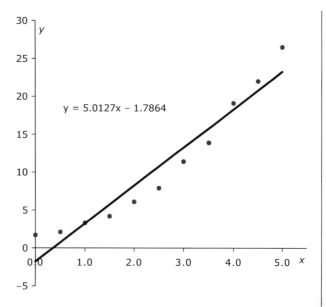

Figure 1.13 Linear function as an approximating function

Choosing a polynomial of degree 2 (that is, quadratic function), a parabola can be fitted to the data set.

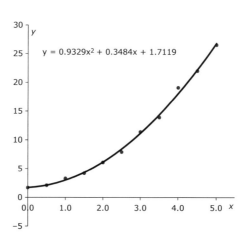

Figure 1.14 Quadratic function as an approximating function

Generating random numbers

Some spreadsheets are equipped with special built-in random number generators. In *Excel*, the functions, "=RAND" and "=RANDBETWEEN(…, …)" are tools that can be used to generate random numbers from a uniform distribution. Figure 1.15 shows how pairs of values (x, y) representing randomly selected points on the Cartesian plane may be generated using the formula for the random number generator in *Excel*.

16 Introducing mathematical modelling

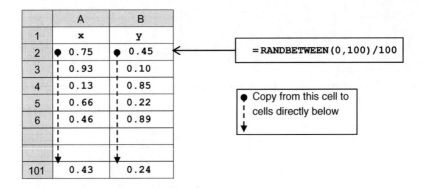

Figure 1.15 Data consisting of 100 pairs of random values

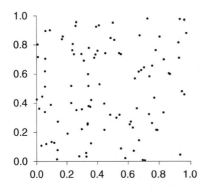

Figure 1.16 Plot of 100 randomly generated points

In this example, 100 randomly generated points inside a unit square are generated and plotted (see Figure 1.16). Since the function "=RANDBETWEEN(a,b)" returns a random integer between a and b, if one wishes to get non-integer random numbers, some manipulation of the returned value is needed (as in the case here).

Table 1.3 Concentration of drugs at various times

Time, t (minutes)	15	30	60	90	120	150	180	240	300
Concentration, x (mg/L)	82	65	43	37	22	19	12	6	2

Examples

Example 1 Drug concentration

In drug therapy studies, experiments in which a dose of drug is introduced into a subject are often carried out to gain a better understanding of how the drugs may diffuse into the body. Measurements of the concentration of the drug in blood samples can be taken at various time intervals. In one such experiment, observations at successive times are made and these are presented in Table 1.3.

A first step in trying to make some sense of the data would be to construct a scatter plot. This may be done quite efficiently using a spreadsheet, such as Microsoft *Excel*. This is shown in Figure 1.17.

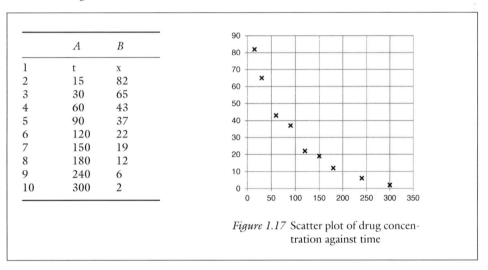

Figure 1.17 Scatter plot of drug concentration against time

From the scatter plot, it can be clearly seen that the concentration of drugs (x) decreases with time (t). It is also clear that the relationship between x and t does not look linear.

We might guess that the concentration of drugs in the bloodstream varies with time in some "exponential decay" fashion. In other words, a possible equation linking x and t could be of the form,

$$x(t) = Ae^{-kt},$$

where A and k are both positive. To complete our model, we will need to find or estimate the values of the parameters A and k.

There are several ways to do this. One quick and easy way is to make use of *Excel*'s "trendline" facility. By right-clicking on any data point in the scatter plot, a menu pops

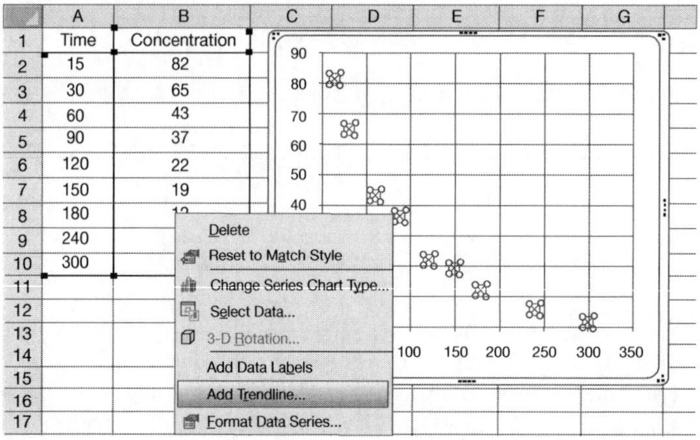

18   *Introducing mathematical modelling*

Figure 1.18 Adding a trendline to the scatter plot

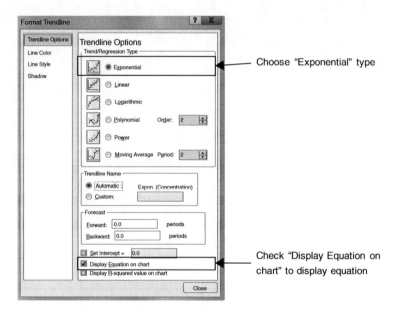

Figure 1.19 Choosing type of trendline and selecting other options

up, and one could choose the "Add Trendline …" option to add a trendline to the plot, as shown in the screenshot in Figure 1.18.

A "Trendline Options" window will then pop up. This window allows the user to choose the type of trend (such as linear, exponential, polynomial, and so on). The other useful option to select is the display of the resulting equation of the trendline. In this case, we would select the "Exponential" type (since we suspect that the data most likely follows an exponential decay curve) and check the "Display Equation" box (Figure 1.19).

Introducing mathematical modelling 19

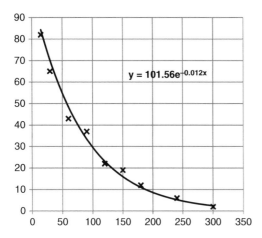

Figure 1.20 Exponential model and data

Once these options are chosen, the curve with its equation will be displayed on the chart. As shown in Figure 1.20, the equation in this case is of the form $y = 101.56e^{-0.012x}$. It is important to note that the variables x and y (in the equation) are default symbols which should be modified accordingly. This means that the data in our model may be approximated by the equation,

$$x(t) = 101.56e^{-0.012t}.$$

In other words, the parameters that we have set out to find are estimated as

$$A \approx 101.56 \text{ and } k \approx 0.012.$$

It can be seen from Figure 1.20 that the data points seem to agree quite well with the exponential curve given by the equation. One question that arises is how well is "quite well"? In other words, can one quantify or measure how well a certain model represents a set of data?

One way to do so is to define some kind of "average error" E by

$$E = \frac{\sqrt{\sum_{i=1}^{n}(x_i - \bar{x}_i)^2}}{n},$$

where x_i and $\bar{x}_i$ are the model and data values respectively, and n is the number of data points. If E is "sufficiently small", then the model equation is good enough to be accepted under the given circumstances. It may not be possible to define what "sufficiently small" means, but in general, we try to find the best possible set of parameter values (in this case, A and k) so that this error is minimised. *Excel* provides a tool to do so, and details can be found in Appendix A.

In the present case, it turns out that $E \approx 0.99965$, which is found to be acceptable.

20 *Introducing mathematical modelling*

This example shows how a simple empirical model can be constructed from known data or observations. It is also clear that such modelling technique requires some knowledge of functions and their behaviour. Skills in using appropriate tools are also important in empirical modelling.

Example 2: Area of a circle

To illustrate the implementation of a simple simulation model on *Excel*, we will look at the problem of finding (or estimating) the area of a circle, without the use of formulae.

The simulation model used is one that involves generating random samplings to simulate the outcomes of an experiment. Models of this kind are commonly known as *Monte Carlo simulation* models.

Consider a circle whose equation is given by

$$x^2 + y^2 = 4.$$

This circle has a radius of 2 units and its centre is at the origin.

To estimate the area of this circle, a square of side 4 units is drawn so that the circle fits nicely in it. This is shown in Figure 1.21.

Suppose points inside this square are now randomly selected. The assumption is that each point is equally likely to be selected. Suppose out of a total of y randomly picked points in the square, x are found to fall within the circle. Then,

$$\text{Area of circle} \approx \frac{x}{y} \times \text{Area of square} = 16\frac{x}{y}.$$

We can simulate the random selection of a (large) number of points inside the square using the random number generator in *Excel*, and then count the number of points accordingly.

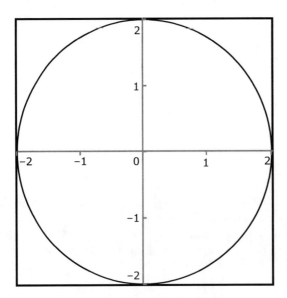

Figure 1.21 Circle is circumscribed by square

Introducing mathematical modelling 21

	A	B	C	D	E	F
1	x	y	Count	Inside	Total	Area
2	0.5778	-0.7413	1	36	50	11.52
3	-1.6215	-1.3755	0			
4	-1.3998	-1.8847	0			
5	-0.0244	-1.9650	1			
⋮	⋮	⋮	⋮			
51	-1.8312	-0.9873	0			

Figure 1.22 Worksheet used in simulation model

An *Excel* worksheet as depicted in Figure 1.22 is first set up. The titles for each column are typed in Row 1. Columns A and B are used to store the values of the x and y coordinates of the randomly selected points respectively. Every point chosen must be inside the square. In Column C, we keep track of whether the point is inside or outside the circle. Cell D2 contains the number of points inside the circle, while Cell E2 contains the total number of points generated. In Cell F2, the formula for estimating the area is used to find an approximate answer.

To randomly select 50 points, we enter the following formula

=4*RAND()−2

from Cells A2 down to A51 and from Cells B2 down to B51. This will generate 50 pairs of numbers ranging from −2 to +2, thus giving rise to the required number of pairs of coordinates in the square.

To check if a point lies inside the circle (of radius 2 and centred at the origin), we enter the formula

=IF((A2^2+B2^2)<=4, 1, 0)

in Cell C2. This formula says that if $(x^2 + y^2) \leq 4$, where the coordinates x and y are stored in Cells A2 and B2 respectively, then Cell C2 takes the value 1; otherwise, it takes the value 0. This formula is copied from Cell C2 down to C51, with relative referencing in force.

Thus, to count the number of points inside the circle, we sum up Column C. Alternatively, we can use the formula

=COUNTIF(C:C, "=1")

and place it in cell, say, D2.

Similarly, the total number of points generated can be counted by entering the formula

=COUNTIF(C:C, ">=0")

22 Introducing mathematical modelling

Table 1.4 Mean values of estimated area using different number of random points

No. of Points	Mean Area	Standard Deviation
50	12.6720	0.8950
100	12.3680	0.6621
250	12.5248	0.4742
500	12.4640	0.4129
1000	12.4384	0.1420
2500	12.5786	0.1326
5000	12.5997	0.0734
10000	12.5829	0.0706

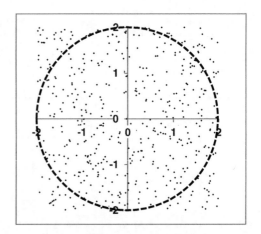

Figure 1.23 Typical scatter plot of simulation model

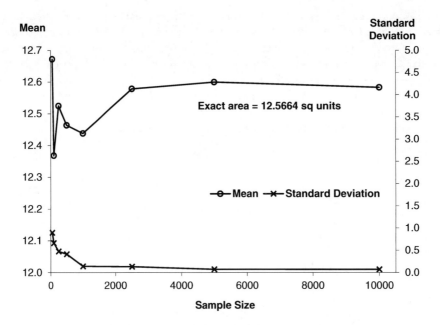

Figure 1.24 Graphs of estimated areas and standard deviations for simulation runs with various sample sizes

in cell, E2, for instance.

To find the approximate area, the formula

=16*D2/E2

is entered in Cell F2. In the case shown in Figure 1.22, out of 50 points randomly selected, 36 are inside the circle. Thus, the estimated area is 11.52 square units. The exact value is about 12.5664 square units.

To visualize the simulation, a scatter plot of the points can be plotted. An example of such a plot using 500 points is shown in Figure 1.23.

Once the worksheet has been set up, a simulation can be executed by pressing the F9 function key. Note that each time the simulation is carried out, the outcome is likely to be different, even if the number of points remains the same. Table 1.4 shows the mean areas estimated for various sample sizes of points. For each sample size, ten simulations are carried out. These results are plotted as graphs in Figure 1.24.

As can be seen from the graphs in Figure 1.24, generally, the estimation using this form of simulation improves with the increase in the sample size. Also, the standard deviation becomes smaller as the sample size increases.

Notes

1 COMAP, see www.comap.com.
2 IMMC, see www.immchallenge.org.
3 "Influenza in a boarding school", *British Medical Journal*, p. 587, 1978.

Bibliography

Ang, K.C. (2006). *Differential Equations: Models and Methods*, McGraw-Hill, Singapore.
Ang, K.C. (2010). Mathematical modelling in the Singapore curriculum: Opportunities and challenges, *Proceedings of the Educational Interfaces between Mathematics and Industry Study Conference*, Lisbon, Portugal (pp. 53–61).
Ang, K.C. (2012). Mathematical modeling as a learning experience in the classroom, *Proceedings of the 17th Asian Technology Conference in Mathematics*, Bangkok, Thailand (pp. 84–92).
Anon. (1978). Influenza in a boarding school, *British Medical Journal*, *4 March* (pp. 587–90).

2 Teaching mathematical modelling

Introduction

Around the world, there are many teachers and mathematics educators who hold differing opinions and views on the practice of teaching mathematical modelling in the classroom. In fact, researchers and mathematics educators do not seem to agree on a precise definition for the term "mathematical modelling". For instance, some mathematics educators define mathematical modelling as simply a process of understanding, simplifying and solving a real-life problem in mathematical terms, while others contend that it is essentially a movement of a physical situation to a mathematical representation. Some researchers are of the opinion that all applications of mathematics are mathematical models, but others view mathematical modelling and applications of mathematics as distinctly different.

Given this backdrop, it is not surprising to find that in different countries or regions of the world, researchers adopt different research paradigms, educators subscribe to different pedagogical principles and teachers engage in different teaching practices in teaching mathematical modelling. It may not be possible, nor is it useful, for the global community in mathematical modelling to agree on any one particular paradigm or pedagogical approach in practical terms as every country is unique: every education system has its own curricular goals, objectives and agenda. Nevertheless, it is good for the teacher to be aware of some of the practices across different parts of the world, as well as to be mindful of the kinds of issues or problems that have confronted teachers from elsewhere. This awareness may in turn be of use to teachers in their design, development and enactment of mathematical modelling lessons.

Mathematical modelling classrooms

In the United States, following the introduction of the Common Core State Standards for Mathematics (CCSSM) initiative, there is an increased and renewed emphasis on mathematical modelling at all grade levels in the recommended mathematics curricula. There is a belief that mathematical modelling is capable of linking classroom mathematics and statistics to real-life situations, and in decision-making. The models that can be tackled in the classroom range from very simple ones, such as using a geometrical shape to describe an object, to more complex and elaborate models involving other disciplines.

The CCSSM document lists examples of possible situations, including designing the layout of stalls at a fund-raising event, modelling of bacterial growth or investment growth, problems in population dynamics and risk analysis in extreme sports or terrorism, and so on. The modelling process, as understood by the CCSSM, is depicted in Figure 2.1. In essence, it is not different from the modelling process described earlier in Chapter 1.

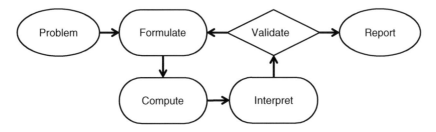

Figure 2.1 The Modelling Cycle (CCSSM, 2010: p. 72)

It is evident that schools across the US are encouraged to adopt the Common Core State Standards and teachers are urged to introduce modelling in the classroom. The document lists the topics to be covered and standards to be attained, and provides examples of the kinds of skills and expected outcomes within each topic at each level. However, while the CCSSM document is a very detailed syllabus document, it is probably not meant to explain or suggest pedagogical approaches or principles, which could explain why there is no mention of how a teacher should teach any particular topic, including mathematical modelling.

Historically, many mathematics teachers in various European countries such as Denmark, Sweden and Germany, have been involved in some form of mathematical modelling, either as part of their university course, or in some professional development programme. For instance, mathematical modelling had appeared in the Swedish curriculum in the mid-1990's, and since then, universities have started to include mathematical modelling in their teacher education programmes (Lingefjard, 2007). However, such programmes are not without problems, and it remains to be seen whether these programmes, while necessary, will be sufficient to prepare teachers to teach mathematical modelling in the classroom.

In Germany, it has been reported that while there had been much emphasis on modelling, teachers continue to hold on to the belief that understanding mathematical concepts and construction of thinking is more important. The idea that mathematics can be useful and applicable in real life appears to play only a minor role in the teachers' perceptions of mathematics and learning of mathematics (Ikeda, 2007).

In the early 1990's, the curriculum reform in the Netherlands saw applications and modelling occupying a central role. However, teachers found a lack of adequate teacher resources, textbooks or assessment material to support them in teaching mathematical modelling. In addition, professional development in this area was also found wanting. It is reported that as a consequence and in response to demands, textbook authors began to write material with tasks that are simpler. The outcome was not as desirable, as these contextual problems are divided into a series of simple questions that does not seem to address the purpose and intention of teaching applications or modelling.

In Australia, mathematical modelling has been an emphasis in the country's school mathematics curriculum since the early 1990's (Geiger, 2015). The inclusion of mathematical modelling may be as a topic for study or an assessment practice, and this is left to each state or territory curriculum authority to decide. However, acceptance across the different states varies widely. For instance, in the state of Queensland, mathematical modelling plays a very important role in the state's mathematics curriculum. In fact, since 1992, mathematical modelling has been made a mandatory aspect of mathematics in the final years of school mathematics in Queensland. In contrast, in the state of New

South Wales, it appears that mathematical modelling is not being featured sufficiently in any manner within the mathematics subjects. Curriculum documents for mathematics in this state do not seem to make any reference to mathematical modelling. Nevertheless, despite the variation of emphasis across the country, Australian teachers and mathematics educators are among the strongest proponents, advocates and practitioners of mathematical modelling in the classroom.

In Japan, it is common to see teachers using applications and modelling to illustrate the utilitarian values of mathematics and of learning mathematical concepts (Ikeda, 2007). However, the process of modelling does not seem to be emphasised or practiced in the classroom. It is believed that this could be due to the focus on entrance examinations, in which modelling tasks seldom appear. Moreover, it is reported that there are not many modelling tasks that have been designed for students to attempt. Yet another reason has to do with the teachers; apart from having little experience in modelling, Japanese teachers are not encouraged to embark on the teaching of mathematical modelling, and there is therefore little incentive for them to want to undertake this task.

In Singapore's mathematics education journey, mathematical modelling has a relatively short history. In fact, it was only in 2001 that Ang first proposed and suggested that mathematical modelling could be introduced in Singapore's secondary schools (Ang, 2001). He argued that since mathematical problem solving is a central theme in the school mathematics curriculum, it is natural to expect some part of the curriculum to focus on applying mathematics in practical and real-life situation.

Coincidentally, the terms "applications and modelling" began to appear in Singapore's national mathematics curriculum framework a couple of years later. Since then, there have been much conscious efforts taken to promote mathematical modelling and the teaching of mathematical modelling in Singapore. Apart from a slate of in-service courses and workshops mounted by the Ministry of Education and the National Institute of Education, Singapore, there have also been other activities to raise awareness among teachers on the essentials of teaching of mathematical modelling. These include Mathematics Teachers' Conference with a focus on mathematical applications and modelling in 2009 and a Mathematical Modelling Outreach programme in 2010. The Singapore International Mathematics Challenge (SIMC) was inaugurated in 2008, and is a biennial international competition that provides opportunities for secondary school students to demonstrate their creativity and mathematical skills in mathematical modelling. In addition, a few local schools have also taken the initiative to run modelling workshops and challenges at zonal or cluster levels.

Despite these valiant efforts to venture into the unknown, many teachers in Singapore remain apprehensive and uncertain about introducing or teaching mathematical modelling. In an examination-oriented environment, with little or no emphasis on mathematical modelling in school assessments, and a lack of sustained support in resources and training, it is understandable if teachers in Singapore do not feel motivated to embark on this journey. It appears, however, that they are not alone; similar issues and problems, in one form or another, seem to permeate across the world. Such concerns that teachers and, indeed, the mathematical modelling community have are universal.

Teacher readiness

From the above discussion, it is clear that there are many concerns that mathematics teachers and educators have in terms of introducing and teaching mathematical modelling in the classroom. These concerns should be addressed if one truly feels that mathematical modelling is a valuable and meaningful activity, and is serious about introducing it to mathematics learners in schools.

While workshops, special events and one-off courses on mathematical modelling may raise awareness among pre-service or in-service teachers, they may not be as useful in helping them take the first step in actually preparing and implementing a modelling lesson or task. It is fair to say that a typical mathematics teacher anywhere in the world faces many challenges in the area of teaching mathematical modelling. These challenges include a lack of ready and relevant resources, a set of good exemplars of modelling problems, and the resistance from students to engage in activities not directly related to or contributing towards examinations and assessment.

Despite these challenges, it is encouraging to note that many teachers are keen and prepared to make an attempt to include mathematical modelling in their teaching curriculum. This can be seen in the positive reports on the state of affairs in terms of mathematical modelling in schools by researchers from various countries at international academic meetings. Perhaps the one important missing piece that mathematics teachers badly and urgently need is a practical framework that can serve as a guide for teachers in preparing mathematical modelling lessons, activities or learning experiences in the classroom.

It must be mentioned that a similar and related framework has been proposed. Stillman and her colleagues outlined a structural framework to support the implementation of mathematical modelling in the Australian schools (Stillman et al, 2007). This framework is based largely on the widely accepted modelling cycle; in essence, it serves as a guide for the teacher to identify possible student blockages moving from one part of the modelling cycle to the next. Although the framework may have been successfully applied by Australian teachers (as reported in Stillman), it appears to be intended more for the researcher, curriculum designer or an experienced teacher to identify particular modelling competencies needed to complete a modelling task. In that sense, such a sophisticated tool may not be suitable for a typical or inexperienced mathematics teacher, who may be a novice or beginner in the teaching of mathematical modelling. In the same way, while the set of design principles proposed and advocated by Galbraith (2006) may be useful for generating real-life modelling problems and tasks, it may prove too advanced a tool for a beginner teacher modeller.

Teachers often have ideas about situations or problems in the real world that could transpire into a modelling task. However, the challenge they usually face is turning these ideas into a modelling lessons suitable for use in the classroom. Therefore, it appears that before teachers can use and apply these principles of design proposed by Galbraith, they need a framework to help them develop their ideas into mathematical modelling tasks as a first step.

Such a framework will also help teachers develop a shared understanding of what it means by teaching mathematical modelling in the classroom. Currently, among teachers, it seems there is a plethora of interpretations of what constitutes mathematical modelling. This can be confusing and it is time we established an understanding that is both useful and practical for schools. In addition, a framework will provide teachers with a common language with which to discuss ideas and deliberate on issues related to mathematical modelling. This can lead to a more structured professional conversation that may in turn lead to improving the current state of affairs.

Levels of learning experience

Before developing the framework for teaching mathematical modelling, it is important to define the scope within which one can properly organize or plan a mathematical modelling lesson in the classroom. Since a mathematical modelling lesson can often be quite different from a typical "mathematics lesson", for the purpose of this discussion, we shall refer to it as a *learning experience*, which can be like a typical lesson, or an activity, or a short project, for students. A novice teacher in mathematical modelling would probably require a more structured approach to planning a successful learning experience in the classroom.

Depending on the readiness of the students, a learning experience in mathematical modelling will need to be pitched appropriately. For the purpose of developing a framework for teachers, classroom learning experiences in mathematical modelling will be classified into three levels, aligned to particular levels of cognitive demands and expectations.

Level 1

At the most basic level (Level 1), the focus is on acquiring skills that may be directly or indirectly related to mathematical modelling. These could be purely mathematical skills presented in a modelling context, or they may be specific skills that are often used in mathematical modelling activities. For example, a lesson on a specific function and its graph applied to a real-life problem (or set in a real-life context) could be considered a Level 1 modelling learning experience.

Another Level 1 modelling activity could be a lesson on curve fitting using a computing or IT tool. In real-life problems, there is often the need to collect data and then to find suitable functions with suitable parameter values that best fit the data. Therefore, skills related to plotting of graphs and finding the best fit can be critical in the success of completing a modelling exercise or task.

Generally, one expects a Level 1 modelling lesson to be trim enough to fit into a one- or two-period lesson.

Level 2

At the next level (Level 2), the focus will be on developing modelling competencies. For the purpose of this discussion, we make a distinction between "competencies" and "skills", the latter having been described above. In contrast, by "competency", we refer to the capacity and capability to apply knowledge specific to mathematical modelling in a modelling problem. Level 2 learning experiences could involve modelling competencies that are inherent in the modelling cycle, such as making assumptions to simplify a problem, identifying factors that influence a dependent variable, or interpreting a mathematical solution in physical terms.

In addition, a Level 2 modelling lesson could be studying and applying known, existing or standard models to a real, physical situation. The related modelling competency here is the ability to recognise the behaviour of a model (or a mathematical function or equation that can potentially be a model) and its use in a real-life problem.

In general, a Level 2 learning experience would take up more instructional time than a Level 1 learning experience.

Level 3

At the highest level (Level 3), students will be expected to tackle a mathematical modelling task. This should involve substantial complexity and would require students to apply various modelling skills and allow them to further develop their modelling competencies. One may expect students to work in groups, and carry out discussions, develop a model, solve the model and make a presentation.

In other words, Level 3 modelling experiences are what researchers and mathematics educators would have commonly called "modelling tasks". Therefore, one would expect a Level 3 activity to take up quite a fair bit of instructional time, possibly a few hours over a few days.

Having a clear idea of the level to pitch a lesson on modelling is an important step in lesson planning. It provides the teacher with a goal and a structure for the lesson. In addition, it will help the teacher in designing and preparing essential scaffolds for students to successfully complete a task or activity. If students are not ready or sufficiently prepared, the teacher could gradually build their capacity by moving from one level to the next over a period of time.

Zone of Proximal Development (ZPD)

Mathematical modelling is more than just applying mathematics; it is also about learning mathematics, both concepts and skills, and appreciating what mathematics can do. As pointed out by Warwick (2007), the first step in this learning process is for the student to "become conversant with the tools of the trade" (Warwick, 2007: p. 34). These include familiarity with mathematical symbols used in the model, algebraic manipulation, computer skills, stages of modelling cycle, and so on. One certainly cannot expect a student with no knowledge of these "tools of the trade" to jump into a modelling task and be successful in carrying out the task.

It is also acknowledged that most modelling tasks are "difficult" for both students and teachers as they are usually cognitively demanding (Blum and Borromeo Ferri, 2009). It is thus unrealistic to expect students (and teachers) to be able to complete a complex modelling task successfully at their first attempt. Therefore, it is important that the teacher recognises the need to devise activities to familiarise students with modelling skills, tools and competencies before embarking on more ambitious tasks. For this reason, an auxiliary to the framework is this concept of mapping an idea to the level of modelling experience.

The conceptualisation of different levels of learning experiences is closely related to the notion of the *zone of proximal development*, or ZPD, as suggested by Vygotsky (Vygotsky, 1978; Kozulin, 2004). The ZPD is roughly defined as the "distance" between what a learner can achieve on his own, and what he can achieve with assistance from a teacher. Recognising the ZPD of learners in a particular learning situation enables the teacher to provide the necessary and appropriate scaffolding to support learning. Similarly, designing modelling activities based on students' readiness, allows the teacher to help students develop the necessary skills or competencies to proceed to a more advanced level. Therefore, the construction of modelling activities at different levels is a deliberate attempt to provide the scaffolding required to take a learner from a level requiring simple, basic skills and knowledge (Level 1) to a level requiring advanced skills and competencies (Level 3).

A framework for teaching mathematical modelling

The three levels of learning experiences in mathematical modelling defined in the previous section facilitates the development of a simple framework that teachers can use when planning or designing a lesson on mathematical modelling.

The structure of this framework is in the form of a set of five questions and is organised in a tabular form as shown below in Table 2.1.

Table 2.1 Framework for planning and designing Mathematical Modelling Learning Experience

Framework Component	Modelling Activity
1. WHICH **level** of learning experience?	Decide which level (Level 1, 2 or 3) of mathematical modelling learning experience that we wish to focus on.
2. WHAT is the **skill/competency**?	List all the specific skills and competencies (mathematical or modelling) that we target in this learning experience; State the problem to be solved, if applicable.
3. WHERE is the **mathematics**?	Write down the mathematical concepts or formulae or equations that will be needed in this learning experience.
4. HOW to **solve** the problem/model?	Prepare and provide plausible solutions to the problem identified in this learning experience.
5. WHY is this experience a **success**?	List factors or outcomes that can explain why this experience is considered successful and look out for them during the activity.

When planning or designing a modelling lesson, a teacher should first decide _which_ level of modelling experience would be most appropriate or suitable that point in time for the students in question. It would not be logical or advisable to plan a, say, Level 3 lesson which requires certain modelling skills or competencies if the target group of students do not have that set of skills or competencies. One could, in fact, "work backwards" and see what is needed in a proposed Level 3 lesson, and plan related Level 2 and Level 1 lessons earlier so that these can serve to support the Level 3 lesson later. In other words, the idea is to build up the skills and competencies using lower levels before getting students to attempt modelling tasks at a higher level.

The next question to ask is _what_ set are the specific skills or competencies that one hopes to develop through this lesson. Skills could include the application of certain mathematical concepts in a problem situation, or the use of some tools, such as a graphing tool or electronic spreadsheet in problem-solving. Competencies related to mathematical modelling, such as identifying factors or variables in a real-world problem, or simplifying a problem by making appropriate and reasonable assumptions, should be clearly identified. It will also be good to write down some details of the problem to be examined or solved in this learning experience. It is important to be able to list these targets as this will eventually help shape the lesson objectives. Doing so will help the teacher focus and scope the learning experience.

The next component in this framework asks _where_ exactly is mathematics applied, used, taught or practised in this lesson. This requires the teacher to think carefully about the problem posed, and to have some idea what kind of mathematical concepts or topics may be useful or can be applied in such a situation. A mathematical modelling lesson or learning experience should involve a certain amount and level of mathematics. It would be even better if the teacher, while planning a modelling lesson, is able to link the mathematics found and used in the activity to the syllabus or curriculum, or the teacher's overall scheme of work.

In order to make sure that the modelling activity provides a problem which is actually solvable and manageable by the target group of students, it is crucial that the teacher must have an idea of _how_ to approach or even to solve the problem or model. By going through the solution process, the teacher would, in some sense, be experiencing the experience before implementing it. This helps the teacher identify possible blockages and prepare suitable scaffolds.

Finally, the teacher needs to know *why* the lesson planned in this way should ensure success. This last step helps one check and look for success factors, and to have the end in mind. Before implementing the lesson or activity, the expected outcomes are listed. If these outcomes are observed or detected during or after the activity, then one could explain why the lesson is considered a success.

Using the framework

In this section, we present examples to illustrate how the framework described in the previous section can be applied. In each example, we begin with an idea, and proceed to use the framework to develop a structure for a modelling lesson or activity or task.

Example 1: Mountain climbing (Level 1)

The main idea in this example is to use a data set obtained from the public domain on atmospheric pressure and altitude (see Table 2.2). Such a phenomenon is often experienced when one climbs a mountain and feels the air getting "thinner" at higher altitudes.

The problem could be to find a plausible relationship between the two variables from the data set, and finding an estimate for any parameter that may appear in the model. It turns out that the relationship may be described by an exponential function and students could practise the skill of parameter estimation.

Given that the main objective of this task is to equip and familiarise the learner with the skill of finding and then fitting a suitable function to the data, it can be positioned suitably as a Level 1 modelling learning experience. Using the framework and answering the five questions, we can write down the following and use it as a guide to plan the lesson.

Framework Component	*"Mountain climbing"*
1. WHICH **level** of learning experience?	Level 1 – about 40 minutes.
2. WHAT is the **skill/competency**?	Knowledge and understanding of the exponential function, and ability to use the Solver tool in *Excel* to find a suitable parameter value.
3. WHERE is the **mathematics**?	Given a set of data, find a function of the form $f(x) = Ae^{-kx}$ that fits the data. Least squares curve fitting, functions and graphs.
4. HOW to **solve** the problem/model?	Use of *Excel*'s Solver tool to find the best value of k that minimizes error between data and model.
5. WHY is this experience a **success**?	Students learn a specific skill, and are able to apply it to a problem with real data.

Example 2: Water warming (Level 2)

In this example, ice-water is left to warm up and its temperature is recorded at regular intervals. The objective is to study the collected data, make some sense of it, and then attempt to develop a possible model that would describe how the temperature of the water changes with time. Data may be collected using a temperature probe on a data-logger and recorded via software such as LoggerPro3 (see Figure 2.2).

32 *Teaching mathematical modelling*

Table 2.2 Atmospheric Pressures at different altitudes above sea level

Altitude (km)	Pressure (mb)
0	1013
1	899
2	795
3	701
4	616
5	540
6	472
7	411
8	356
9	307
10	264
11	226

The problem may be suitably posed as a Level 2 modelling activity in which students are expected to list factors in the problem and make some assumptions about these variables or factors. By inspecting the set of data, one could also propose a possible function that describes how the temperature of the warming water varies with time, and apply a method of estimating any model parameters that may arise from the modelling process.

Alternatively, students may directly apply Newton's law of cooling/warming to explain the observed phenomenon, and complete the solution of the problem by estimating the rate of cooling/warming for this case.

As students collect data, they will make some observations. Based on these observations, they may be asked the following questions:

(1) What are the factors (variables) that can influence or affect the temperature of the water?
(2) What happens near the beginning and near the end of the experiment?
(3) What assumptions do we need to make about the warming process?
(4) How quickly or slowly does the temperature change at different times?
(5) What can you say about the rate of change of the temperature? Write down a word equation that describes the rate of change.
(6) Write down a differential equation that describes how the temperature changes with time.

These questions serve to help them think more deeply about the warming process. In principle, students at different stages of their mathematics education should be able to tackle most of the questions above. However, depending on their cognitive development, they may answer these questions differently, with varying degrees of mathematical sophistication. For instance, a pupil in the primary (elementary) school may be able to handle the more basic questions like (1), (2) and (3), whereas a secondary (high school) or pre-university (senior high school) student should be able to handle all the questions, including higher order ones like (4), (5) and (6).

From these questions, hopefully, students can be led to "discover" that the rate of warming (or cooling) of an object is directly proportional to the difference between its temperature (θ) and that of the surrounding (S).

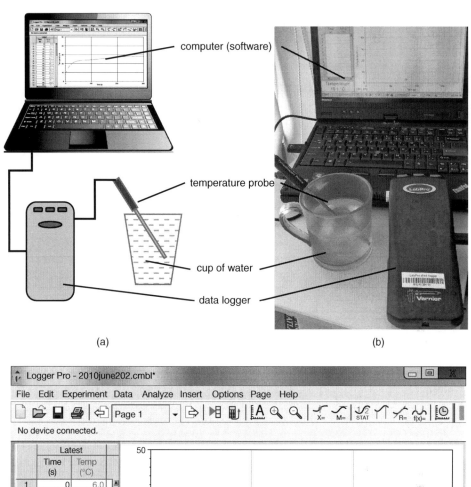

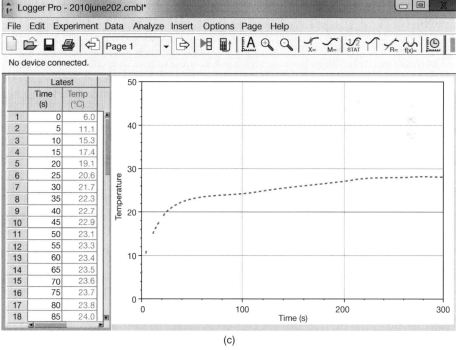

Figure 2.2 Recording temperature of ice-water warming up to room temperature: (a) Schematic diagram showing the set up of the data collection equipment, (b) Temperature probe and data-logger used to collect data, and (c) Snapshot of LoggerPro 3 showing variation of temperature of water with time

34 *Teaching mathematical modelling*

Based on this idea, the basic framework for a Level 2 modelling lesson could be drawn up as follows.

Framework Component	"Water warming"
1. WHICH **level** of learning experience?	Level 2 – about 1 hour, with homework.
2. WHAT is the **skill/competency**?	Listing variables or factors in a model. Finding suitable equations and estimating model parameters.
3. WHERE is the **mathematics**?	Functions and graphs. First-order differential equations (for students with Calculus background).
4. HOW to **solve** the problem/model?	A data-logger is used to collect data. Either: Guess from the behaviour of the points that a possible relationship could be $$\theta = S + (\theta_0 - S)e^{kt}$$ where θ_0 is the initial temperature; <u>Or:</u> Apply Newton's law of cooling/warming and the differential equation $$\frac{d\theta}{dt} = k(\theta - S)$$ and use the data-set to estimate the unknown parameter, k.
5. WHY is this experience a **success**?	This lesson helps students to learn to: • identify variables in a real problem, • list assumptions in modelling, • collect and work with data, • make some sense of data, • apply a known model to real data, • apply a method of parameter estimation.

Example 3: Accident at the MRT Station (Level 3)

A tragic incident happened at one of Singapore's Mass Rapid Transit (MRT) stations in April 2011. As was reported in the local news, a teenage student from Thailand had fallen onto the tracks and was run over by a train approaching the station. She lost both her legs.

In one particular news article, it was reported that the girl could have fallen onto the tracks because "she had a dizzy spell while waiting on the platform".[1] The accident happened at around 11am on a Monday, and one would expect that some people would be waiting for the train at that time. Is it possible for a person to be walking randomly (under a "dizzy spell") and falling onto the tracks without being noticed? How many steps would such a random walker take before he/she falls off the platform?

Based on this scenario, a simulation model may be constructed to study and examine the claim made by the girl. One would first need to make some assumptions about the dimensions of the platform, the starting position of the random walk, the rules governing the random walk and so on. A schematic diagram showing the plan for this simulation is shown in Figure 2.3. We use the numbers 1, 2, 3 and 4 to represent the 4 possible directions of each step a random walker may take.

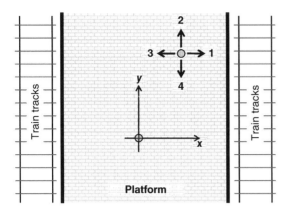

Figure 2.3 Simulating a random walk on a train station platform

The model would then consist of a set of simulation steps, and if possible, these are implemented on the computer. A possible way to handle this problem is to implement a simulation on an *Excel* worksheet. Using *Excel*'s random number generator to produce integers 1, 2, 3 and 4 to represent four possible directions in which a person can randomly walk, one could construct a simulated random walk and plot the path taken (see Figure 2.4).

The complexity of the problem makes it suitable as a Level 3 modelling task meant for students who have been introduced to probability and the idea of experimenting with chance, and have had experience with *Excel*'s random numbers. Using the framework proposed, we can check the various components as follows.

Framework Component	*"MRT accident"*
1. WHICH **level** of learning experience?	Level 3 – over at least two sessions, possibly with students working in small groups.
2. WHAT is the **skill/competency**?	• Listing variables or factors in a model. • Making assumptions about real physical situation and simplifying problem. • Designing and carrying out a simulation.
3. WHERE is the **mathematics**?	• Probability. • Random numbers and the use of a random number generator. • Coordinate geometry.
4. HOW to **solve** the problem/model?	• Decide on the dimensions of the platform. • Let the walker begin his random walk from the origin. • Generate random numbers 1, 2, 3 and 4 using a computer tool, to represent a step in four different directions. • Compute distance from origin at each step. • Run simulation and see on average how many steps are taken to reach edge of platform.
5. WHY is this experience a **success**?	As a small-group modelling activity, this task allows students to: • work as a group to communicate ideas, • list and agree on suitable and reasonable assumptions, • consolidate conceptual understanding of experimental and theoretical probability (and random numbers), • practise generating random numbers using a computing tool, • design a plausible simulation model.

36 *Teaching mathematical modelling*

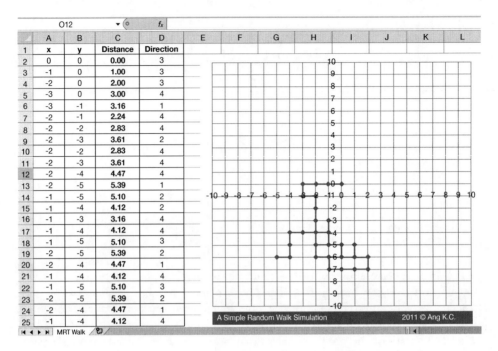

Figure 2.4 A typical run of the simulation on random walk implemented on *Excel*

Concluding remarks

The framework described above allows the teacher or curriculum designer to transform an idea or a real situation into a classroom activity on mathematical modelling. Of course, not every idea is suitable, but one could use the framework as a guide to identify the modelling skills or competencies that could be taught, practised or developed.

Another important aspect of the framework is its emphasis on the mathematics needed for the problem solution and the solution process. Apart from getting students to go through the modelling process and cycle, it is also highly desirable for students to learn how to use and apply mathematics to some real-life situations. Using the suggested framework to plan a lesson, the teacher will be forced to think through the mathematics and the model solution process. One might argue that doing so may result in the teacher focussing on just one solution and stifling students' creativity during implementation. However, as long as the teacher is aware that the mathematics used and solution designed are just one way or one approach to the problem, it should not be a hindrance to the plan. In fact, knowing what mathematics can be applied and how it can be applied would give teachers added confidence when implementing or facilitating the activity.

The hierarchical nature of the framework means that the teacher is able to move from one level to the next, depending on the ability and readiness of the students. It also helps the teacher plan a longer term programme or series in mathematical modelling activities, starting with cognitively less demanding lessons at Level 1, and advancing towards more challenging modelling tasks.

It is worth mentioning that when applying the framework, one should keep the modelling experience in focus and not be too enmeshed or carried away in trying to list and unpack the information. The main purpose of the framework is to guide the teacher in developing an idea further and to provide a structure to a mathematical modelling lesson.

The framework described in this chapter provides the teacher with a structured way of selecting an appropriate approach of designing a modelling lesson or activity. This could be an important first step towards developing more sophisticated modelling exercises, activities or projects. The framework advocates a more systematic and organized way of planning modelling lessons, and provides a practical set of guidelines for the teacher, step by step.

It should be noted that the framework does not attempt to include all aspects, elements or components of mathematical modelling in any one particular lesson as this is not the objective. More competencies can be built up over time, and as the teacher becomes more familiar and confident. The framework serves mainly as a way of guiding a novice modeller in moving a possible modelling idea in the real world to a possible modelling lesson or activity in the classroom. In time and with practice, it is hoped that eventually, the teacher will no longer need the framework as thinking through the questions in the framework becomes second nature to the teacher modeller.

A lesson plan on a modelling activity on warming of iced water (discussed earlier in Example 2), complete with a student handout and teacher guide, is provided as a sample in Appendix B. This is by no means a "model answer" but it does serves as a reference for teachers.

Note

1 The Straits Times, "Thai teen loses both legs after being hit by MRT train", 2011, April 4, news article by Jaleah Abu Baker.

Bibliography

Ang, K. C. (2001). Teaching mathematical modelling in Singapore schools. *The Mathematics Educator*, 6(1), 63–75.

Ang, K. C. (2015). Mathematical modelling in Singapore schools: A framework for instruction. In N. H. Lee and K. E. D. Ng (Eds.). *Mathematical Modelling: From Theory to Practice* (pp. 57–72). Singapore: World Scientific.

Blum, W. and Borromeo Ferri, R. (2009). Mathematical modelling: Can it be taught and learnt? *Journal of Mathematical Modelling and Applications*, 1(1), 45–58.

Galbraith, P. (2006). Real world problems: Developing principles of design. In P. Grootenboer, M. Chinnappan and R. Zevenbergen (Eds.), *Identities, Cultures and Learning Spaces: Proceedings of the 29th Annual Conference of the Mathematics Education Research Group of Australasia, Canberra, Australia* (Vol. 1, pp. 229–36). Adelaide: MERGA.

Geiger, V. (2015). Mathematical modelling in Australia. In N. H. Lee and K. E. D. Ng (Eds.). *Mathematical Modelling: From Theory to Practice* (pp. 73–82). Singapore: World Scientific.

Ikeda, T. (2007). Possibilities for, and obstacles to teaching applications and modelling in the lower secondary levels. In W. Blum, P. L. Galbraith, H-W. Henn, and M. Niss (Eds.). *Modelling and Applications in Mathematics Education* (pp. 457–62). Boston: Springer.

Kozulin, A. (2004). Vygotsky's theory in the classroom: Introduction, *European Journal of Psychology of Education*, 19, pp. 3–7.

Lingefjärd, T. (2007). Mathematical modelling in teacher education: Necessity or unnecessarily. In W. Blum, P. L. Galbraith, H-W. Henn, and M. Niss (Eds.). *Modelling and Applications in Mathematics Education* (pp. 333–40). New York: Springer.

National Governors Association Center for Best Practices and Council of Chief State School Officers (2010). *Common Core State Standards for Mathematics (CCSSM)*. Retrieved from www.corestandards.org/Math/Content/HSM/.

Stillman, G., Galbraith, P., Brown, J. and Edwards, I. (2007). A framework for success in implementing mathematical modelling in the secondary classroom. In J. Watson and K. Beswick (Eds.), *Mathematics: Essential Research, Essential Practice: Proceedings of the 30th Annual Conference of the Mathematics Education Research Group of Australasia, Hobart, Tasmania* (Vol. 2, pp. 688–97). Adelaide: MERGA.

Vygotsky, L.S. (1978). *Mind in Society: The Development of Higher Psychological Processes*. Cambridge: Harvard University Press.

Warwick, J. (2007). Some reflections on the teaching of mathematical modelling. *The Mathematics Educator*, *17*(1), 32–41.

3 Empirical modelling

Introduction

Many mathematical models are built with the aid of data obtained by experiment, observation or surveys, and such models are called empirical models. In empirical modelling, one often collects or obtains data for a problem, and then studies them before making an attempt to see if some function, equation, concept, or known model may be applied in the situation. It should not be seen as merely curve-fitting; rather, it is about making sense of the data, and making a connection between what has been observed and the concepts or theory surrounding the real situation.

At times, an empirical model is used to make predictions, although one has to be aware that the model built using one set of data may not always apply to another set. At other times, an empirical model is used to explain observed phenomena, or to obtain essential or important parameter values in another model. Whatever it is, empirical modelling involves making observations, taking measurements, and making sense of data to construct a mathematical model.

Playing detective

Problem situation: A footprint or shoeprint found at a crime scene, such as that shown in Figure 3.1, can yield very useful and important information about the perpetrator of the crime. Police detectives often team up with forensic scientists to solve crimes and the analysis of footprints or shoeprints is an important part of the forensic investigations.

The size of a shoeprint can tell us something about the height of the wearer of the shoe. The depth of the print (if found in soft mud) can also indicate the person's weight quite well, assuming that the weight is evenly distributed throughout the shoes. In this problem, we will focus on the task below.

The task: A footprint (or shoeprint) was discovered at a crime scene. How tall is the perpetrator or suspect?

Teacher notes

To motivate this modelling activity, the teacher could show students a shoeprint or footprint imprinted on a piece of paper, and claim that the person the print belongs to is of a certain height. Alternatively, the video called "CSI: State College, Clue 3" available on YouTube (StateCollegeSpikes, 2009) that describes how a "detective" deduces that the suspect is about 6 feet tall (approximately 182cm) as the shoeprint came from a shoe of US

40 Empirical modelling

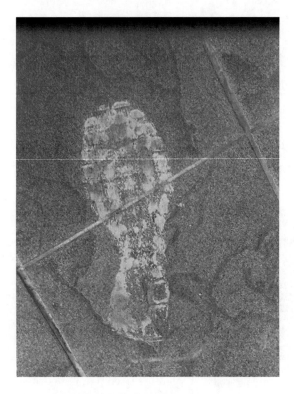

Figure 3.1 Example of a shoeprint

size 13 (assumed to be around 29.4cm). The teacher may ask the students to investigate if the deduction is correct, and to think about the variables involved in a problem such as this. It should not be hard for students to figure out that the variables involved are a typical person's height and the size of his foot (or shoe). In this instance, the shoe sizes of interest are the lengths of shoes.

To solve the problem, students will need to construct a model that describes the relationship between a person's height and his shoe length. In order to do so, they will first need to collect data, that is, find the heights and shoe lengths of a number of people.

Students should be reminded to be as precise and accurate as possible when obtaining data. For example, a person should stand upright (say, against the wall) when the height is being measured, and a shoe can be traced on paper before its length is measured. In addition, the thickness of the shoes, as well as how well they fit, may also affect the accuracy of the model. Therefore, students will need to be aware that certain assumptions about the thickness and fit of the shoes will have to be made. Moreover, different races, ages and genders of individuals, as well as the measurement of right or left foot, may affect the relationship between heights and shoe lengths of people. Thus the relevant assumptions can be made and the right or left foot can be consistently used during data collection.

Based on reports by other researchers, a person's shoe length is roughly 15% of his/her height, for both males and females (Giles and Vallandigham, 1991; Robbins, 1986).

A suggested approach

The students in a class may work in pairs to measure their partners' heights and shoe lengths. The measurements can be collated into one set of data, and the whole class may then work on this one set. Using the data collected, an *Excel* spreadsheet may be employed to generate a scatter plot similar to that shown in Figure 3.2.

Since the points lie roughly in a straight line, one may deduce that a linear function could be a suitable function to represent the relationship between the two variables. Using the "Add Trendline" function, a line of best fit for this data set can be found, and it is plotted as shown below.

For a given data set, suppose that $y = mx + c$ represents the equation of the line of best fit obtained, where y refers to height and x refers to shoe length. Then to obtain the approximate height of any person, one just needs to input the corresponding shoe length into the equation.

The task is essentially completed when a relationship is obtained. However, one should also check the validity of the equation using other data values. Whether a model (equation) is considered good enough will depend on the error tolerance (difference between actual height and height obtained from the equation). Note that the model may not be valid for shoe lengths that fall outside the range of the data used. Also, the parameter, c in the linear equation does not have any specific physical meaning.

If the scatter plot shows very little correlation between height and shoe length, the simplifying assumptions may need to be revisited and the data collection may have to be re-examined. For example, the number of male and female subjects may have an influence on the overall trend. A bigger set of data values may improve the fit or the model. Alternatively, different models can be constructed for males and females separately.

As the mathematical concepts and skills required in this problem are rather basic, it can be posed to students from the lower secondary levels onwards. Teachers can use the following framework to structure their modelling activities.

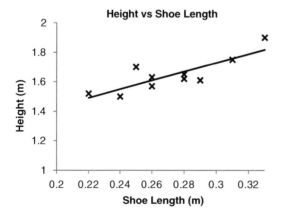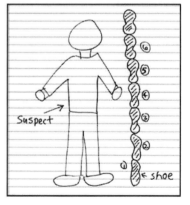

Figure 3.2 Relationship between a person's height and shoe length (in metres)

42 *Empirical modelling*

Using the framework

Framework Component	"Playing detective"
1. WHICH **level** of learning experience?	Level 1.
2. WHAT is the **skill/competency**?	• Identify the variables involved in the problem. • List assumptions. • Collect data. • Construct a model. • Use of a graphing tool. • Validate the model.
3. WHERE is the **mathematics**?	• Functions and their graphs (linear functions).
4. HOW to **solve** the problem/model?	• Find out the heights and shoe lengths of several people. • Construct a scatter plot of "height versus shoe length" using *Excel* or a graphing calculator. • Plot the line of best fit and obtain the equation of the line. • The height of the suspect can then be found by entering the shoe length into the equation.
5. WHY is this experience a **success**?	In this lesson, students learn about: • collecting real data accurately, • using a graphing tool to find a relationship between two variables, • how to defend their models.

Possible discussion points

To assist students in undertaking the task, the teacher may facilitate the process and discuss with students using the following questions to guide their thinking at different stages of the model construction process:

- How can we find the height of a person given the length of his footprint or shoeprint?
- What are the variables involved in this problem?
- What do we need to do to find a relationship between these variables?
- What are the assumptions that we need to make in order to simplify our problem?
- How can we go about collecting data on the heights and shoe lengths of different people accurately?
- How can we use all these data to find the relationship between the two variables?
- From the plot of data points, what function type may be suitable to represent the relationship between heights and shoe lengths of people?
- How can we use the function obtained to solve the problem?
- Is the model or function good enough? Is there a way to check?
- If the model is not appropriate, how can we improve it?

Similar problems

A variant of this problem is the "Giant Shoes" problem and is described by Blum and Borromeo Ferri (2009) as follows,

> "In a sports centre on the Philippines, Florentino Anonuevo Jr. polishes a pair of shoes. They are, according to the Guinness Book of Records, the world's biggest, with a width

of 2.37 m and a length of 5.29 m. Approximately how tall would a giant be for these shoes to fit? Explain your solution."

If a model representing the relationship between a person's shoe size and height is obtained or available, then, it would not be difficult to answer the question.

Another similar problem which involves the relationship between a person's waist and neck sizes, was used by some teachers. The problem, which appeared in an unpublished thesis (Tan, 2015: p. 168), is as follows,

> "Lulu went out to meet her friends for dinner last weekend. On the way to the restaurant, she saw her favourite boutique having a sale! She saw the red skirt that she had been eyeing for weeks on a huge discount. She rushed in, grabbed the skirt and headed to the changing room. However, there were long queues at the changing room but she was too lazy to queue up. Suddenly, Lulu put the waistband of the skirt around her neck, smiled and headed to the cashier. How was Lulu able to determine the size of her skirt?"

Again, to answer the question, one may need to establish a model that describes the relationship between the two variables in the problem.

In deep water

Singapore is a tiny island located at the southern tip of the Malaysian peninsula. The bridge that connects Johor, the southern-most state of Malaysia, to Singapore is known as the Causeway. As Singapore is resource-scarce and has few water catchment areas, water supply to the people living in the country has always been an important issue. The two countries have signed agreements at various times, stipulating that Singapore would be able to import water from Johor. One of these agreements had allowed Singapore to construct a dam across *Sungei Linggiu* to facilitate the extraction of water from the Johor River. In the meantime, Singapore has been striving to become less reliant on imported water.

Problem situation: The drought across the Causeway is raising serious concerns in the country. With the water level in Linggiu Reservoir in Johor rapidly falling to historic lows, the scenario where Singapore would be unable to import any water from its neighbours before the country becomes self-sufficient in 2060 is not as far-fetched as it may seem, experts say. Currently, water from Johor River helps to meet half of Singapore's water needs. Under the 1962 Water Agreement between Singapore and the Johor state government—which expires in 2061—Singapore can draw up to 250 million gallons of water per day (mgd) from the river ("Malaysia to Work with Singapore", 2016).

The task: Will Singapore be able to wean herself from a condition of water dependency to one of self-sufficiency and sustainability?

Teacher notes

Water sustainability may be roughly thought of as being achieved if the supply of water must be greater than or equal to the demand of water over a period of time. For this task, therefore, we wish to investigate if water supply will meet water demand from the present time to 2061, in the event that Malaysia stops supplying Singapore with water before the agreement expires.

44 *Empirical modelling*

Table 3.1 Water supply and usage in Singapore in 2016

Water demand (about 430 million gallons/day)	Water supply	Population and usage
Domestic: 45% Non-domestic: 55%	Local catchment and Imported water: at least 45% of demand NEWater: up to 30% of demand Desalination: up to 25% of demand	5,607.3 million Per capita domestic daily consumption: 151 L

Table 3.2 Projected water supply and usage in Singapore in 2060

Water demand (double that in 2016)	Water supply	Population and usage
Domestic: 30% Non-domestic: 70%	Local catchment and Imported water: at least 15% of demand NEWater: up to 55% of demand Desalination: up to 30% of demand	6.68 million Per capita domestic daily consumption: 140 L (by 2030)

The mathematical problem can be formulated by considering these two questions: (a) how much water will Singapore residents use from now to 2061?; and (b) how much water can they obtain from Malaysia between now and 2061? Students can search online for information on the sources of water supply and water demand in Singapore, and for any relevant data. For instance, the projected data on water sources can be obtained from various publications posted by the Public Utilities Board (PUB), Singapore's National Water Agency (see for instance, the March 2017 or 24 October 2017 reports). The current and projected data on water demand and supply obtained from the PUB are given in Tables 3.1 and 3.2.

The sources of water supply for Singapore, commonly known to the people in that country as the "Four National Taps", are imported water, local catchment water, *NEWater* and desalinated water. Imported water and local catchment water is water that Singapore buys from Malaysia and water from the local reservoirs or from rain, respectively. *NEWater* is the term used in Singapore for recycled water, of course, after undergoing very advanced treatment. Desalinated water comes from the seawater through the desalination plants built across the island.

Water supply and demand for water are affected and influenced by many important factors. Based on the water sources, students can identify and justify their choices of the important factors for water supply. For example, changes in the climate could affect the frequency and quantity of rainfall. The water levels in *Linggiu* Reservoir and Singapore's water-catchment areas will also be affected by rising temperatures (which cause more extensive evaporation of water). The country's water-catchment areas currently occupy about two-thirds of the island's land area, and the government hopes to expand this to 90 per cent by 2060.

Though there are plans to increase the production of *NEWater* and desalinated water, the costs of production, which include energy costs, manpower costs, costs of land and capital, may also rise. Meanwhile, Singaporeans are encouraged to reduce their daily consumption of water, and water conservation measures are also encouraged in the non-domestic sector (for industrial and commercial uses). Nonetheless, demand for water will continue to increase in tandem with population and economic growth, since the effect of any reduction in domestic daily consumption or non-domestic consumption on the water demand may not be as significant.

A suggested approach

First, we can study the data on water demand and water supply in the recent years (in Table 3.3) to examine the trends. Past data on domestic and non-domestic sales of water, and past data on water supply (amount of used water treated) can be retrieved from the PUB's 2016 report (see the 26 September 2016 report). Assuming that "Used water treated" refers to the water supplied over the years, a plot showing the supply and total demand data can be constructed using *Excel*.

For simplicity, we can assume an overall linear increasing trend for both demand and supply data in the plot in Figure 3.3. Note that the lines of best fit for the two data sets have been inserted using the "Add Trendline" function in *Excel*.

Based on the trend for water demand between 2008 and 2015 as shown above, we can assume a linearly increasing demand trend from 2016 to 2060 (when the projected demand roughly doubles the amount in 2015). Suppose that, despite possible increasing costs of production, Singapore is still able to increase the production of *NEWater* and desalinated water up to the projected amount (85% of demand) in 2060 due to improved technology and sufficient funds. In addition, we can assume a linear trend to simplify the variation of *NEWater* and desalinated water produced with time. If Malaysia is unable to

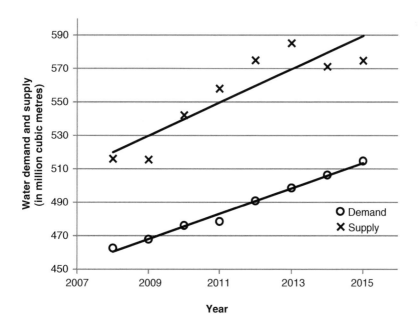

Figure 3.3 Water demand and supply data (2008 to 2015)

46 Empirical modelling

Table 3.3 Water supply and water demand in Singapore from 2008 to 2015

Sales of water (million m³)	2008	2009	2010	2011	2012	2013	2014	2015
Domestic	271.4	277.8	281	281.3	284.4	286.7	291.2	297.1
Non-domestic	191.2	190.1	195.1	197.2	206.5	211.9	215.1	217.6
Total	462.6	467.9	476.1	478.5	490.9	498.6	506.3	514.7
Water supply (million m³)								
Used water treated	516	515.5	542.1	558	575	585.2	571.1	574.8

supply Singapore with the stated amount of water due to a worsening drought or for any other reasons, it can be assumed that the supply decreases linearly to zero between 2016 and 2060 (when Singapore is targeted to be self-sufficient), for simplicity. In addition, if the water collected from expanding local catchment areas can increase steadily over the years to cover about 15% of the demand in 2060 (as projected), there would be an overall increase in supply to meet the demand. The water supply is assumed to follow an approximately linearly increasing trend similar to that seen from 2008 to 2015, based on these assumptions.

For this problem, students mainly need to handle some statistical data and understand some basic ideas about water demand and supply in Singapore. As many factors may affect water demand and water supply, and as there are numerous uncertainties in this problem, it is not possible to predict what will happen exactly and solve the problem entirely. Nevertheless, one main objective of this modelling task is to provide opportunities for students to develop some modelling competencies. In this respect, the following framework is suggested.

Using the framework

Framework Component	"In deep water"
1. WHICH **level** of learning experience?	Level 2.
2. WHAT is the **skill/competency**?	• Understand a real-world problem. • Formulate a mathematical problem. • Identify factors that affect the problem. • Collect/find data. • List and justify assumptions. • Construct a model. • Use of a graphing tool.
3. WHERE is the **mathematics**?	• Statistics. • Functions and their graphs (linear functions).
4. HOW to **solve** the problem/model?	• Obtain the water demand and supply data of past years to see the trend. • Make an assumption on linear increase in demand. • Assume linear trends on the water supply from the different sources. • Discuss the possibility of supply meeting demand in future years.
5. WHY is this experience a **success**?	In this lesson, students learn about: • representing a real-world problem in a mathematical form, • identifying factors and making simplifying assumptions, • interpreting real data and constructing approximating functions to data points.

Possible discussion points

It may not be easy for students to formulate the mathematical problem in this task and to devise a solution method without exploration or some form of intervention and facilitation by the teachers. Teachers can guide students using the discussion points below:

- Discuss what it means to have water self-sufficiency and water sustainability.
- How can we formulate the mathematical problem?
- Identify the sources of water demand and water supply.
- What are the important factors that influence water demand and water supply?
- Why will the demand for water increase as projected?
- Is the supply of *NEWater* and desalinated water likely to increase (as projected)?
- Will the supply from local catchment areas increase or decrease over time?
- How can we use the data available online?
- State and justify any assumptions made.
- Is the water supply likely to meet the demand in future with changes in the amount of imported water?
- What is a possible mathematical model to represent future water demand and supply?

The problem of ensuring that a country's water supply is sufficient to meet its demand is never a trivial one. Certainly, it is unlikely that a huge, national problem such as this can be solved by students in a classroom. Nonetheless, the point in this modelling task is to expose students to real-life issues and problems, and to see how simple ideas in mathematics can help one understand and appreciate these problems better.

Growing mould

Problem situation: Mould is a form of fungi that may start to grow on bread after a few days of exposure to a humid environment. Bread mould typically appears as a green or black substance. It can grow easily on bread because bread retains moisture and is often stored at room temperature. One should discard mouldy food as eating it can cause illnesses like nausea, vomiting and also respiratory problems (if inhaled). Now, how quickly does mould grow on bread? Factories producing bread can use the growth rate of bread mould to estimate the amount of preservatives needed to stop mould from growing, or to estimate the expiry dates of their products. In this section, we are interested in the following task.

The task: Construct a mathematical model for the growth of mould on a piece of bread.

Teacher notes

An empirical approach may be used to tackle the problem in this task. The way in which mould grows on bread may first be studied by actually growing mould on some pieces of bread, and taking measurements of the amount of mould that has grown over a period of time. The collected data should provide some idea on what kind of function may be used to represent the growth, and the relevant parameters in the model can then be estimated. The model may be refined later if necessary.

The amount of mould on the bread may be recorded by taking pictures of a piece of bread each day as mould grows on it, and measuring the areas covered by the mould.

48 Empirical modelling

Factors that may affect the growth of mould include the environment, and the size, weight, volume and type of bread. During data collection, we need to ensure consistency in the measurements. In addition, some assumptions need to be made. For example, environmental factors such as the amount of light, heat and dampness should be (or are assumed to be) constant throughout the period of data collection.

Assuming that the areas of bread mould are the same on both sides of the bread slice, we only need to obtain data using one side of the bread. If the task was to be extended to compare the growth rates of different bread types, then all other variables (size of bread, surrounding temperature, etc) should be the same for the different types. Another possible extension or variation of the task above is to investigate the effect of temperature on the growth rate. That is, mould is grown on different slices of bread of the same type and size at different constant temperatures to observe that a higher temperature leads to faster mould growth. Bags containing mouldy bread should not be opened and if students were to touch mould accidentally, they should wash their hands thoroughly.

A suggested approach

The process of growing mould on bread should take place over a sufficiently long period of time (typically, say, 10 to 14 days) to ensure that there is sufficient data available to construct a meaningful model. To prepare, sprinkle some water onto a fresh piece of bread and leave it exposed for a few hours. This could help the fungi spores in the air to settle on the bread and produce results more quickly and readily.

Next, place the bread in a sealable plastic bag, seal it and leave it in a warm, damp place (for example, under the kitchen sink). Using a square grid placed on the bread, the total area of the bread may be estimated. Pictures of the bread with the grid should be taken every day at around the same time of the day, to serve as a record of the changes in the bread. The area covered by the mould may be estimated from these pictures, and these will correspond to the amount of mould that has grown on the piece of bread.

As an example, the circled portion in Figure 3.4 is enlarged in Figure 3.5 (taken from Ang, 2012). For this portion, the area covered by mould is estimated to be around $2\,\text{cm}^2$. Using the collected data, a model may be constructed.

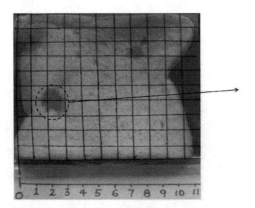

Figure 3.4 Estimating the amount of mould

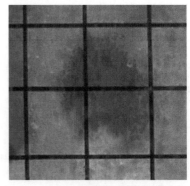

Figure 3.5 Example of an estimate

Suppose that we denote the time in days by t (the independent variable), and the amount of area covered by mould (in cm^2) at time t is denoted by $x(t)$ (the dependent variable). That is, $x(t)$ represents the *population* of the mould at time t. We can first plot the graph of $x(t)$ against t using *Excel* and discuss what we can interpret from the graph (in Figure 3.6).

From the set of data shown in Figure 3.6, it can be seen that the area of bread covered by mould (representing the "population" of mould) increases slowly in the first two days. After that, it increases rapidly over the next few days, and towards the final days of the experiment, the increase slows down, and the amount of mould seems to tend towards a constant.

This growth pattern is quite typical for populations of micro-organisms in an environment constrained by space and nutrient resource. In this case, mould starts to grow slowly, and then rapidly and later as resources are depleted, the growth slows down. This is a characteristic of the *logistic growth* model.

Therefore, a possible way to fit the data points is to use a logistic equation $g(t) = \dfrac{N}{1 + Ae^{-kt}}$, where k is the growth rate and N is the carrying capacity (the maximum sustainable population). The logistic equation is a well-known model used in population dynamics studies. As discussed in Chapter 1, using the Solver tool in *Excel*, we can find the values of the parameters, A, k and N that best fit the set of data points. In this case, the values are found to be $A = 62.0$, $k = 1.2295$, $N = 94.5$ and the graphs of the data points and the model are plotted as shown in Figure 3.7.

Students may not have any knowledge of the logistic equation, but it is possible to highlight to them the different ways in which populations are modelled prior to the modelling activity. The two most common models are the exponential growth and the logistic growth models. There are extensive online discussions on these models. If students are familiar with first-order differential equations, then the approach could be from the construction of first-order differential equations that model the logistic growth.

As the mathematical concepts and skills required in this problem are of a slightly higher level than that seen in the two problems discussed earlier, teachers may wish to use this activity only for students who have a slightly higher level of mathematical knowledge; for instance, students in Grade 10 and above. Teachers can use the following framework to structure their modelling activities.

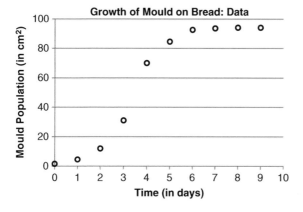

Figure 3.6 Plot of data collected over ten days

50   Empirical modelling

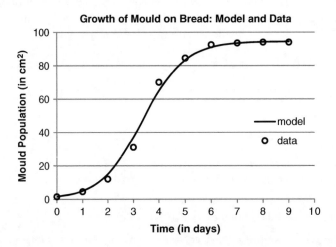

Figure 3.7 Graph of data points and the logistic model

Using the framework

Framework Component	"Growing mould"
1. WHICH **level** of learning experience? 2. WHAT is the **skill/competency**?	Level 2. • Identify the many factors affecting the problem. • List several assumptions. • Collect data carefully. • Interpretation of data. • Construct a model. • Use of a graphing tool.
3. WHERE is the **mathematics**?	Logistic function $(t) = \dfrac{N}{1 + Ae^{-kt}}$, which is the solution of a differential equation of the form $\dfrac{dx}{dt} = ax(1 - bx)$.
4. HOW to **solve** the problem/model?	• Collect data by recording the area of bread mould formed over days. • Plot the population of bread mould vs time in *Excel*. • If the logistic model is to be used, employ the Solver tool in *Excel* to find the parameters that give a good fit, and discuss the physical meaning of the parameters.
5. WHY is this experience a **success**?	In this lesson, students will have the opportunity to learn the following: • conditions affecting population growth, • the way to grow mould on bread, • graphing skills or use of the Solver tool in *Excel*, • understanding/using a model for population growth.

Possible discussion points

For this task, students need to carry out an experiment to collect data and to analyse the results. From the data collection process to formulating the mathematical model, they may require some assistance from the teachers. The following guiding questions could facilitate the process:

- What is bread mould?
- Why would we want to investigate how it grows?
- What are some factors that should be considered when studying its growth?
- What reasonable assumptions can we make?
- How can we measure the amount of mould over time as accurately as possible?
- What can we interpret about the mould growth over time from the plotted data?
- What kind of functions can be used to approximate the data?
- Do the parameters in the constructed model have any physical meaning?

While investigating the growth of bread mould provides a good introduction to the study of population dynamics, it can be quite challenging. There are other modelling activities that can also be considered. For instance, one could try to model the growth of beansprouts by first measuring their heights over time, and then finding a suitable function to represent the data. The key is to get students to take measurements and collect data in a real physical setting before using them to construct a suitable mathematical model.

Pass it on

One of the most critical parts of a relay race is the passing of the baton from one runner (preceding) to the next (succeeding).

Problem situation: The school's sports day is around the corner. You and your friends are participating in the 4 × 100 m relay race event, in which four runners in the team will complete 100 metres each and then pass a baton to the next runner. You would like to use mathematics to improve the time taken to finish a race, which depends on many factors (Smith and Radford, 2002). These factors include the following:

(a) the 100 m completion times of the individual runners,
(b) the running order of the athletes,
(c) the position where a preceding runner should be when the succeeding runner starts their sprint,
(d) the method of baton passing used, and
(e) the distance between the preceding and succeeding runners at each of the baton exchanges (or free distance).

In this activity, we will focus on answering the question stated below.

The task: At what point should a preceding runner be when a succeeding runner starts his sprint so as to achieve a better overall timing for a 4 × 100 m relay race?

Teacher notes

Students can first be introduced to this activity by being shown a video clip of an actual relay race (for instance, YouTube video posted by Olympic, 2012), with focus on a video segment where a group of succeeding runners start running until they obtain the batons from their preceding runners. It is common to see each succeeding runner begins running

52 *Empirical modelling*

from his position when he sees the preceding runner reaching some point behind him, that is, a check mark.

There are three common ways to pass a baton in a relay race. The *upsweep* method, in which the preceding runner passes the baton up into the succeeding runner's hand. The *downsweep* method where the receiving arm is extended with the hand almost like a V-shape, with baton landing between the thumb and first finger. The *push pass* method, where the receiving arm is extended out parallel to the ground with the thumb pointing down. Transferring of the baton in such a race must be done in an exchange zone, which is usually marked by coloured lines or triangles and is 20 m long. The distance between the standing position of each succeeding runner and the start of the respective exchange zone is usually fixed at 10 m.

The position of the check mark depends on the "running profiles" of the preceding and succeeding runners and the free distance. A running profile shows how one's speed varies with time. For an athlete in a race, it can be a "distance-time" graph starting with the runner accelerating from rest before maintaining a maximum constant speed and then decelerating (in many cases). It is assumed that the preceding runner will approach the check mark at his maximum constant speed and the succeeding runner will accelerate from rest. The placement of the check mark will therefore determine whether the runners can exchange the baton "at the same speed" inside the exchange zone to ensure a smooth baton pass and to improve the overall race timing. If the succeeding runner starts too early, he will have to run at a slower speed to accommodate the preceding runner. If the succeeding runner starts too late, clearly the overall race timing will also be increased.

The mathematical problem is thus to determine an optimal position for the check mark, so that the succeeding runner will achieve a speed that matches the top speed of the preceding runner, while staying within the exchange zone.

A suggested approach

Everyone has his own unique "running profile" – that is, we accelerate from rest, and achieve our top speed in a sprint differently. It therefore seems logical to first establish the running profiles of each individual team member in order to tackle this problem. An exercise can be carried out to construct the running profiles of the chosen preceding and succeeding runners in their respective groups. Markers can be placed at regular intervals (for example, 10 m for the preceding runner and 2 m for the succeeding runner) and videos can be recorded of the preceding runner doing a 50 m sprint and the succeeding runner doing a 30 m sprint. We assume that an average secondary school student may take about 50 m to reach his maximum speed. The students can then use the two running profiles to determine the check mark. Assuming that the preceding runner is at his maximum constant speed starting from the time when the succeeding runner starts his sprint (for simplicity), we may obtain running profiles similar to those shown in Figure 3.8.

If we were to assume further, a free distance of 0m and that the runners exchange the baton at the same speed within the exchange zone, we can then match the two graphs. This is as shown in Figure 3.9. That is, insert a tangent line at the point on the running profile of the succeeding runner that is parallel to the running profile of the preceding runner, and obtain its y-intercept. The distance between the check mark and the standing position of the succeeding runner is then obtained and the students can validate their solution in the field.

An exchange zone and standing position of a succeeding runner can be marked and students can try different check marks and do several trial runs with baton exchanges using the same chosen baton passing method, to understand the problem better. The students can

Empirical modelling 53

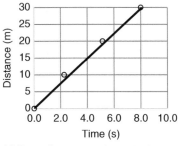
(a) Preceding runner at constant maximum speed

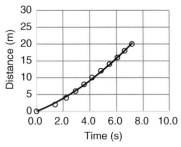
(b) Succeeding runner starting from rest

Figure 3.8 Distance-speed graphs of the preceding runner at maximum speed and succeeding runner starting from rest

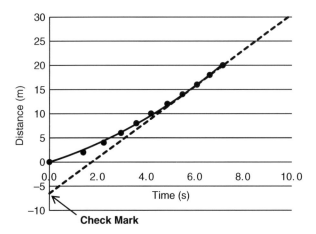

Figure 3.9 Top speeds of the preceding and succeeding runners

use this running profile to get an average speed (say, by plotting the line of best fit over an interval when the speed does not change much) and then use it to obtain his approximate running profile over the 30 m.

For this problem, the required mathematical concepts and skills of students are quite basic. Hence, we recommend that it be posed to students from the lower secondary levels onwards. The following framework can guide teachers in structuring their modelling activities.

Using the framework

Framework Component	*"Pass it on"*
1. WHICH **level** of Learning Experience?	Level 3.
2. WHAT is the **skill/competency**?	• Identify the various factors involved.
	• Consider important assumptions.

54 Empirical modelling

Framework Component	"Pass it on"
	• Collect data accurately using teamwork. • Use of a graphing tool. • Construct a model. • Validate the model.
3. WHERE is the **mathematics**?	• Polynomial graphs (e.g., linear and quadratic) and their tangents lines. • Graphical relationships among distance, speed, and acceleration with time.
4. HOW to **solve** the problem/model?	• Collect data to find the running profiles of the preceding and succeeding runners over 50 m and 30 m respectively. • For the preceding runner, use his maximum speed to obtain his approximate running profile over 30 m (from the standing position of the succeeding runner to the end of the exchange zone). • Find a point on the running profile of the succeeding runner that has a tangent line parallel to the running profile of the preceding runner, and obtain the y-intercept of this tangent line.
5. WHY is this experience a **success**?	In this lesson, students learn about: • factors affecting a relay race, • teamwork involved in modelling, • careful data collection, • some graphing skills and interpretations of graphs, • testing if the solution obtained is suitable.

Possible discussion points

Though this modelling activity does not involve high-level mathematics, it is nevertheless non-trivial to solve the problem. We suggest that teachers provide guidance through some points of discussion similar to the following:

- What are the factors that affect relay race timings?
- State your observations from the video segment when a group of succeeding runners starts their sprint to when they do the baton exchanges.
- What factors affect the position of a check mark?
- How does the chosen check mark affect overall timing?
- How can a baton exchange be done?
- Can a baton exchange occur if the runners are at different speeds?
- What does the "running profile" of a person commonly look like?
- What may the running profiles of the preceding and succeeding runners from the standing position of the succeeding runner to the end of the exchange zone be like?
- How can we formulate the problem mathematically?
- What assumptions can we make in finding the check mark?
- How can we use the running profiles to determine the check mark?

- Is the solution obtained suitable?
- In what way(s) can we improve on the solution obtained?

This activity requires students to do some physical activity, namely, running or sprinting. For some, it would be a good break from having lessons in the classroom, but for others, they may not be keen to participate as it can be physically demanding. In addition, mathematics teachers may not be trained in carrying out Physical Education (PE) activities. One suggestion is for the mathematics teacher to collaborate with a PE teacher in this task, so that the entire activity can be meaningfully carried out and in a safe manner.

To cross or not to cross?

Problem situation: Marked pedestrian crossings are placed on busy roads at locations where pedestrians need assistance to cross the road safely. These are usually at roads where vehicle numbers, vehicle speeds or road widths make it vulnerable for road users (such as children and the elderly) to cross the road, or where there is a huge volume of pedestrian traffic. At times, pedestrian crossings may also be created to slow down heavy road traffic intentionally. Some examples of pedestrian crossings are push button crossing, zebra crossing, pedestrian overhead bridge, and pedestrian underpass.

The task: Consider a situation where the road in front of a school currently does not have any pedestrian crossing. Construct a model for deciding whether a pedestrian crossing for a road in front of a school is necessary, and if so, where should it be placed.

Teacher notes

There are many factors determining whether we should introduce a pedestrian crossing, the location for a crossing and the type of crossing to construct. In addition, there are usually certain government guidelines to adhere to. For example, according to the Land Transport and Authority (LTA) guidelines in Singapore, the effect of proposing any pedestrian crossing along a road on the traffic flow will be analysed, and other crossings such as an overhead bridge or underpass will be considered if they are deemed more appropriate. In this way, there can be a balance between ensuring road safety for pedestrians and maintaining smooth traffic for motorists. In addition, there should be provision for pedestrian crossings to bus stops and mass rapid transit stations. However, a pedestrian crossing along a road should not be located too close to an entrance or exit of a development, or to uncontrolled junctions (say between a main road and a side road). This is to ensure, for example, that drivers have adequate time to see a crossing and to brake safely. Furthermore, in deciding on the location for a crossing along the road, pedestrians must be able to see approaching traffic. Visibility should not be obscured by, for example, parked vehicles or trees. Additional, care should be taken when considering wheelchair users and school children.

For simplicity, suppose that the relevant guidelines above have been adequately considered and a suitable location for any pedestrian crossing (if necessary) can be found. We can then focus on the following condition: *Pedestrians can cross if and only if the time t between two successive vehicles passing point P is greater than the time T taken to cross the road*. Figure 3.10 illustrates the situation.

56 Empirical modelling

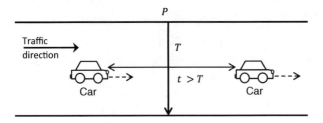

Figure 3.10 A diagrammatic representation of the condition for safe crossing

This condition translates into the mathematical statement: a pedestrian crossing is needed if and only if $t < T$. The time t depends on the speed and arrival times of vehicles at the point, and the time T depends on the width of the road and the walking speed of pedestrians. Therefore, these factors will determine the necessity of a pedestrian crossing.

A suggested approach

We can start by making some assumptions to simplify the problem. For example, assuming that pedestrians cross the road at a constant average speed v, and w is the width of the road considered, the time $T = \dfrac{w}{v}$ can be easily found. To illustrate this, suppose that the width of a small street is 2.8 m and pedestrians walk at an average speed of about 1.73 m/s. Then, we will obtain $T \approx 1.62$ s.

Further, if we assume that vehicles travel at a constant speed (for instance, equal to the speed limit for that street) and they arrive at regular time intervals based on the *safe distance* between them. The safe distance between vehicles depends on the reaction time (time for a driver to react to a situation) and the braking distance (actual distance taken to stop after the brakes are applied). Assuming that the speed limit of motor vehicles travelling along an ordinary road in a residential area is 50 km/h (or 13.89 m/s). The safe distance corresponding to this speed is 23 m. Hence we can take the safe distance to be 23 m here for simplicity. The time t can then be calculated to be approximately 1.66 s. Based on these values of T and t, it appears a pedestrian crossing is probably not necessary.

However, taking into consideration the fact that in general, school children walk at a slower speed than an average person, and that the difference between T and t is just 0.04 s, the decision may require some re-thinking. This approach, therefore, may be too simplistic and therefore unrealistic, and not very useful.

The model can be improved by looking at real data. For example, the amount of time taken by different students to walk a distance equal to the road width can be collected and T can be the average time taken. We shall assume that a pedestrian crosses a road at his usual walking speed. In addition, students can monitor the road traffic in front of their school over a certain peak period, to obtain the shortest time interval between successive vehicles passing a certain point (that is suitable as a location for a pedestrian crossing). Using this as the value of t, they can then check if a crossing is necessary.

Another possible improvement is to use the model suggested by Berry and Houston (1995: pp. 12–15). As proposed, it can be assumed that a pedestrian crossing will be installed if p, the probability of a gap of time interval greater than a certain value, is less than some pre-determined value, p_0. That is, let us assume that a time interval between two successive vehicles greater than 2 s is deemed safe for pedestrians to cross. Then students can use their data on time intervals between vehicles to obtain the value

$$p = \frac{\text{number of time intervals greater than 2 s}}{\text{total number of time intervals}},$$

and check if it is smaller than p_0 (an acceptable minimum probability below which crossing will not be installed).

If students have deeper knowledge in Probability and Statistics, a more realistic solution can be developed by modelling the arrival times of vehicles and pedestrians, say using a Poisson distribution, and considering the waiting times of pedestrians (e.g., see Mesterton-Gibbons, 2011: pp. 187–89).

We can see from the above that there can be several approaches to study the problem, and only basic concepts in speed, time, distance, probability and statistics are needed for simple models. Therefore, teachers can pose this problem to students from lower secondary level onwards. The following framework can assist teachers in structuring their modelling activities.

Using the framework

Framework Component	"To cross or not to cross"
1. WHICH **level** of Learning Experience?	Level 3.
2. WHAT is the **skill/competency**?	• Translating a real-life problem into a mathematical problem. • Identify the many factors involved. • Consider simplifying assumptions. • Carry out data collection. • Construct a mathematical model.
3. WHERE is the **mathematics**?	• Basic distance, speed, time concepts. • Basic probability and statistics (use of averages).
4. HOW to **solve** the problem/model?	• A model can be constructed by first collecting data on the times taken by students to walk a distance equal to the width of road considered. The average of these times can be used as f. • Students can then collect data on the time intervals between successive vehicles in front of their school to find the shortest time interval between successive vehicles, and use it as t. • Recommend the installation of a pedestrian crossing if $t < f$. • If students are familiar with basic probability, data on time intervals between successive vehicles can be used to find p, the probability of a gap of time interval greater than a certain value (e.g., a "safe" time needed by pedestrians to cross a road). A pedestrian crossing can then be introduced if p is less than some p_0.

Framework Component	"To cross or not to cross"
5. WHY is this experience a **success**?	In this lesson, students learn about: • the many realistic and safety issues surrounding a pedestrian crossing, • working with quantifiable factors to formulate a mathematical model, • making assumptions and understanding the limitations of a model formed based on the assumptions, • careful data collection, • validation of models (e.g., if the first simple model was constructed, real data can be collected to see if the solution was reasonable), • refinement of models.

Possible discussion points

There is a good chance that students will be able to relate the walking speeds of an average person to the average speeds of vehicles when looking at this problem. However, they probably require some assistance in actually formulating the problem properly. Teachers can facilitate the discussions in this modelling task by asking the following questions:

- What are the factors or variables in this problem?
- What would be a condition for safe crossing by a pedestrian?
- List the assumptions made for your mathematical model.
- What data do we need to collect?
- Is the result obtained reasonable?
- What are some limitations of your model?
- How can your model be improved on?

A note of caution: if teachers do want students to collect real data outside, the saftey of the students' should be of paramount importance. To avoid having too many school children standing by the side of the road doing data collection, one suggestion is to have a couple of representatives with cameras set up to capture the traffic along the road. Students may then view the video and estimate the relevant and required values.

Bibliography

Ang, K.C. (2012). Mathematical modelling as a learning experience in the classroom. *Proceedings of the 17th Asian Technology Conference in Mathematics*, Bangkok, Thailand (pp. 84–92).

Berry, J. and Houston, K. (1995). *Mathematical Modelling*. London: Edward Arnold.

Blum, W. and Borromeo Ferri, R. (2009). Mathematical modelling: Can it be taught and learnt? *Journal of Mathematical Modelling and Application*, 1(1), 45–58.

Giles, E. and Vallandigham, P.H. (1991). Height estimation from foot and shoeprint length. *Journal of Forensic Sciences* 36(4), 1134–51.

Malaysia to work with Singapore to honour share of water under 1962 agreement: Najib. (2016, December 13). *TODAYonline*. Retrieved from www.todayonline.com/singapore/malaysia-work-singapore-honour-share-water-under-1962-agreement-najib.

Mesterton-Gibbons, M. (2011). *A Concrete Approach to Mathematical Modelling.* Hoboken: John Wiley and Sons, Inc.

Olympics. (2012, August 10). *Men's 4× 100m round 1 highlights – Jamaica & USA win – London 2012 Olympics* [Video file]. Retrieved from www.youtube.com/watch?v=JYsusrFHGdg.

Public Utilities Board, Singapore's National Water Agency. (2016, September 26). *Sales of potable water* [Data file]. Retrieved from https://data.gov.sg/dataset/sale-of-potable-water?view_id=385c3411-2e46-47ec-9664-b55f5acf0403&resource_id=c5aba1a6-f3e2-4ed4-882e-0a4ce14ef9ed.

Public Utilities Board, Singapore's National Water Agency. (2016, September 26). Water supply – used water treated [Data file]. Retrieved from https://data.gov.sg/dataset/water-supply-used-water-treated?view_id=e3e33f51-36f6-42d4-83a1-fa789cbfeac9&resource_id=7f3539ee-13b0-477d-85d7-1f8483d3eb3a.

Public Utilities Board, Singapore's National Water Agency. (2017, March 15). *Our water our* future. Retrieved from www.pub.gov.sg/Documents/PUBOurWaterOurFuture.pdf.

Public Utilities Board, Singapore's National Water Agency. (2017, October 24). *Singapore water story.* Retrieved from www.pub.gov.sg/watersupply/singaporewaterstory.

Robbins, L.M. (1986). Estimating height and weight from size of footprints. *Journal of Forensic Sciences, 31*(1), 143–52.

Smith, A.J. and Radford, P.F. (2002). A mathematical analysis of the 4 × 100 m relay. *Journal of Sports Sciences,* 20, 369–81.

StateCollegeSpikes. (2009, July 9). *CSI: State college, clue 3* [Video file]. Retrieved from www.youtube.com/watch?v=YgBpCfQVfzE&feature=youtu.be.

Tan, L.S. (2015). *Professional Development for Teachers of Mathematical Modelling in Singapore.* Unpublished thesis, submitted for the degree of Doctor of Philosophy, Nanyang Technological University, Singapore.

4   Deterministic modelling

Introduction

Many situations in life involve factors or variables that are related by some formula in some way. Sometimes, it is possible to study the dynamics of the variables, and then construct an equation, a formula, a table or an algorithm that could possibly help us solve certain problems. In a decision-making model, for instance, the idea is to find a way to make the best decision based on whatever knowledge we have of the factors that influence the decision. Such a model could be in the form of an equation, or just a decision table. There could also be physical phenomena that we wish to understand better through a mathematical model. In fact, the well-known Newton's laws of motion are mathematical models for the motion of particles in an ideal environment.

A model constructed by examining the relationships among the variables of the problem, and creating equations, formulae or rules based on these relationships is called a deterministic model. In some sense, given a set of values for the independent variables, the model yields a result or outcome that addresses the problem. In other words, once the model is fixed, the outcome is more or less determined by the values of the variables in the model.

Correct me if I'm wrong

Problem situation: A correction tape is a piece of stationery used to erase and cover erroneous printed or handwritten text. After application, the area covered can usually be written over immediately. Many school children and students use correction tapes to correct mistakes when doing their schoolwork. There are many different brands and designs of correction tapes, and they come in different shapes and sizes, as depicted in Figure 4.1. For example, they can come in pen-style with ergonomic designs, as paper-based or polyester film-based tapes, and as those with gear or belt mechanisms. With so many different brands and types of correction tapes in the market, one natural question to ask would be: which is the *best* correction tape?

The task: Construct a model that can be used to decide on the *best* correction tape.

Teacher notes

To approach this problem, we first need to decide on what is meant by the *best* correction tape. The factors or variables that affect the choice of a correction tape include its price, availability, aesthetic appeal, ease of use (for example, ergonomic design, smooth application or tear resistant) and effectiveness (which could include blocking of the ink and ease

Deterministic modelling 61

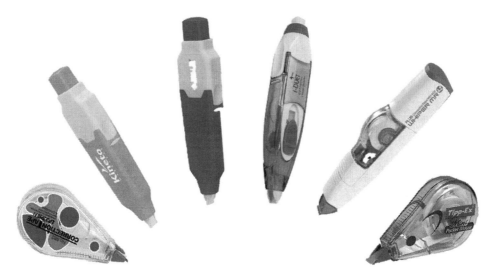

Figure 4.1 Examples of correction tapes

of writing over covered parts). Teachers may motivate the activity by first asking students to share what correction tapes they are using, where the correction tapes are purchased and their reasons for choosing a particular type or brand. They can collate the information in groups and share the information with the whole class, and then discuss the factors that contribute to their choice. This process would help students to *identify the factors* in the problem. Following the discussion, students will then try to find a way to quantify the factors, with a view to constructing a mathematical model to decide on the best correction tape.

A suggested approach

For simplicity, let's assume that a correction tape's price, availability, ease of use and effectiveness are the four chosen factors or criteria that would determine the selection of the best correction tape among, say, six brands of tapes (most commonly used by students). Here we are assuming that the "best tape" is among the most popular ones and all the factors are equally important. Students can collect data relevant to each of the chosen factor and rank the tapes accordingly.

To quantify the factors, points for each factor are given to each brand of correction tapes based on the ranks. For instance, if we are considering six brands, the top ranked brand for a certain factor may be given 6 points for that factor. The next highest ranked brand gets 5 points, and so on, with the points decreasing in a linear fashion. Brands with tied ranks may be given the same points.

As an illustration, consider the price of correction tapes. Let's assume that the prices of correction tapes do not vary across different stores or shops. A simple survey would reveal that correction tapes do come in different lengths, and some may be sold with a refill as a set; therefore, care needs to be taken when comparing prices. One way to overcome such differences is to calculate the price of each correction tape based on its *price per unit length*,

62 Deterministic modelling

or unit price. Therefore, the correction tapes can be ranked in terms of their unit prices, with a cheaper brand allocated a higher rank for the price factor. Table 4.1 shows the points scored by the six brands, A to F, of correction tapes based on their ranking in terms of unit prices.

As another illustration, consider availability. The correction tape that is sold in more stores can be ranked higher in terms of availability. Students may be asked to look for these brands of correction tapes in their local bookstores, including their school bookstore. Table 4.1 shows a sample of tabulated findings for six brands of correction tapes and four bookstores (namely, the school bookstore, *Popular Bookstore*, *Kinokuniya* and *Times*). An "NA" in the table entry indicates that that brand of correction tape is not available in the corresponding bookstore.

Let's denote the points for the brands of correction tape in the different categories by p_{xy} where the subscript x represents the factor or category, and the subscript y denotes the brand. For example, suppose factor 1 refers to "unit price" and factor 2 represents "availability", then the points for correction tape A in terms of these factors are $p_{1A} = 5$ and $p_{2A} = 3$ respectively.

To rank the correction tapes based on the other two factors (ease of use and effectiveness), students can try using all the six brands of tape and rank them accordingly. One needs to be mindful that a criterion like "ease of use" can be subjective and may depend on several factors. For example, while some may focus on the smoothness when the tape is used, others may consider the amount of pressure required to run over the paper. All these could contribute to some variance in the data collected, but in general, if the sample size is large enough, the data can provide useful information for one to do some ranking.

A correction tape's effectiveness can be assessed or judged by the amount of "bleeding" that occurs after it has been applied over the erroneous writing. Here, "bleeding" refers to the condition in which the ink (or printed material) can still be seen through the correction tape. An effective correction tape would be such that the erased (or "correction-taped") words or writing are completely covered and blocked. In addition, the tape should dry up quickly enough to be written on or typed over.

When the rankings in all the factors for all the brands are tabulated, the final total points for any particular brand can be computed as a sum of all the points. For instance, for Brand A, the total, P_A is

$$P_A = p_{1A} + p_{2A} + p_{3A} + p_{4A}.$$

Table 4.1 Unit price (price per metre) of tapes in stores and the ranks

Store \ Brand	A	B	C	D	E	F
School bookstore	NA	0.380	NA	NA	0.290	0.264
Popular bookstore	0.287	0.383	0.290	0.361	0.290	NA
Kinokuniya	NA	0.383	NA	0.363	NA	0.271
Times	0.287	0.382	NA	NA	0.291	0.271
Lowest price	0.287	0.380	0.290	0.361	0.290	0.264
Points (unit price)	5	1	4	2	4	6
Points (availability)	3	6	1	3	5	5

Deterministic modelling 63

Table 4.2 Ranking of tapes corresponding to each factor and the final ranking for each brand of tape

Factor \ Brand	A	B	C	D	E	F
Price	5	1	4	2	4	6
Availability	3	6	1	3	5	5
Ease of use	1	5	4	6	3	2
Effectiveness	2	5	3	6	4	1
Total Points	11	17	12	17	16	14

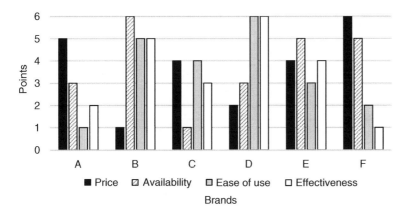

Figure 4.2 Comparison of points scored by each brand, for each factor considered

The brand of correction tape with the highest total would then be the best tape. All the results can be tabulated. A sample is shown in Table 4.2.

To compare the points scored by each of the six brands of correction tapes in the four factors, a bar chart as shown in Figure 4.2 can be plotted. In this case, it is evident that Brands B and D have emerged with higher points, and the clear "loser" is Brand C.

To improve the model, we note that certain factors may be considered more important than others. For instance, effectiveness may be seen as a more important factor to consider than the unit price. Students can rank the importance of the factors and place heavier emphasis on the more important ones in a refined model. This could be done by multiplying p_{xy} by some weights.

For example, suppose that w_i $(i = 1,...,4)$ represents the weighting of factor i, with $\sum_{i=1}^{4} w_i = 1$. The weighted points for Brand A is then

$$P_A = w_1 p_{1A} + w_2 p_{2A} + w_3 p_{3A} + w_4 p_{4A}.$$

A similar formula can be obtained for all the other brands and the brand with the highest weighted total points would then be the best brand of correction tape.

To find a solution to this task, students need some elementary statistical knowledge. Thus this problem can be posed to students from lower secondary level onwards. Teachers can make use of the following framework to design their modelling activity.

Using the framework

Framework Component	"Correct me if I'm wrong"
1. WHICH **level** of learning experience?	Level 2.
2. WHAT is the **skill/competency**?	• Identifying the many factors or variables involved. • Finding a mathematical representation of a task. • Making reasonable assumptions to simplify a problem. • Different data collection methods. • Use of *Excel* in data representation. • Model refinement.
3. WHERE is the **mathematics**?	• Statistics (e.g., use of averages, data representations and statistical analysis).
4. HOW to **solve** the problem/model?	• Choose the factors that determine the best tape. • For each factor, rank the tapes using collected data, with a higher rank corresponding to lower price, greater availability, easier usage and better coverage of errors. • Calculate the final (total) rank for each tape and pick the tape with the highest rank.
5. WHY is this experience a **success**?	In this lesson, students learn about: • how to quantify factors or variables, • teamwork in careful data collection and analysis, • appropriate forms of data representation, • revisiting of assumptions and improving on models.

Possible discussion points

This modelling activity does not require high-level mathematical knowledge. However, it is still important for teachers to provide some guidance to students in constructing the model. Some of the following questions could be used to guide students:

- What are the possible factors that affect our decision on the "best" correction tape?
- How can we quantify the factors to formulate the problem mathematically?
- What data do we need to collect with regards to each factor? How can we collect it?
- What assumptions do we need to make?
- How can we rank the correction tapes in a fair way?
- How can we represent the data meaningfully?
- Is the solution reasonable? Is there any way to improve on it?

The correction tape activity is a modelling task that can be handled by students in Grades 5 or 6. If students stop at constructing the table and then using the table as a decision-making tool, they may not even realise it is a model. While a table as a mathematical construct certainly qualifies as a mathematical model, it may be useful to point out to students that a simple equation (the sum of all the points) can be derived. In the equation form, the model can be modified (with weights) as one moves to refine and improve the model. This activity, though simple in concept, is rich enough to include the different aspects and components of the process of mathematical modelling.

(a) Parallel parking and 90° parking (b) Angled parking

Figure 4.3 Examples of different types of parking lots

Design and park

If we examine a typical car park, say, in the school compound, we may find that the parking lots are probably demarcated with lines. Here, we use the term "parking lot" to refer to the space occupied by a parked car, and the entire area used for parking cars, usually consisting of many parking lots, is known as the car park. There are many ways to design a car park and mark out the parking lots. For example, a car park could have parallel parking and angled parking lots. The choice of these designs depends on the space available, as well as other factors. Figure 4.3 shows some examples of the different types of parking lots commonly seen.

Problem situation: Consider a space in the school that can be converted to a car park to accommodate the cars parked in the school. Is there a way to design the car park and the layout of the lots as to optimise the space? The following questions can be considered:

- How many cars can be parked side by side along the kerb?
- How much space is needed to accommodate traffic within the car park?

The task: Develop a mathematical model that optimises the use of car parking spaces.

Teacher notes

The common factors or variables that contribute to the design of car park lots include sizes of types of vehicles likely to be parked in these parking lots, space between parking lots, and the dimension of the parking aisle or driveway (for cars to move and turn in to the parking lots). In addition, the layout of car parking lots and parking aisles must be consistent with the requirements specified by the local authorities. For instance, in Singapore, one needs to abide by the guidelines set out by the Land Transport Authority (LTA). As an example, there are minimum dimensions for angled parking lots and parallel parking lots. There is also a minimum requirement for the width of parking aisles corresponding to 30°, 45°, 60° and 90° angled parking lots, based on whether one-way or two-way traffic is allowed, and whether there are parking bays on one or two sides of the car park. In general, the width of parking aisles required increases with the angle as more space is needed for cars to turn in to the parking lots. For educational institutions, there is a minimum number of parking lots required, and this is based on the number of classrooms, staff members and student

66 Deterministic modelling

numbers. For more details, the reader can refer to the code of practice on vehicle parking provision provided by Land Transport Authority (2011). Additional data that students can collect for this task include the following:

- Dimensions of the common vehicles that will require car parking lots in the school.
- The space needed for a driver or passenger to open a door and get in or out of a vehicle comfortably.
- The average distance between parallel parked cars.
- Dimension of the entire car park.

The modelling method for this problem may not be one of those commonly used. One strategy is to do the relevant calculations corresponding to a few possible designs before making a comparison to obtain the *best* design.

A suggested approach

We can calculate the maximum possible number of car parking lots along a given kerb, corresponding to parallel parking lots and 30°, 45°, 60° or 90° angled parking lots, and the distances occupied by the lots perpendicular to the kerb. These designs are considered due to the standard requirements stated in the LTA guidelines. For simplicity, let the average length and width of cars (only) commonly parked in a school compound be L and W respectively, and suppose D is the estimated distance between two parallel-parked cars necessary for entering or exiting a parallel car parking lot (as shown in Figure 4.4). In addition, let f be the space at both sides of the car to allow the driver or passenger to stand beside the vehicle, as shown in the figure.

The dimension of such a parallel parking lot would then be $L + D$ by $W + 2f$. Furthermore, it is not hard to see that the maximum number of parallel parking lots along a given length of kerb is simply

$$\frac{\text{Total length of kerb}}{L + D}.$$

For angled parking lots, suppose that θ is the parking angle, where $0 < \theta \le 90^\circ$, and $x_1 + x_2$ is the width occupied by a lot along the kerb (as shown in Figure 4.5). Let m denote

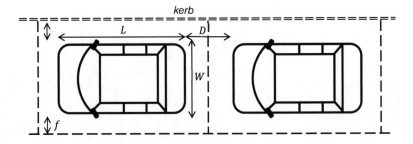

Figure 4.4 Plan view of parallel parking lots

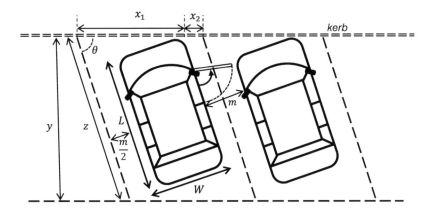

Figure 4.5 Plan view of angled parking lots

the estimated space required by a driver or passenger to enter or exit a vehicle, perpendicular to the length of a car. We can then obtain

$$x_1 = \frac{W + \frac{m}{2}}{\sin \theta} = \frac{2W + m}{2 \sin \theta} \text{ and } x_2 = \frac{m/2}{\sin \theta} = \frac{m}{2 \sin \theta}.$$

The maximum number of angled parking lots along a given kerb is then
$$\frac{\text{Total length of kerb}}{x_1 + x_2}.$$

Next, we calculate y, the perpendicular length of the parking lot measured from the kerb, as shown in the figure, to find the actual space occupied by an angled parking lot. To do so, we obtain the length of the parking lot given by z in Figure 4.5. It is not hard to see that $z = L + x_1 \cos \theta$. Solving for y, we obtain

$$y = z \sin \theta = (L + x_1 \cos \theta) \sin \theta.$$

Using the above formulae for parallel parking lots and angled parking lots with 30°, 45°, 60° or 90° angles, and taking into account the minimum dimensions required of the different parking lots and the minimum width of parking aisles, we can then proceed to compare some or all of the five designs to decide on the optimal design and layout. In addition, cases where one-way or two-way traffic are allowed may need to be considered. A combination of different types of lots can also be considered, though the calculations involved will be more complex.

To build a mathematical model to solve this problem, students need to have a good understanding of trigonometry, taught typically in the lower secondary level. Teachers involved in conducting classes from lower secondary level onwards can use the framework below as a guide.

68 *Deterministic modelling*

Using the framework

Framework Component	"Design and park"
1. WHICH **level** of learning experience?	Level 2.
2. WHAT is the **skill/competency**?	• Identifying the many factors or variables involved. • Making reasonable assumptions to simplify a problem. • Collecting the variety of data. • Drawing figures to help in visualizing a problem. • Constructing a mathematical model.
3. WHERE is the **mathematics**?	• Geometry and Measurement, particularly the use of trigonometric ratios.
4. HOW to **solve** the problem/model?	• Construct appropriate diagrams and consider the necessary measurements for some chosen designs. • Find the size of a lot for a given design using trigonometry and obtain the maximum number of parking lots that can be constructed along a kerb. • Given the vertical distance occupied by a lot, the width of the car park and the minimum width of parking aisles, consider if parking bays on one or two sides of the car park can be constructed for each of the chosen designs. • Compare the number of possible lots for the different designs and choose the best design.
5. WHY is this experience a **success**?	In this lesson, students learn about: • geometrical representations of a problem, • careful data collection and use of simplifying assumptions, • intricate trigonometric calculations, • understanding the limitations of a model.

Possible discussion points

The mathematics concepts and skills required for this task involve a fair amount of trigonometry. In addition, students need to understand how car parking lots may be arranged or laid out, and the local rules and regulations related to designs of car parks. Teachers can facilitate the modelling process using the discussion points below:

- What is the current design for the car parking space in your school compound?
- What does it mean to optimise the space in a car park?
- List the factors or variables that affect the optimum use of space in a car park.
- Are there any government guidelines that we must follow?
- What are the possible designs for the parking lots?
- What kind of data do we need to solve the problem?
- What are the assumptions?
- What mathematical concepts are involved in your model?
- Is your solution reasonable?
- How can you improve on your model?

There are some other factors to consider in this mathematical model. For example, in reality there is usually some space allocated to the front and rear of a car in an angled-parking lot, which is not discussed here. The actual physical dimension and shape of the area will pose another constraint. Moreover, in some countries or cities, only certain angled lots are allowed (for example, only 60° angled-parking). The teacher may need to check these rules or guidelines, which are usually stipulated by the relevant local authorities in the country or city, before carrying out this activity.

A draining experience

Problem situation: Flash floods, especially when they spill onto roads, can cause severe traffic disruptions. In countries where sudden heavy downpours are common, this can be a serious problem. For instance, it was reported that in Singapore one Saturday evening (Dec 24, 2016), following heavy rains, traffic came to a standstill at the junction of two major arterial roads, due to some cars stalling, and oil drums and debris were seen floating at the location ("Flash Floods Across Singapore", 2016). The local authorities take every flood incident seriously, and the government has made attempts to address the problem. One of the key strategies for flood management is continual drainage improvement, as drains reduce flash floods by rapidly funnelling the rainwater and channelling to other locations, and containing as much of the rainwater as possible. In other words, these channels or drains must be both effective and efficient.

The task: How should a drain (technically called an open channel) be constructed or designed to make drains more effective and efficient?

Teacher notes

Flash floods are localised flooding which typically subsides within an hour. However, if the drainage system is effective and efficient, then the water may be channelled to other locations (such as bigger drains, canals, rivers or to the sea) more quickly, and reduce the impact of flash floods. The drainage system in the area therefore plays a very important role in flood management. The factors to consider in designing drains include the availability of land, rainfall intensity, allowable drain depth and the permissible slope (which affects water flow velocity).

Two common cross-sectional shapes of drains are the U-shaped and trapezoidal cross-sections, as shown in Figure 4.6. Though it is clear that having larger drains and canals can help to reduce flash floods, there is a limit to how wide drains can be as there could be physical constraints. There is also a limit to digging deeper drains as a minimum gradient is required for effective conveyance of storm-water (surface water in abnormally large quantity resulting from heavy falls of rain) to the reservoirs. The ground conditions and existence of any underground obstructions also affect the possible depth of drains.

Normally, it is required that drains should be designed to have discharge capacities (Q_c) adequate to cope with the estimated peak runoffs (Q_r). That is, $Q_c \geq Q_r$. The runoff (surface water runoff) is the flow of water that occurs when excess storm-water, melt-water, or other sources flow over the Earth's surface. The peak runoff (Q_r) is the maximum rate of runoff per unit time, and is calculated using a certain formula (for instance, the *Rational Formula* is used by the Public Utilities Board, or PUB, Singapore). The size, geometry and

70 *Deterministic modelling*

(a) U-shaped cross section of drain   (b) Trapezoidal cross-section of drain

Figure 4.6 Cross-sectional shapes of commonly seen drains

slope of a drain determine the discharge capacity of the drain, calculated using Manning's equation. That is,

$$Q_c = AV, \text{ where } V = \frac{R^{\frac{2}{3}} \times S^{\frac{1}{2}}}{n}.$$

V is the cross-sectional average flow velocity (in m/s), A is the cross-sectional area of the flow (m^2), R is the hydraulic radius (m), S is the channel slope, and n is Manning's roughness coefficient. The hydraulic radius, $R = \frac{A}{P}$, where P is the wetted perimeter (perimeter of the cross-sectional area that is "wet" as a result of contact with the water, in m). Manning's roughness coefficient is a fixed value depending on the flow surface of the drain. A key assumption in the use of Manning's equation is that uniform steady flow exists.

In most cities, the local authority will decide on certain minimum and maximum restrictions on the velocity of flow in a drain. That is, it should not be too low for self-cleansing action to take place, and should not be too high to cause excessive scouring or hydraulic jumps. For instance, Singapore's PUB has certain guidelines and the reader may to their 2011 report for details.

Based on Manning's equation, the mathematical problem for the design of drains is then to maximize the discharge capacity Q_c so that it is at least equal to the estimated peak runoffs Q_r, subject to certain restrictions on the size of the drain and the corresponding average flow velocity.

A suggested approach

For this task, students will need to quantify the quality of a drain design in terms of its cross-sectional area and the cross-sectional average flow velocity, and understand the trade-offs between using different designs. For example, though a circular cross-section is good for the drain to enable a smoother water flow, its cross-sectional area may not be the largest. In

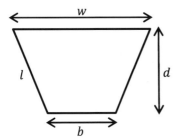

Figure 4.7 An isosceles trapezoid

contrast, a combination of the two shapes, for example, a trapezoid or a "depression" at the bottom of a rectangular drain may be more desirable.

Since many factors are included in Manning's equation, students may need to simplify the problem with suitable assumptions when examining plausible designs for the cross-sectional shapes of the drain. For example, they can assume that the top width and cross-sectional area of the drain is fixed due to constraints in land use and availability, and that the channel slope is constant. If the surface flow of the drain is given or fixed, then Manning's roughness coefficient will also be fixed. The problem is then reduced to producing a design that leads to a lower wetted perimeter (than those of some current designs), which in turn increases the hydraulic radius and elevates the average flow velocity. For simplicity, we can also assume that the depth of the drain is fixed at some allowable value when comparing some possible designs.

As an illustrative example, consider an "isosceles trapezoidal drain" where the cross-sectional area, top (surface) width and depth of are fixed at A, w and d respectively. Figure 4.7 shows the cross-section with the symbols representing the various dimensions.

Area of isosceles trapezoid is $A = \frac{1}{2}(b+w)d$. Given that A, w and d are fixed, we obtain $b = \frac{2A}{d} - w$. Thus $l = \sqrt{d^2 + \left(\frac{w-b}{2}\right)^2}$ and the wetted perimeter is $b + 2l$ (assuming that rainwater fills the drain up).

In an actual implementation of this task, the teacher could ask students to take measurements of drains around the school area, do the relevant calculations and make comparisons before discussing possible improvements to the drainage designs. An example of a design proposed by some secondary students given a similar modelling task is as shown in Figure 4.8. Here, the students examined the possibility of re-shaping the base of the trapezoidal drain in an attempt to improve the water flow, based on Manning's equation.

For this modelling task, simple mathematical concepts like areas and perimeters of different geometrical shapes are required. The derivation of Manning's equation, while important, may be not be necessary, but a good understanding of the equation in determining optimal solutions would be useful. Therefore, students from the lower secondary levels onwards should be able to handle in this modelling activity. The following framework should serve to guide teachers in structuring a lesson based on this task.

72 *Deterministic modelling*

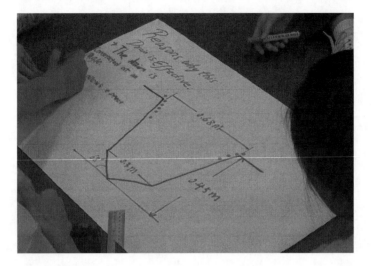

Figure 4.8 A cross-sectional shape proposed by some students

Using the framework

Framework Component	"A draining experience"
1. WHICH **level** of learning experience?	Level 3.
2. WHAT is the **skill/competency**?	• Formulate a mathematical problem. • Identify the many factors that affect the drain design. • Making reasonable assumptions. • Constructing different mathematical models.
3. WHERE is the **mathematics**?	• Geometry and Measurement, particularly areas and perimeters of different shapes.
4. HOW to **solve** the problem/model?	• Assume that some factors contributing to Manning's equation are fixed. For example, the cross-sectional area and the channel slope. • Construct designs that have lower wetted perimeters than some common ones. In doing so, we can assume that the top width and depth of the drain are fixed, for simplicity.
5. WHY is this experience a **success**?	In this lesson, students learn about: • a new equation (Manning's equation), • visual representations of a problem, • importance of simplifying assumptions, • defending a model.

Possible discussion points

At the first contact with this problem, students may not immediately think that the shape of the cross section of drains will have such an impact on effective and efficient drainage. To assist students, the teacher could engage them with the following discussion points or questions:

- State some designs of drains that you have seen.
- What are the government guidelines on drainage design?
- Formulate the mathematical problem for this task.
- List the factors that affect the drain design.
- State and justify some assumptions to simplify the problem of the drain design.
- Formulate and solve the mathematical models for your drain designs.
- Compare your recommended drain designs with some commonly used designs.
- How can you improve your model?

Although the main governing equation in this modelling task is the Manning's equation, which students may not be familiar with, the task can be simplified by making some assumptions to fix certain variables. Doing so reduces the problem to something that secondary school students can handle. Such techniques are often used in the teaching of mathematical modelling; it is good for teachers to learn to look at a problem, search for the relevant mathematics to tackle it, and then simplify or structure it so that it is accessible to their own students.

Cover up

Problem situation: In a certain school, whenever it rains, students have to brave the rain and run from the school gate (where most of them would be dropped off by their parents) to the school building. It was proposed that a covered pavement (or "covered walkway" as is commonly called in some countries, like Singapore) be constructed between the school gate and the building to provide shelter to students during the rainy days.

The task: What is the *best* design for the cover of a pavement? That is, what is the best design for a covered walkway?

Figure 4.9 shows some designs of such covered walkways in Singapore.

Teacher notes

Students should first be encouraged to identify the factors or variables that should be considered in the design of covered walkways. These variables should include the width of pavement (p), the horizontal span of cover (s), the height of the vertical supports (h) and the angle of strike of rain from the horizontal (θ), as shown in Figure 4.10. The width of the pavement and height of the supports are easy to understand. By the "horizontal span of cover", we mean the distance between the two ends of the cover measured horizontally as shown in Figure 4.10. Naturally, we expect the span to be longer than the width of the pavement so that the edges of the cover extend beyond the sides of the pavement.

Rain will typically strike the ground at some angle. For simplicity, we shall assume a two dimensional situation in which rain falls along a plane that is perpendicular to both the surface of the pavement and the sides of the pavement. Given this simple situation, the angle of strike is as shown in Figure 4.10.

Students can take photographs of covers in the neighbourhood when it rains to observe the angle of strike of the rain. The other factors that could be considered are the cost of building the cover, the type of material to use and perhaps the aesthetic appeal of the design. However, we could focus our objective in this case on using mathematics to decide the "best" cover based on the *effectiveness* of the cover in protecting a person from the rain.

Figure 4.9 Examples of covers of a walkway found in Singapore, showing different designs

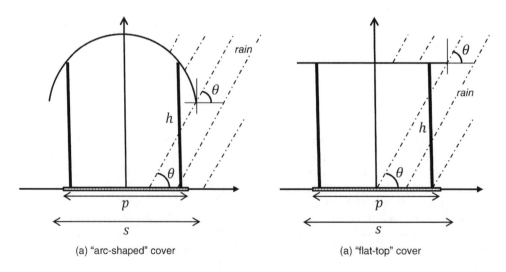

(a) "arc-shaped" cover   (a) "flat-top" cover

Figure 4.10 Two possible cross-sectional shapes of shelters for covered walkways, and the variables involved in the modelling task

Deterministic modelling

That is, given a certain design, with everything else (such as building cost and so on) being equal, how effective is it compared to another design?

A suggested approach

If we focus on the effectiveness of a cover, then the mathematical question that we wish to answer would be "what should the shape of a cover be in order to provide the most effective shelter from rain?" To keep the problem simple as a first model, we shall consider only the cross section of the covered walkway. To keep the problem tractable, we make some assumptions on certain dimensions of the cover and on the angle of strike of the rain. With the size of the pavement, span of the cover and the height of the supports fixed, and given the angle of strike of the rain, we can compare the effectiveness of the covers of different shapes. For instance, assuming that an "arc-shaped" cover and a "flat-top" cover have similar spans, and are held in place by vertical supports of the same height over a pavement of the same width, we may then make a fair comparison of their effectiveness. From Figure 4.10, it can be seen that the "arc-shaped" cover (a) provides more cover than the "flat-top" cover (b) from rain with the same angle of strike. The objective is then to minimize the portion on the pavement which gets wet during rain, given fixed values of s, h, p, and for a given value of θ. If the cross-sectional shape of the cover is represented by some function, $f(x)$, and "placed" symmetrically on the supports covering the pavement, it may be possible to determine some optimal values for parameters that appear in the function.

As an illustration, suppose the cross-sectional shape of the cover is represented by a quadratic function $f(x) = ax^2 + b$. That is, we want the cover to be of this particular shape. The question is, what values of a and b do we choose in order to provide the best cover (that is, for it to be most effective)? This situation is illustrated in Figure 4.11.

In Figure 4.11, x, $\dfrac{p}{2}$ and $\dfrac{s}{2}$ are points the horizontal axis of a coordinate system with the origin placed at the midpoint of the pavement. Therefore,

$$\frac{s}{2} - x = f\left(\frac{s}{2}\right)\tan\left(\frac{\pi}{2} - \theta\right) \text{ or } x = \frac{s}{2} - f\left(\frac{s}{2}\right)\tan\left(\frac{\pi}{2} - \theta\right).$$

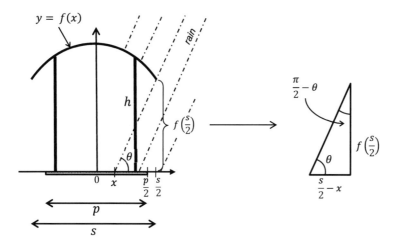

Figure 4.11 Cross-sectional view of the shelter (covered walkway) and the variables involved

76 Deterministic modelling

Therefore, the objective is to choose a and b so that the length $\frac{p}{2} - x$ is minimised, or, alternatively, to increase x to be as close as possible to $\frac{p}{2}$.

Substituting the form of $f(x)$ into the equation above, we obtain

$$x = \frac{s}{2} - f\left(\frac{s}{2}\right)\tan\left(\frac{\pi}{2} - \theta\right) = \frac{s}{2} - \left(\frac{as^2}{4} + b\right)\tan\left(\frac{\pi}{2} - \theta\right).$$

Using the fact that $f\left(\frac{p}{2}\right) = h$, that is, $\frac{ap^2}{4} + b = h$ or $b = h - \frac{ap^2}{4}$, we further obtain

$$x = \frac{s}{2} - \left(\frac{as^2}{4} + h - \frac{ap^2}{4}\right)\tan\left(\frac{\pi}{2} - \theta\right).$$

From the last equation, it is clear that only the varying a will result in different values of x, given that s, h, p and θ are fixed. A dynamic geometry software, such as Geometer's Sketchpad or Geogebra, may be used to visualize and determine the functional form of the cross-section of the cover as a changes, and the impact this will have on x.

From the discussion above, it is evident that once the problem is formulated mathematically, only basic concepts and ideas from topics such as coordinate geometry, functions and graphs, and trigonometry are required to deal with the problem. Hence this problem is suitable for students with these pre-requisite knowledge and skills. The following framework can serve as a guide for teachers in planning a lesson based on this modelling activity.

Using the framework

Framework Component	"Cover up"
1. WHICH **level** of learning experience?	Level 3.
2. WHAT is the **skill/competency**?	• Identify all factors or variables that affect the task. • Formulating a mathematical problem. • Making assumptions and simplifying a problem. • Use of a dynamic geometry software (such as Geometer's Sketchpad) to find suitable parameters. • Use of a graphing tool.
3. WHERE is the **mathematics**?	• Coordinate Geometry. • Functions and their graphs. • Trigonometry.
4. HOW to **solve** the problem/model?	• Construct a cross section of the covered walkway. • Find an expression for the portion on the pavement that will get wet when it rains. • Minimize the size of this portion based on the function for the shape of the cover.
5. WHY is this experience a **success**?	In this lesson, students learn about: • the need to make assumptions to simplify the problem and abstract the physical situation, • connecting topics taught in class, • geometrical representations of a problem.

Possible discussion points

This modelling task is rather open-ended and may be a challenge for many students. The task requires a fair amount of abstraction – seeing what is in the real world and simplifying the situation so that some mathematical concepts become relevant and can be applied. To guide students in attempting this activity, the teacher may consider the following questions as discussion points:

- What are the different factors that should be considered in the design of the covered walkway?
- How do we quantify these factors or variables?
- What does it mean to have the "best" design mathematically?
- What are different shapes that we can use for the cover?
- Is it possible to solve the problem by considering all the factors or variables together?
- How can the problem be simplified through suitable assumptions?
- How does the cross-section of a covered walkway look like?
- Mathematically, what does it mean when a cover is "effective"?
- What sort of function can we use to represent the cross-sectional shape of the cover?

If teachers are interested in carrying out this activity, it may be necessary to do a bit of homework before planning the activity. This could include looking around the neighbourhood of the school for covered walkways, and taking pictures of them, which may be used to motivate the lesson. It will be useful also to show a video of rain coming down one of these covered walkways, to demonstrate how effective or ineffective these covers or shelters may be. The idea is to see if students are able to use basic school mathematics such as elementary geometry and trigonometry, to view the problem mathematically. This activity provides an excellent opportunity for students to connect an everyday, familiar problem with basic mathematics.

Let's dart

Problem situation: It is common for schools to organise carnivals or fairs, sometimes with an aim to raise funds. One common game stall in the carnival would be the Dart Board Game. The standard dart board is as shown in Figure 4.12, and the scores are based on the rules set out by national and international groups, such as the National Darts Association.

The standard dart board may prove to be difficult for an amateur to score points, and possibly not as interesting as the game could be. In this task, students are required to design a new dart board and the corresponding game rules. The cost incurred in producing the props for the game and providing the rewards must be recovered using money collected from players at the carnival. Therefore, the net profit will be the difference between the revenue collected and the cost of running the game stall. In designing the game, it is necessary to provide rewards that are sufficiently attractive to players while ensuring that the stall will have the best chance of making a profit.

The task: Design a new dart board and the corresponding game rules to maximise the profit.

Teacher notes

For this modelling task, students need to formulate a mathematical model for a new dart board game by quantifying their designs in terms of estimated profits. That is, the mathematical problem is to design a new dart board game with the highest revenue and lowest

78   *Deterministic modelling*

Figure 4.12 A standard board for the game of darts

expenditure possible. As a start, they need to consider the factors and variables that contribute or are related to the revenue collected, the fixed cost incurred and the expected pay-out to players of the dart game. Examples of these factors and variables are the prizes awarded, amount charged per game, the demand for the game, the dart board design, the materials used to make the board and the darts, the height of the board above the ground, the distance between the board and the throwing line, and other game rules. In testing the viability of a board design and the associated game rules, students can play the game repeatedly to estimate the probability of landing darts in different regions of the board and deem the attractiveness of the game. However, this can be tedious and time-consuming.

Alternatively, students can be asked to design the dart board and the game rules in a way where it is not difficult to calculate the required probabilities. However in their calculations, some assumptions may be necessary to simplify the situation. For example, a dart thrown onto a dart board will not drop or bounce off, the height from the floor to the board and the distance between the board and the throwing line do not affect the scoring probabilities. Considering a psychological factor of game play in their dart board game designs, that is, when there is a very attractive pay-out, people will participate even if there is a small chance of winning, students can design a dart board in such a way that makes it very challenging or near impossible to win the grand prize. Logically, then, a higher score (and hence a bigger pay-out) will correspond to a region on a board with a lower probability of landing a dart.

The materials that can be used to make a dart board and the darts include foam boards, cardboards, corrugated boards, coloured papers and pins. A survey can be conducted among students to study the demand for a dart game in relation to different prices charged and the rewards offered. This could help in determining a reasonable price to set for each game. As it can be difficult to estimate the demand for the dart game during the carnival, students may assume a certain total number of games in their calculations. At the end of the initial discussions, students should have some preliminary ideas of the following:

- Basic design (a drawing) of the new dart board, and reasons for the design.
- Corresponding game rules.
- Assumptions to be made.
- Information on the fixed cost and expected pay-outs to players.
- Pricing of each game.
- Likely profit.

A suggested approach

Some teachers, who participated in a professional development programme in mathematical modelling in Singapore, had tried this modelling activity with students in their schools. Here, we describe two samples of students' attempts at tackling this problem.

SAMPLE 1

The dart board suggested here consists of a grid with letters in each cell, as shown in Figure 4.13.
   Players pay $3 per game for 4 darts
   Total number of games: 100
Game Rules:

- To win, throw the darts to form either a three or four letter word
- Letters need not be in order and must not be repeated.

Assumptions:

- Darts that are thrown will land on the board
- Different darts that are thrown will land on different letters
- The 100 games will be sold out via pre-sale of tickets.

Calculations of game revenue:

For this set of letters, there are seven 4-letter words and eighteen 3-letter words (see http://wordsolver.net).

Expected number of prizes for getting 4-letter words with the 4 darts $= \dfrac{7}{9P_4} \times 100 \approx 1$

X	Q	U
W	G	C
J	E	A

Figure 4.13 Dart board with letters, designed by a group of students

80   *Deterministic modelling*

Expected number of prizes for getting 3-letter words with the 4 darts

$$= \left(\frac{18}{9P_4} \times 4P_3 \right) \times 100 \approx 15$$

Cost = cost of darts + cost of board + cost of top prize + cost of 15 second prizes
= $5 + $5 + $10 + 15 × $4 = $80

Profit = 100 × $3 − $80 = $220

Refine model:
   Relax the assumption that different darts that are thrown will land on different letters.

SAMPLE 2

Rules:

- Player pays $3 for each game, which consists of 3 darts
- Following competition standards, the dart board is hung so that the centre of the bullseye is 1.73m from the floor. The throwing line (or toeline) is located 2.37m from the face of the dartboard, measured horizontally
- The dartboard is as shown in Figure 4.14
- For each game, player scores points for each dart that hit the dartboard according to the points indicated on the board. The total scores of the 3 throws shall determine the rewards as follows.

Points	Rewards
150	$6.00 worth of prizes
	The first to hit 3 bullseyes will get $20 worth of prizes!
100–149	$2.00 worth of prizes
50–99	$1.00 worth of prizes
20–49	$0.50 worth of prizes
0–19	No prize

Points cannot be accumulated and rewards are to be claimed within each game

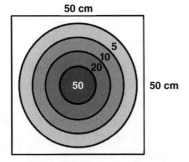

Figure 4.14 Dart board with points, designed by another group of students

Deterministic modelling 81

Assumptions:

- Each player will throw all 3 darts
- 100 games are played
- Players are amateurs and not skilled in throwing darts
- A dart can land on any point on the dart board with equal chance.

The expected profit calculated was $207.

This modelling activity differs from others previously discussed as it involves the construction of a game and maximizing of profits. We note that a higher expected profit does not necessarily mean that a "better solution" is obtained. There are other factors to consider, and it is also necessary to examine the viability of the game in detail. Clearly, the basic concepts in probability, geometry and measure are required of students undertaking this modelling task, from lower secondary level onwards. The framework below can guide teachers in planning this modelling activity.

Using the framework

Framework Component	"Let's dart"
1. WHICH **level** of learning experience?	Level 3.
2. WHAT is the **skill/competency**?	• Identifying various factors and variables involved.
	• Making reasonable assumptions.
	• Careful data collection and calculations.
	• Clear and detailed presentation of a model.
3. WHERE is the **mathematics**?	• Probability.
	• Geometry and measure.
4. HOW to **solve** the problem/model?	• List down the factors and variables that affect revenue and expenditure.
	• Determine some necessary simplifying assumptions.
	• Decide on a design and game rules and calculate the probabilities of players getting different prizes.
	• Choose materials that can make a dart board and darts, and rewards corresponding to different probabilities of winning. Calculate the costs incurred.
	• Conduct a survey to estimate a reasonable price to charge players for each game.
	• Calculate the expected profit.
5. WHY is this experience a **success**?	In this lesson, students learn about:
	• revenues, costs and profit maximization,
	• the need for simplifying assumptions,
	• creating a game and setting rules,
	• justification of a model.

Possible discussion points

For this modelling activity, students need to be familiar with a range of concepts and consider many factors and variables related to the task. Teachers will need to provide sufficient guidance through the modelling process. Some of the following questions could serve to facilitate the process:

82 Deterministic modelling

- What is the mathematical problem to be solved?
- What makes up the expenditure on a dart board game?
- What are the factors and variables that contribute to the revenue and expenditure of running the game stall?
- What are some standard dart game rules?
- What mathematics do you need in designing your dart board?
- Can a dart board take other shapes?
- Is it feasible to consider all the factors and variables in your design?
- What assumptions can be made to simplify the problem?
- What sort of prizes can we offer in a game?
- How can we price each game?
- What is a possible demand for the game (total number of games that will be played)?
- Can you justify your dart board design and the game rules? What is your estimated profit?

There are many examples of game stalls at school carnivals. Although the modelling activity described here is about designing a dart board for a game stall, the idea can be extended to other kinds of games that involve probability and pay-outs, and in which the objective is to maximise the chances of making a good profit. For instance, a game could involve dropping a certain number of balls onto a board with holes and depending on which holes the balls fall into, points could be scored, or prizes could be given, and so on. If decisions on the design are made arbitrarily, or simply by following past designs, the profits or gains may not be as desirable. This modelling idea, therefore, provides students with the opportunity of examining a typical scenario, casting it into a mathematical problem, formulating a model to solve it, and then testing the model on the ground.

Bibliography

Flash floods across Singapore cause massive traffic disruptions. (2016, December 24). *TODAYonline*. Retrieved from www.todayonline.com/singapore/flash floods across-singapore-cause-massive-traffic-disruptions.

Land Transport Authority. (2011, December 5). *Code of practice on vehicle parking provision in development proposals*. Retrieved from www.lta.gov.sg/content/dam/ltaweb/corp/Industry/files/VPCOP2011.pdf.

Land Transport Authority. (2016, December 5). *Architectural standards*. Retrieved from www.lta.gov.sg/content/ltaweb/en/industry-matters/development-and-building-and-construction-and-utility-works/architectural-standards.html.

National Darts Association. (n.d.). *Official rules of play*. Retrieved from www.ndadarts.com/rules/general-rules-play.

Public Utilities Board, Singapore's National Water Agency (2011, December). *Code of practice on surface water drainage*. Retrieved from www.pub.gov.sg/Documents/COP_Final.pdf.

5 Simulation modelling

Introduction

Simulation, or more commonly, computer simulation, has been used as a form of mathematical model in many real-life applications and as a teaching tool in mathematics classrooms. In many real-world problems, the situation can be very complex, and may not lend themselves to deterministic modelling as easily. Sometimes, it can also be difficult to obtain data related to the situation or problem. In such cases, simulation models may be a better way to study or investigate these problems. Very often, computer simulations are used to model a phenomenon or situation when it is either impossible or impractical to construct real, physical experiments to study it.

In a typical simulation model, a set of rules or an algorithm will control how a certain state of situation flows to another, and this is often implemented as a computer program or by means of some technological tool. The rules that control the model are usually a result of interpreting the way a certain process or a phenomenon normally evolves or progresses. It is based on these rules that the computer program is written and then executed. The outcomes of the interactions of the variables or components in the model are then generated. It is therefore implicit that in order to perform a simulation, a technological or computing tool is required. This is because calculations of the values of variables in the model are performed iteratively, rapidly and even continuously throughout the simulation process. While many tools and computing languages are available, in terms of teaching in the school, one has to take into account the accessibility of these tools to the learner, and the teacher. For this reason, in this chapter, the tool that is used is Microsoft *Excel*. Though some may argue that it may not be the best tool, *Excel* does provide the convenience of a spreadsheet and graphing features, and programming capabilities through its Visual Basic Applications (VBA) facility.

Break it up

Problem situation: If we bend a dry spaghetti stick until it breaks, we will find that it usually breaks into more than 2 pieces. The question is, if a stick of spaghetti is broken at two random points, what is the probability that the three resulting segments will form a triangle?

This problem is the well-known *Broken Spaghetti Problem*.

The task: Investigate the probability that three segments of a spaghetti stick of arbitrary lengths can form a triangle.

84 *Simulation modelling*

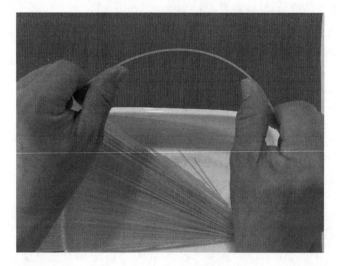

Figure 5.1 Bending a spaghetti stick could break it at one or more points

Teacher notes

The Broken Spaghetti Problem is an elementary problem in geometric probability. That is, it is a problem in probability but it also involves a geometric problem. This modelling task differs from those described in the last two chapters in that it is used to guide students in discovering a well-known result in geometry and in investigating the probability of obtaining an outcome through a simulation. One may argue that strictly speaking, this is not modelling since there is no "real-life problem" that we want to solve. However, it is introduced here to explain and illustrate the steps that one needs to go through to develop a simulation. If nothing else, at least it is an activity that requires and develops certain skills and competencies that are useful in simulation modelling.

We can determine if a triangle can be formed given any three side lengths using *the triangle inequality theorem*, which states that any side of a triangle is always shorter than the sum of the other two sides. Proofs of the theorem are available in various sources, such as from the online resource at basic-mathematics.com (see link in the bibliography at the end of the chapter). In addition, it can be shown that if the sum of the lengths of the two shorter sides of a triangle is larger than the length of the longest side of the triangle, then the sum of the lengths of any other pair of sides of the triangle will be larger than the length of the remaining side. This means that we only need to do one check to see if a triangle can be formed. In other words, given the lengths of the three segments, we first determine the longest one. Then, if this length is smaller than the sum of the other two lengths, a triangle can be formed. Otherwise, it is not possible to form a triangle. There is no need to perform any other further checks.

To calculate the probability that three segments of a spaghetti stick can form a triangle, the length of the stick does not matter. For simplicity, we shall assume that the stick is of unit length. Then the problem is equivalent to choosing two numbers at random between 0 and 1. The two random numbers will then represent the points on the stick (of unit length)

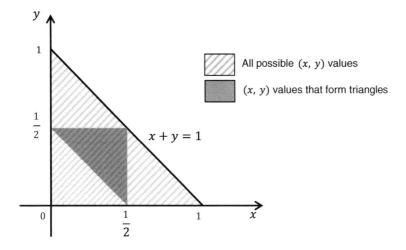

Figure 5.2 Region of all possible (x, y) values and region of (x, y) values that can form triangles

where the stick breaks into three parts. Let the lengths of two of these pieces be x and y, and the length of the third piece will have to be $(1 - x - y)$. The region formed by the inequalities, $x > 0, y > 0$ and $x + y < 1$ corresponds to all the possible lengths x and y when a stick is broken into three pieces (shaded region in Figure 5.2).

It is possible to form a triangle when x, y and $1 - x - y$ satisfy the triangle inequality. That is, the three cases are

$$x + y > 1 - x - y \Rightarrow x + y > \frac{1}{2}$$

$$x + (1 - x - y) > y \Rightarrow y < \frac{1}{2}$$

$$y + (1 - x - y) > x \Rightarrow x < \frac{1}{2}.$$

The grey area within the shaded region in Figure 5.2 is formed by all these three inequalities. Thus the probability that a triangle can be formed from three arbitrary segments of a spaghetti stick is

$$\frac{\text{Area of shaded region}}{\text{Area formed by all possible outcomes}} = \frac{0.5 \times 0.5 \times 0.5}{0.5 \times 1} = \frac{1}{4}.$$

A suggested approach

After posing the problem to students, they may be asked to explore the conditions for the lengths of the three segments of a broken spaghetti under which a triangle can be formed. This may mean guiding them towards the triangle inequality theorem through some trial and error process, to uncover the required conditions. They may then investigate

86 Simulation modelling

the probability that three arbitrary line segments can form a triangle by devising some form of simulation. Using sticks of spaghetti, students can carry out the following process:

1) With a pen or pencil, randomly choose and mark any two points on a stick of spaghetti
2) Carefully break the stick at the two marked points to obtain three segments
3) Try and form a triangle using the three segments
4) Measure the lengths of all the three sticks, as accurately as possible and record the measurements from smallest to largest
5) Find the sum of the lengths of the two shorter segments and state whether a triangle can be formed or not
6) Repeat Steps 1 to 5 a few times, and record all the results obtained in a table.

Based on the results, students can try to find a relationship between the sum of the lengths of two shorter segments and the length of the longest segment for a triangle to be formed.

We can simulate the outcomes of the above experiment using an electronic spreadsheet such as *Excel*. For simplicity, we assume that each spaghetti stick is of length 1 unit. An *Excel* worksheet similar to that depicted in Figure 5.3 can be set up.

Consider, say, 1000 trials in each simulation, as listed in Column A of the worksheet. The randomly marked points are simulated by generating random numbers r1 and r2 using *Excel*'s formula "=RAND()". These are recorded in Columns B and C as shown for each corresponding trial. From the two marked points, the lengths of the individual segments, denoted by x, y and z are calculated and recorded in Columns D, E and F respectively, as follows. First, the smaller of the two random numbers, r1 and r2 is found and x is set to this value. Next, the difference between r1 and r2 is calculated, and we let y take this value. Finally, we take away the larger of r1 and r2 from 1, and set this value to z. In other words, for the first trial (Row 3), the formulae for the relevant cells are as follows. For Cell D3, enter "=MIN(B3,C3)"; for Cell E3, enter "=ABS(B3-C3)"; and for Cell F3, enter "=1-MAX(B3,C3)".

	A	B	C	D	E	F	G	H
1	No.	Random number between 0 and 1		Segments			Longest minus sum of other two	Triangle if difference is negative
2		r1	r2	x	y	z	Difference	Test
3	1	0.9812	0.1241	0.1241	0.8571	0.0188	0.7142	0
4	2	0.5329	0.9190	0.5329	0.3861	0.0810	0.0658	0
⋮	⋮	⋮	⋮	⋮	⋮	⋮	⋮	⋮
1002	1000	0.2981	0.7476	0.2981	0.4495	0.2524	-0.1009	1
1003								
1004							Total	246
1005							Probability	0.246

Figure 5.3 Simulation to find probability of forming a triangle from three line segments

Column G is used to record the result of the formula,

length of longest segment-(sum of lengths of other two segments)

for each trial. This is done by finding the sum of all the segments and then taking away the length of the longest segment from it. This gives us the sum of the lengths of the two shorter segments, which is then taken away from the length of the longest segment to yield the required result. For instance, in Cell G3, for the first trial, the formula, "=MAX(D3:F3)-(SUM(D3:F3)-MAX(D3:F3))" is entered.

From this point, it is easy to check if a triangle can be formed from the segments. If the value in Column G3 is negative, we have a triangle. Otherwise, we do not. This test is performed using *Excel*'s "COUNTIF" formula and recorded in Column H. For instance, in Cell H3, we enter the formula, "=COUNTIF(G3,"<0")", which returns 1 if the value in Cell G3 is negative, and 0 otherwise.

To generate the simulation run for the rest of the trials, the formulae in Columns B to H are copied down the rows, bearing in mind that relative cell referencing should be in place. The total number of "1"s recorded in Column H for all the trials will represent the number of triangles that can be formed. This is found easily by summing; for instance, in Cell H1004, enter "=SUM(H3:H1002)" and the experimental probability is computed by dividing this sum by the total number of trials. The value of 0.246 given in Figure 5.3 is the result of a simulation executed. In *Excel*, hitting the F9 function key will re-calculate the cell values, and therefore represent a fresh run of the simulation. The simulations (and for different sample sizes) can be run repeatedly, and an average value can be obtained which may be used as an estimate of the required probability.

This modelling activity is suitable for students from the lower secondary level onwards, who have been introduced to probability, elementary concepts in geometry and measure, and basic *Excel* skills. The framework below can guide teachers in their planning of this activity.

Using the framework

Framework Component	"Break it up"
1. WHICH **level** of learning experience?	Level 1.
2. WHAT is the **skill/competency**?	• Understanding the problem.
	• Making assumptions to simplify the problem.
	• Careful data collection.
	• Designing and executing a simulation.
3. WHERE is the **mathematics**?	• Probability.
	• Random numbers and the use of a random number generator.
	• Geometry and measure.
4. HOW to **solve** the problem/model?	• Guide students to discover the triangle inequality theorem by doing an experiment using spaghetti sticks.
	• Use *Excel* to set up a simulation:
	• generate random numbers for the two break points,
	• compute the lengths of the three resulting segments,
	• determine if triangles can be formed,
	• calculate the number of triangles formed in a given sample and the corresponding probability.
	• Repeat the simulations and obtain an estimate of the required probability.

Framework Component	"Break it up"
5. WHY is this experience a **success**?	In this lesson, students learn about: • a new geometrical result, • deeper understanding of randomness, • experimental and theoretical probability, • use of a computing tool to construct a simulation.

Possible discussion points

Though this task does not require a high level of mathematical knowledge or skills, the modelling process and simulation of experimental outcomes may be a new challenge for some. It will certainly help if teachers discuss some of the following points with the students while embarking on this task at different stages of the activity:

- What does it mean to break a spaghetti stick at two random places?
- Can we ensure that we choose two points on a stick independently and randomly?
- Do the lengths of spaghetti sticks matter in our investigation?
- What assumptions can we make to simplify the problem?
- How can we estimate the probability of forming a triangle? How many sticks is enough?
- How can we simulate the outcomes of the experiment? For example, what are the random values to generate and what calculations do we need to make? What sample size(s) can we use?
- What is a reasonable estimate for the probability based on the simulations?
- Can you prove the theoretical probability using the triangle inequality theorem (for more advanced students)?

As mentioned earlier, although this modelling activity does not appear to be one that is aimed at solving a real-life problem, it provides opportunities for students to explore the basics of simulation modelling. Important aspects of simulation models such as random numbers, the law of large numbers, and more advanced topics like the Monte Carlo methods are involved.

A walk in the park

Problem situation: Suppose that a person (possibly drunk) begins walking at some starting point along a sidewalk. For each step taken, he is unable to decide whether to take a step forward or backward. That is, the direction (forward or backward) taken for each step is random and there is an equal chance for either direction.

The task: Develop a simulation model to represent this "random walk" and see how far from the starting point the man would have gone after taking, say, 50 steps.

Teacher notes

The situation described is commonly known as a *one-dimensional random walk* since the assumption here is that the steps are taken along one straight line. We can think of a one-dimensional (or simple) random walk as being carried out in the following manner. Starting at some origin, a person will take a step either forward or backward by first tossing a coin. If the coin shows heads, he takes a step forward. If it shows tails, he takes a step backward.

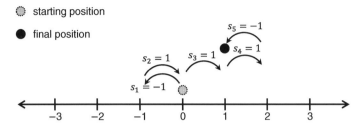

Figure 5.4 An example of a one-dimensional random walk

Assuming that the coin is unbiased, there is an equal chance of getting heads or tails in each toss. Figure 5.4 illustrates the situation for a few steps.

Suppose that the starting position is at the origin, and step i ($i = 1, 2, ...$) is represented by s_i and each step is of unit length. That is, $s_i = 1$ if step i is a step in the forward direction (to the right, in the figure) and $s_i = -1$ if step i is a step backward (to the left in the figure). The position of the person starts at 0, and reaches 1 after 5 steps in the example shown in Figure 5.4.

Clearly, the distance travelled from a starting point after N number of steps (where N is any positive integer) may vary every time we repeat the experiment. Nonetheless, because each s_i has an equal chance of being 1 or −1, if the experiment is repeated a sufficiently large number of times, it turns out that on the average, a random walker will end up near the starting point. This may be explained by analysing the process and by first considering simpler cases.

Consider the probability that a walker arrives at a particular position, say, x, after N steps, and let this probability be denoted by $f_N(x)$. For each N, the sum of probabilities for all values of x must equal 1, and, assuming that the starting position is at $x = 0$, then the furthest positions are $-N$ and N. For simple cases when $N = 0$ and $N = 1$, it is not hard to see that $f_0(0) = 1$ and $f_1(-1) = f_1(1) = \frac{1}{2}$. For the case when $N = 2$ (that is, the walker takes two steps), we can obtain the probabilities by considering all the possible end positions and what kind of coin toss outcomes will lead to them. There are only three possible final positions, namely, −2, 0 and 2. There are a total of $2^2 = 4$ possible coin toss outcomes, namely, Heads-Heads, Tails-Tails, Heads-Tails, Tails-Heads, and two of them will lead to 0 as the final position, one of them to −2 and the last one to 2. Therefore, we have $f_2(0) = \frac{1}{2}$ and $f_2(-2) = f_2(2) = \frac{1}{4}$.

In general, we can find the probability distribution function for the final position of the walker after N steps using a binomial distribution, with the probability of going forward and going backward as p (probability of "success") and q (probability of "failure") respectively. In this case, we assume that $p = q = \frac{1}{2}$. In addition, the central limit theorem entails that if the number of steps is sufficiently large (tends towards infinity), the probabilities approach a normal distribution. For details, the reader may refer to Dougherty (1990) and Dworsky (2008).

In this modelling problem, we wish to construct a simulation of a one-dimensional random walk and find out the position of the random walker from a starting point after taking a certain number of steps. We shall assume each step is of the same size. The model,

90 Simulation modelling

of course, can also be extended to include different or random sizes of steps taken, or unequal probabilities of the walker moving in different directions. If students have sufficient knowledge in probability distributions, they can be guided to work out the probability distribution function for the location of the walker after a certain number of steps.

A suggested approach

To help students better understand the one-dimensional random walk, they can construct outcomes of the walks by physically acting out the process. They could toss coins and walk forward or backward based on the outcome of the toss, and track the movements of their walks on paper, for a reasonable number of steps. However, to carry out such a physical simulation with a high number of steps many times would be time-consuming and tedious. Hence, a computer simulation would be a logical and reasonable approach. Here we will simulate one-dimensional random walks of 50 steps using *Excel*. Figure 5.5 shows a sample of an *Excel* worksheet and a typical graphical output for a given simulation run of the one-dimensional random walk.

Column A lists the steps taken from 0 to 50 in this example. We simulate the coin tossing for each step in Column C using the formula "=RANDBETWEEN(1,2)", with 1 representing heads and 2 representing tails. The outcome of the formula will determine the direction in which the next step will be taken. This will be calculated and stored in Column D.

For example, we enter the formula "=IF(C2=1,1,IF(C2=2,-1))" in Cell D2. That is, if the value in Cell C2 is 1, then the next step should be 1 unit forward; if the value is 2, then the next step should be 1 unit backwards (thus −1). This formula is copied from Cell D2 down to Cell D52, with relative referencing in place. Finally in Column B, the position at each step (from step 1) is computed, with the starting position at step 0 being at the origin. In Cell B3, we enter the formula "=B2+D2"; that is, we simply add to the current position the value stored in Cell D2 (which will be either positive 1 or negative 1, depending on the direction determined by the simulated coin toss). This formula is copied down in the same column to B52, with relative referencing in place. For this simulation run, we see that the final position of the walker is at $x = -4$. We can repeat the simulation to see some possible walk patterns and obtain an average value of the final position after 50 steps. For example,

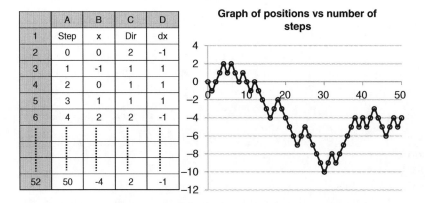

Figure 5.5 Simulation of one-dimensional random walks with 50 steps taken

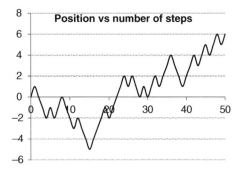 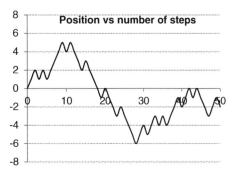

Figure 5.6 More examples of simulated random walks of 50 steps

Figure 5.6 shows that the final positions of two other simulated walks after 50 steps are at $x = 6$ and $x = -2$, respectively.

This problem can be suitably framed as a modelling task for students who have been introduced to probability and the idea of experimenting with chance, from the lower secondary level onwards. Teachers can plan this activity using the following framework as a guide.

Using the framework

Framework Component	"A walk in the park"
1. WHICH **level** of learning experience?	Level 2.
2. WHAT is the **skill/competency**?	• Understanding the problem. • Making assumptions to simplify the problem. • Planning and carrying out a simulation.
3. WHERE is the **mathematics**?	• Probability. • Random numbers and the use of a random number generator.

4. HOW to **solve** the problem/model?	• Ask students to construct a simple random walk of a reasonable number of steps using flipped coins.
	• Set up a simulation on *Excel*:
	  • assume that the starting point is at the origin,
	  • generate random numbers (either 1 or 2) to represent steps going forward or backwards,
	  • compute the distance to move (either 1 or -1) at each step,
	  • find the position of the walker at each step.
	• Repeat the simulation to obtain some possible walk patterns and find the average final position after 50 steps.

5. WHY is this experience a **success**?	In this lesson, students learn about: randomness and generating random numbers, experimental and theoretical probability, designing simulation models using *Excel*.

Possible discussion points

Students may be familiar with ideas such as coin tossing and probability, but may not have come across a problem such as random walk. They may also wonder how to design a simulation to model such a process. Doing a physical experiment (that is, acting out by actually tossing a coin and walking) may help. It will also be useful for teachers to facilitate the model construction process using the following discussion points as a guide:

- How can we construct a one-dimensional random walk?
- What assumptions can we make to simplify the problem?
- What object can we use to give us an equal chance of going forward or backwards?
- Can you think of some possible applications of random walks?
- How can we simulate a random walk using *Excel*? For example, what are the random values to generate and what calculations do we need to make?
- From your *Excel* simulation, what is the average position of the walker after 50 steps?
- How can you extend your model to other random walk simulations?
- Can you work out the probability distribution function for the location of the walker after a certain number of steps (for more advanced students)?

There are many applications of random walk models or processes in physics, biology, ecology and medicine. For example, random walks can predict how heat dissipates or diffuses in a solid, model the dispersal and population redistribution of animals and micro-organisms, and be applied to the context of cell migration leading to blood vessel growth. They are also related to Brownian motion, that is, the random motion of particles in a fluid resulting from their collision with atoms or molecules in the gas or liquid. Another application of a random walk is an interesting phenomenon called the gambler's ruin: a persistent gambler with a finite amount of money will eventually and inevitably go broke when playing a fair game against a bank with an infinite amount of money. The gambler's money will perform a random walk until it reaches zero at some point, and the game will be over.

Pick a door

Problem situation: The *Monty Hall problem* is a well-known problem based roughly on an American television gameshow, "Let's Make a Deal", and after the host of the gameshow. In this game, a contestant is shown three doors labelled 1, 2 and 3. A grand prize, say, a car is behind one of the doors and booby prizes, called "goats" are behind the other two doors. The contestant's objective, obviously, is to win the grand prize. The rules of the game are as follows.

- A contestant must first choose one of the doors that he thinks hides the grand prize.
- Monty Hall, the gameshow host, opens one other door with a booby prize behind it.
- The contestant is then asked whether he wants to stay with his original choice, or switch to the other unopened door.

The task: When playing the Monty Hall game, should a contestant switch doors or stick to the original choice to increase or maximise his chances of winning the grand prize?

Teacher notes

A video on the Monty Hall problem can first be shown to students to introduce them to the game rules (see for example, Newcombe, 2007). Actually playing the game using a simple set-up like that shown in Figure 5.7 can help gain students interest and bring the problem to life.

Figure 5.7 Playing the Monty Hall game using a simple set-up

Besides adding some fun to the lesson, playing the game in class can also get students to talk about the best strategies and help frame the problem. Alternatively, rather than using physical props, teachers may also use online versions of Monty hall simulation games (see the bibliography for link to an example of an online game) to play the game and motivate the lesson.

The logic behind the strategy to tackle the Monty Hall problem may sound a little counter-intuitive at first. Consider this: suppose that a contestant's initial choice is random, and the host randomly picks one of the two remaining doors to open if there is a booby prize behind each unopened door, and all the rules of the game are satisfied. It may appear that switching or staying with the initial choice will not make any difference since everything is random. However, since the gameshow host knows where the grand prize is, and he opens a door behind which is *not* the grand prize, the process is not quite random. The probabilities we obtain from switching or sticking to the original choice are therefore not the same. In essence, the gameshow host has *improved* the contestant's chances of winning by "removing" one booby prize!

We can analyse the situation in the following way. Suppose that in a game, the contestant's first choice is not the right choice (that is, behind the door chosen is not the grand prize). The host will have no choice but to open the only other door with a booby prize behind it. This implies that if the contestant switches, he will win. However, if the contestant's first choice is the grand prize and he switches, then he will lose. Therefore, if the contestant always switches, then *he wins if and only if his first choice is not the right choice*, which is an event with probability $\frac{2}{3}$. We can obtain this probability by multiplying the probability of not having picked the grand prize initially, that is, $\frac{2}{3}$, to the probability of picking the car after switching, which is $\frac{1}{3-1-1}=1$.

However, if the contestant never switches, then *he wins if and only if his first choice is the right choice*, which is an event with probability $\frac{1}{3}$. This means that the contestant should **always** switch since the chance of winning will be twice the chance if he chooses to stay with his original choice.

Another approach to analysing the Monty Hall problem is to use a probability tree similar to that explained in the video by Mark Lehman (2013).

94 Simulation modelling

A suggested approach

A simulation to find some computational or experimental solution of the Monty Hall problem could be one that evaluates the frequencies of winning or not winning the grand prize while assuming one of the two strategies, namely either "Always Stay" or "Always Switch". Such an approach can help students gain insight into the problem and guide them in learning the relevant probability theory. Here, we will suggest two ways to develop the simulation model.

Method 1

In this method, a normal worksheet as shown in Figure 5.8 is given to students. This worksheet consists of a table with many rows to be filled, and some instructions. The class should be divided roughly into two groups, Group A and Group B. Students in Group A will adopt the "Always Stay" strategy while those in Group B shall adopt the "Always Switch" stance for this exercise. Each row in the table represents a trial. To start, all students will be asked to randomly pick a "winning door" (that is, the door behind which lies the grand prize) for each trial, and mark an "X" in the appropriate column in the corresponding row. For instance, for trial 1, we may choose Door 3, for trial 2, Door 1, and so on, until every row contains an "X" in one of the three columns for the doors.

The teacher would then use a spinner (or other tools) with 3 outcomes, "1", "2" or "3", to randomly determine the door that would first be chosen by a contestant for each trial. This will be marked with an "O". For each row, if the "O" coincides with the "X", then the trial would result in a success for those with the "Always Stay" strategy and the student would put a tick in the last column. If the "O" and "X" appear in different columns, then those with the "Always Switch" strategy would have won the grand prize and should put a tick in the last column. When all trials are completed, that is, when the rows are all filled, students will count the total number of ticks (successes) and share with the rest of the class.

1. Choose a door and place the prize behind it by marking it with an X.
2. Use a spinner to randomly choose a door - mark it with a O.
3. Either always stay or always switch and then count successes.

No.	Door 1	Door 2	Door 3	Always Stay / Always Switch
1				
2				
3				
⋮				
⋮				
100				

Figure 5.8 Worksheet with instructions, used in a simulation method 1

Method 2

In the second method, students may be guided in constructing a simulation for the Monty Hall game using an *Excel* worksheet set up in a fashion similar to that shown in Figure 5.9. In this worksheet, we use Column A to list the number of trials, Columns B and C to record the door to the grand prize and the door first chosen by the contestant respectively. Columns D and E indicate which strategy ("Stay" or "Switch") results in the contestant winning the grand prize. Each row represents a trial of the game, and at the bottom, the number of wins for each strategy is computed.

In Column B, the door with the prize for each trial is randomly chosen and this can be simulated by entering the formula "=RANDBETWEEN(1, 3)" in Cell B3 or the first trial. This is copied down in the column to other cells in Column B. We use the same formula for each of the entries in Column C to represent the first door randomly chosen by the contestant. Then in Column D, we assume that the strategy "Stay" is adopted. The formula "=IF(C3=B3, "Win", "")" entered in Cell D3 basically says if the "grand prize door" and the "first chosen door" are the same, then enter the text "Win" in the cell. This represents the case when the contestant who "stays" gets the grand prize. As before, the formula is copied down the column to other cells in Column D.

Column E records the "wins" when the strategy to switch doors results in the contestant getting the grand prize. In Cell E3, the formula "=IF(C3<>B3, "Win", "")" ensures that if the door first chosen by the contestant is not the same as that with the grand prize, then the contestant wins the grand prize since he will switch doors. This formula is copied down the column to fill up Column E.

The formulae "=COUNTIF(D3:D102, "Win")" and "=COUNTIF(E3:E102, "Win")" are entered in Cells D104 and E104 respectively, to count the number of wins based on the two strategies. As shown in the example in Figure 5.9, in this particular simulation run, the contestant wins 34% of the time if he does not switch, but 66% of the time if he switches. The simulation can be repeated (and for different sample sizes) to estimate the required probabilities.

	A	B	C	D	E
1	No.	Grand Prize Door	First chosen door	Stay	Switch
2					
3	1	1	1	Win	
4	2	2	1		Win
5	3	3	2		Win
6	4	1	1	Win	
⋮	⋮	⋮	⋮	⋮	⋮
102	100	1	2		Win
103					
104			Total Wins =	34	66

Figure 5.9 Worksheet used in a simulation method 2

96   Simulation modelling

Students with more mathematical maturity or higher ability can attempt to work out the theoretical probabilities, using what they know from the experimental probabilities obtained through the simulations.

This modelling activity could be introduced to students with basic knowledge of probability. The following framework serves as a guide for teachers in planning this activity.

Using the framework

Framework Component	"Pick a door"
1. WHICH **level** of learning experience?	Level 3.
2. WHAT is the **skill/competency**?	• Understanding the problem, together with the associated rules and assumptions. • Designing and executing a simulation. • Validate the experimental results (for more advanced students).
3. WHERE is the **mathematics**?	• Probability. • Random numbers and the use of a random number generator.

4. HOW to **solve** the problem/model?	• One way is to set up a simulation on *Excel*,
	  • for each of 100 trials (for example), generate a random number between 1 and 3 for the door with a grand prize behind, and another for the first chosen door,
	  • determine if the contestant wins under the strategies "Always Stay" or "Always Switch",
	  • find the total number of wins of the grand prize under the two strategies,
	  • repeat the simulation and obtain estimates of the required probabilities.

5. WHY is this experience a **success**?	In this lesson, students learn about: an interesting counter-intuitive statistics puzzle, randomness and non-randomness, experimental and theoretical probabilities, constructing simulations using worksheets or excel.

Possible discussion points

As the probability concepts involved in the Monty Hall problem may not be obvious to some students, it may not be easy for them even to begin thinking about how best to develop a strategy or a simulation to study the problem. Teachers can facilitate the modelling process by guiding students through the questions and discussion points given below:

- What are the assumptions in the Monty Hall problem?
- Do you think a contestant should switch doors or stay with the original choice? Why?
- Will the gameshow host's action of opening a door affect the chances?
- How can we simulate the outcomes of the game? What variables are involved in a simulation? For example, what random values do we need to generate? How do we determine if the contestant wins?
- From your simulation, what are the likely probabilities of winning under the two strategies?

Simulation modelling

- Which strategy should we always choose when playing the game?
- Can you work out the theoretical probabilities of winning under the two strategies (for more advanced students)?

Although this problem is essentially about simulating a game rather than solving a real-life problem, it provides an excellent platform for learning about constructing a simulation model to study or investigate a situation where a decision has to be made. In this case, the decision to be made is the strategy that one should adopt when faced with a situation whose outcome depends very much on the strategy. If analytical methods are known or accessible to students, then the simulation could provide some form of experimental verification and may serve to convince students of the analytical results.

Drop the needle

Problem situation: Buffon's Needle experiment is a well-known problem in the field of geometrical probability. Consider a surface marked with equidistant parallel lines and a needle is randomly thrown onto this surface. Figure 5.10 shows an illustration of several needles dropped onto such a surface. What is the probability that the needle will cross one of the lines?

Remarkably, we can use this probability to estimate the value of π.

The task: Construct a simulation model to study and investigate the Buffon's Needle experiment. Develop the simulation further to obtain an estimate of the value of π.

Teacher notes

In the simplest case of the Buffon's Needle experiment, a needle of length, say, L cm is thrown onto a piece of paper with parallel lines drawn at a distance, also L cm apart.

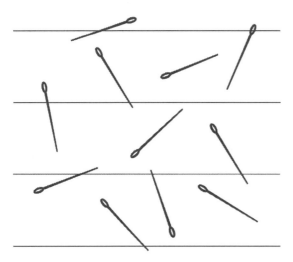

Figure 5.10 Illustration of the Buffon's Needle experiment

98 Simulation modelling

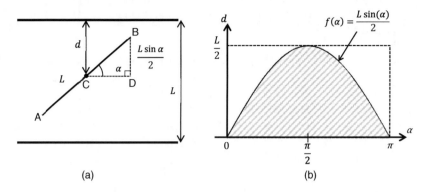

Figure 5.11 Buffon's Needle experiment: (a) typical position of needle between two parallel lines, and (b) graph of *d* against α, and the $(L/2 \times \pi)$ rectangle

The needle falling down on the paper may or may not cross (or touch) any of the parallel lines. This is repeated many times and the number of times the needle crosses or touches any line is counted. The length and thickness of the needle, the way the needle is thrown, the thickness of the parallel lines drawn and the distances between them, are factors to consider in the experiment. For simplicity, we assume that the thickness of the needle and lines are negligible, and the needle is randomly dropped or thrown onto the paper. Though the height from which the needle is dropped is not an important factor, the needle should be dropped from a reasonable height so that the dropping process is random. In other words, the needles should really be dropped, and not simply "placed" onto the paper.

The Figure 5.11(a) shows a typical position of a needle labelled AB that lies between a pair of parallel lines. In this diagram, the point C is the midpoint of AB, and point D is the foot of the perpendicular dropped from B such that CD is parallel to the pair of parallel lines. The variables involved here are α, the angle that the randomly dropped needle makes with the parallel lines, and *d*, the perpendicular distance between the midpoint of the needle and any line closest to it.

Obviously, the angle α can vary from 0° to 180°, and it is also clear that $0 \le d \le \frac{L}{2}$.

Using basic trigonometry, we obtain $BD = \frac{L \sin(\alpha)}{2}$. From the diagram in Figure 5.11(a), we observe that the needle will touch or cross a line if $d \le \frac{L \sin(\alpha)}{2}$. To examine the frequency of this happening, consider the graph of *d* against, and the rectangle with the dimensions as shown in Figure 5.11(b). For any given orientation (or value of α) of a needle AB, the distance *d* can take any value (and hence any point) inside the rectangle. However, if the needle crosses or touches a line, then the value of *d* is less than or equal to $f(\alpha)$ and the point representing its location in the graph is in the shaded region. Therefore, the probability of the needle touching or crossing a line is the ratio of the shaded area to the entire rectangle with length π and width $\frac{L}{2}$.

$$\text{Area of the shaded part } = \int_0^\pi \frac{L\sin(\alpha)}{2}\,d\alpha = -\frac{L}{2}\bigl[\cos(\alpha)\bigr]_0^\pi = L.$$

The required probability is $\dfrac{L}{\pi L/2} = \dfrac{2}{\pi}$. Since this probability can also be obtained from the ratio, $\dfrac{\text{total number of needles crossing/touching lines}}{\text{total number of needles dropped}}$, we can conclude that $\pi \approx \dfrac{2 \times \text{total number of needles dopped}}{\text{total number of needles crossing/touching lines}}$.

There are extensions of the above Buffon's Needle experiment, including the cases where the distance between the parallel lines is not the same as the length of the needle. The reader may refer to Wolfram Alpha LLC (2017) for some of these extensions.

A suggested approach

To help students understand the concepts involved in this modelling activity, teachers could get them to carry out the process of throwing toothpicks (in place of needles as a safer option) onto a piece of cardboard with parallel lines drawn equidistant apart. The following steps should provide sufficient guidance for this hands-on activity:

1) Measure the length of the toothpick, and let it be denoted by L (in cm, for instance)
2) Draw parallel lines L cm apart on a piece of cardboard, and place it on a flat surface
3) From a height of about 15 to 20 cm, drop the toothpick onto the cardboard and take note of whether or not it crosses or touches any line
4) Repeat Step 3 for about 50 times
5) Calculate the experimental probability of the toothpick crossing or touching a line.

There are online simulation tools that can also be used to introduce the Buffon Needle experiment to students. For example, the Office for Mathematics, Science, and Technology Education, University of Illinois (see reference below) has developed one such tool that is publicly available.

The outcomes of the experiment described above can be simulated using a simple electronic spreadsheet such as *Excel*, set up as shown in Figure 5.12 below. The value of π can then be estimated using the relationship between the probability (found experimentally) and π as discussed earlier. For simplicity, we assume that the length of the needle, $L = 1$ cm, which is also the distance between successive parallel lines. In the illustration in Figure 5.12, a simulation run consists of 100 trials or 100 needles dropped.

Column A lists the trials, with each trial consisting of a needle dropped onto the plane of parallel lines. In Column B, we record values of d using the formula "=0.5*RAND()", which returns a randomly chosen real number between 0 and 0.5, since in this case, $0 \leq d \leq \dfrac{1}{2}$. In a sense, this random chosen value of d determines the random position of the needle when dropped. This is because we can identify the location of the needle by its midpoint, and fixing the midpoint is equivalent to fixing the value of d, the perpendicular distance between the midpoint of the needle and the nearest parallel line.

100 Simulation modelling

	A	B	C	D	E	F
1	No.	d	α	$\frac{1}{2}\sin\alpha$	$d \leq \frac{1}{2}\sin\alpha$	Total no. of "Yes"
2	1	0.102288	2.575129	0.268325766	Yes	62
3	2	0.449425	2.740124	0.195385522	No	
4	3	0.132641	1.020916	0.426293413	Yes	$\pi \approx$
5	4	0.470165	2.008593	0.452843884	No	3.225806452
6	5	0.451606	3.115338	0.013126001	No	
⋮	⋮	⋮	⋮	⋮	⋮	
101	100	0.215357	2.682672	0.22149021	Yes	

Figure 5.12 A simulation of the Buffon's Needle experiment implemented on a spreadsheet

To simulate the randomly chosen orientation of the needle, we let the angle α take a random value between 0 and π. This is achieved using the formula, "=PI()*RAND()" entered in Column C. The corresponding values of $\frac{1}{2}\sin\alpha$ to be stored in Column D may be obtained using the formula, "=0.5*SIN(C2)", for instance in Cell D2 and then copying the formula down to other cells in the same column.

In Column E, we check if $\leq \frac{1}{2}\sin\alpha$, for the corresponding values in Columns B and D. The formula "=IF(B2<=D2, "Yes", "No")" performs the checking, and if d in Cell B2 is not greater than the value of $\frac{1}{2}\sin\alpha$ in Cell D2, then the answer is "Yes". Otherwise, "No" will be recorded in Cell E2. As before, the formula is copied down the same column to other cells. A "Yes" constitutes the case when the needle crosses or touches any one of the parallel lines. Therefore, counting the number of "Yes" in Column E will provide information on the number of times, among this given number of trials, that a needle crosses or touches a line.

To obtain the total number of "Yes", the formula "=COUNTIF(E2:E101,"Yes")" is entered in Cell F2. With this value, the experimental probability of the needle crossing or touching a line can be calculated. For example, as shown in Figure 5.12, the probability obtained from this simulation is 0.62. The formula "=2*100/F2" in Cell F5 is used to find an approximation to the value of π. In the illustration shown in Figure 5.12, the result of a simulation run results in an estimated value of about 3.226 for the value of π. The simulation may be repeated, and done so for different number of trials, and an average value for the approximation to π can be computed.

Teachers can conduct this modelling activity for students from the upper secondary level onwards, who are familiar with basic concepts in geometry, trigonometry and probability theory. For students who are familiar with calculus, particularly integration, they can be guided to derive the theory behind the experiment. Teachers can use the following framework as a guide in planning the activity.

Using the framework

Framework Component	"Drop the needle"
1. WHICH **level** of Learning Experience?	Level 3.
2. WHAT is the **skill/competency**?	• Visualization of the problem. • Identify the factors and variables involved. • Make simplifying assumptions. • Understanding the mathematical problem. • Collecting data carefully. • Designing and executing a simulation.
3. WHERE is the **mathematics**?	• Geometry and measure, in particular trigonometry. • Probability. • Random numbers and the use of a random number generator. • Calculus, particularly integration (for more advanced students).

4. HOW to **solve** the problem/model?	• One approach is to set up an *Excel* simulation:
	  • consider a sample of 100 trials and set $L = 1$ cm for simplicity,
	  • generate random values of d between 0 and 0.5, and random values of α between 0 and π,
	  • check if $d \leq \frac{sin(\alpha)}{2}$ for each set of randomly generated values of d and α,
	  • collate the total number of hits in the 100 trials and obtain the required probability,
	  • repeat the simulations and take an average of the estimated probabilities for higher accuracy,
	  • for more advanced students, they can also obtain an approximation to π.

5. WHY is this experience a **success**?	In this lesson, students learn about: • randomness and non-randomness, • experimental and theoretical probabilities, • simulation using physical tools or *Excel*, • an interesting way to estimate π (for more advanced students).

Possible discussion points

This modelling activity may be challenging to many students because of the level of mathematics required and the skills involved. It would therefore be helpful if teachers could guide students along using some of the questions suggested below:

- What are the factors that should be considered in the Buffon's Needle experiment?
- Can we simplify the problem by making some assumptions?
- How can we ensure that the needle is thrown randomly on the paper?
- What are the variables involved here? Are there any restrictions on their values?
- How can we simulate the experiment? If using *Excel*, what sample size should we use, what random values must we generate and how can we obtain the total number of hits?
- From your simulations, what is the estimated probability of a needle touching a line?
- How does your estimated value compare with the theoretical value of $\frac{2}{\pi}$?

102 Simulation modelling

- From your simulations, what is a possible estimate of π (for more advanced students)?
- Can you work out why π can be estimated this way (for more advanced students)?

Like previous examples on simulation models, it may appear that there is no practical, real-life problem to solve in this particular mathematical modelling activity. However, the activity stresses on the use of mathematics to study and examine a problem or a given situation, and more specifically, the use of simulation to investigate a problem. The process of thinking through the steps for the simulation of the Buffon's Needle experiment, and constructing a spreadsheet to implement the simulation will help develop important skills required in simulation modelling.

Who do we hire?

Problem situation: A company would like to hire a secretary, but will need to do so under the following conditions:

- There is a known number of candidates, say, n, who have applied for the job.
- The candidates are ranked, from best to worst without ties.
- The candidates are interviewed sequentially in a random order, and each order is equally likely.
- Immediately after the interview, the interviewed candidate is either accepted or rejected.
- The decision to accept or reject a candidate is based only on the *relative ranks* of the candidates interviewed so far.
- Candidates who have been rejected cannot be recalled.

The goal is to hire the top-ranked candidate.

The task: Propose a way to maximise the probability of choosing the best secretary.

Teacher notes

In this problem, we need to develop or find a strategy that will help us hire the best candidate, and then construct a model that we can use to test it out. The goal here is to try and hire the best candidate. Clearly, it would not sound right that we simply offer the job to the first candidate who steps in for the interview. On the other hand, we do not wish to wait until the last candidate is interviewed, since we will be forced to accept this last candidate. Therefore, a reasonable method could be to reject a certain number, for example, $k-1$ of the candidates (where $1 \leq k \leq n$), and then choose the first candidate that is better than all the previous candidates from this point on. If no such candidate exists, then we accept the last candidate (implying that we have failed). If $k = 1$, we choose the first candidate; if $k = n$, we select the last candidate. This is illustrated in Figure 5.13. The selected candidate is randomly distributed on $\{k, k+1, \ldots, n\}$. We will refer to this strategy as *strategy k*. The probability of success $p_n(k)$ using strategy k with n candidates can be calculated, for small n.

For example, if there are three candidates ($n = 3$), the 6 permutations of $\{1, 2, 3\}$, representing the order in which the candidates are sequenced for the interview, can be listed. The candidate that is eventually hired based on all possible strategies can be identified and the total number of successes for the different strategies can then be collated (as shown in Table 5.1). Here, the numeral in {1, 2, 3} represent the actual rank of candidate, with 1 being the highest rank.

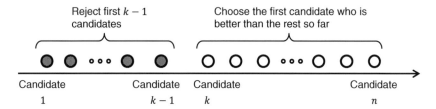

Figure 5.13 An illustration of a strategy to choose the best secretary

Table 5.1 Computation of number of successes for different strategies

Permutation	k = 1	k = 2	k = 3
(1, 2, 3)	1	3	3
(1, 3, 2)	1	2	2
(2, 1, 3)	2	1	3
(2, 3, 1)	2	1	1
(3, 1, 2)	3	1	2
(3, 2, 1)	3	2	1
Total no. of successes	2	3	2

The probabilities of successes for the different strategies are $p_3(1) = \frac{2}{6}$, $p_3(2) = \frac{3}{6}$ and $p_3(3) = \frac{2}{6}$, and we should use strategy 2 to maximize the probability of hiring the best candidate.

It can be shown that it is optimal to interview and reject about $\frac{1}{e}$ (about 37%) of the applicants (especially for large n), and then select the first candidate that is better than all of the previous candidates. If no such candidate exists, then the last candidate is chosen. The probability of finding the best secretary is also about 0.37. Readers may refer to the article by Ferguson (1989) for details.

A suggested approach

Teachers may wish to facilitate students' understanding of the Secretary Problem by acting out the situation, not unlike playing a game. For instance, we could get a group of, say, 10 students to be candidates attending the job interview. Each candidate is given a card indicating his "rank" and will appear before the rest of the class in some random sequence. As each candidate is presented to the class, he will reveal where he stands (in terms of his rank) in relation to those who have already been interviewed and rejected. The class will decide whether or not to "hire" the candidate. Obviously, the first candidate will say he ranks as number 1, as no one else had appeared before him. This "game" may be repeated several times, and the class may be asked if they could think of a more systematic or strategic way of doing things. The teacher could guide students into realising or noticing that it is probably more logical to reject a certain number of candidates before looking for the next best one.

104   *Simulation modelling*

The Secretary Problem (with 4 Candidates)

	Permutations of order				Reject0	Reject1	Reject2	Reject3
1	1	2	3	4	✓			
2	1	2	4	3	✓			
3	1	3	2	4	✓			
4	1	3	4	2	✓			
5	1	4	2	3	✓			
6	1	4	3	2	✓			
7	2	1	3	4		✓		
8	2	1	4	3		✓		
9	2	3	1	4		✓	✓	
10	2	3	4	1		✓	✓	✓
11	2	4	1	3		✓	✓	
12	2	4	3	1		✓	✓	✓
13	3	1	2	4		✓		
14	3	1	4	2		✓		
15	3	2	1	4			✓	
16	3	2	4	1			✓	✓
17	3	4	1	2	✓		✓	
18	3	4	2	1				✓
19	4	1	2	3		✓		
20	4	1	3	2		✓		
21	4	2	1	3			✓	
22	4	2	3	1			✓	✓
23	4	3	1	2			✓	
24	4	3	2	1				✓
Total No. of successess								

Figure 5.14 A worksheet to determine the success rates of different strategies

Teachers may then help students derive the actual outcomes of using different strategies, using a worksheet with a table as shown in Figure 5.14. In this worksheet, four candidates are considered. Students are to list down the 24 different permutations of $\{1, 2, 3, 4\}$ and put ticks in boxes corresponding to successes in hiring the best candidates, under the four different strategies. The total number of successes (ticks) obtained under each strategy is collated and the relevant probability of success in choosing the best secretary is found. The completed table for four candidates is shown in Figure 5.14. The reader may verify that the probabilities of successes for the different strategies are $p_4(1) = \frac{6}{24}$, $p_4(2) = \frac{11}{24}$, $p_4(3) = \frac{10}{24}$ and $p_4(4) = \frac{6}{24}$. Therefore, Strategy 2 will maximise the probability of choosing the best secretary in this case.

In reality, if the company intends to interview more than four candidates, it would be too tedious to obtain the probabilities of successes under different strategies by hand calculations. In this case, a simulation using an electronic spreadsheet such as *Excel* could be implemented to study the problem and work out the probabilities instead. As the entire spreadsheet for this simulation is quite large, involving several steps, in the description below, it is described and presented in two parts before putting them together.

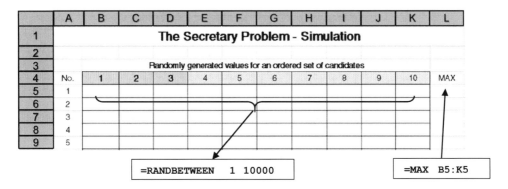

Figure 5.15 Setting up the Secretary Problem simulation

As an example, let $n = 10$ and assume we reject the first, say, three candidates. In the first part of the simulation, we set up the candidates by randomly assigning values to each of the 10 candidates. These "values" represent the "worth" of the candidate – one with a higher value is a better candidate and ranks higher than one with a lower value. In order to reduce the chance of having ties, the values assigned are randomly chosen integers from the interval [1,10000]. Figure 5.15 below shows how this part can be set up.

In the example shown, the numbers in Row 4 from Columns B to K shows the candidate number, which is also the order in which the candidates are interviewed. In Row 5, Cells B5 to K5 store the values of the candidates obtained randomly using the formula "=RANDBETWEEN(1,10000)" in the first trial of our simulation. The largest of these values is found using the formula "=MAX(B5:K5)", and stored in Cell L5. This represents the value of the best candidate in this instance. Row 5 is the first trial, and the next row is the second trial, and so on. These formulae can be copied down the respective columns up to the number of simulation trials desired.

In the second part of the simulation, we set up a corresponding table and use various *Excel* formulae to help find the best candidate after rejecting a fixed number of them. In this example, we shall assume that the strategy is to reject the first three candidates. This is illustrated in Figure 5.16 below.

In the part of the worksheet shown in Figure 5.16, the entries of the value "0" in the entire Column M indicate that Candidate 3 and those before are rejected. The other rows are assigned formulae to find the best candidate after the first three are rejected. The case for Row 5 (first trial) is described below.

In Cell N5, the formula, "=IF(MAX(M5:M5)=0,IF(E5>=MAX(B5:D5),E5,0),0)" is entered. The formula is a "nested IF" statement – meaning that there is an "IF" statement contained inside another. The outer "IF" statement merely says that if the largest value of all those who have been interviewed is zero (meaning we have not found or accepted a candidate), then we go on to see if the next one is to be chosen (in the inner "IF" statement); otherwise, we set the current cell to zero. The inner "IF" statement compares the value of the current candidate with the maximum value of all previously considered candidate to see if it should be accepted. For instance, in the case of the first trial in Row 5, if the value of Candidate 4 (which is stored in Cell E5) is higher than the maximum value of the previous three candidates (whose values are stored in Cells B5, C5 and D5), then Cell N5 takes

106 *Simulation modelling*

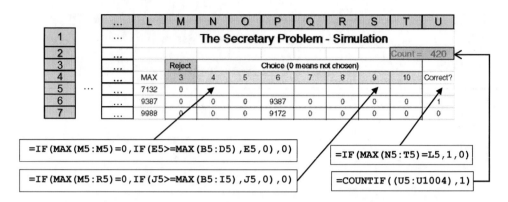

Figure 5.16 Implementing simulated runs of the strategy for solving the Secretary Problem

the value of Cell E5; otherwise, it takes the value 0. This would mean that Candidate 4 is chosen.

As another example, for Candidate 9 (whose value is stored in Cell J5), we enter formula "=IF(MAX(M5:R5)=0,IF(J5>=MAX(B5:I5),J5,0),0)". This means that all the candidates before Candidate 9 are not chosen (checked by the outer "IF" statement), and if the value of Candidate 9 is larger than the highest value of the previous eight candidates, then the value of the candidate is placed in Cell S5; otherwise the value 0 is entered.

In Column U, from Row 5 onwards, for each row, we check if the maximum of the values stored in Columns N to T is the same as the maximum for that simulated run. If so, a value "1" is entered and if not, "0" is entered. We can then count the number of "1"s, which will be the number of times the best candidate was successfully picked. This value is stored in Cell U2, as shown.

Figure 5.17 depicts part of a worksheet with 1000 simulated runs.

As this modelling activity requires a certain level of understanding of probability concepts and a certain degree of mathematical maturity from students, it would be more meaningful as an activity for students who are in higher grades or who have achieved a higher level in their mathematical content knowledge. The following framework can guide teachers in planning the activity.

Using the framework

Framework Component	"Who do we hire?"
1. WHICH **level** of learning experience?	Level 3.
2. WHAT is the **skill/competency**?	• Understanding the problem, together with the associated assumptions. • Understanding the limitations of a problem and its solution due to the assumptions made. • Ability to formulate strategies to solve a problem. • Designing and executing simulations.
3. WHERE is the **mathematics**?	• Probability (including permutation concepts). • Random numbers and the use of a random number generator.

The Secretary Problem - Simulation

	A	B	C	D	E	F	G	H	I	J	K	L	M	N	O	P	Q	R	S	T	U
1																					
2																					Count = 377
3				Randomly generated values for an ordered set of candidates								MAX	Reject		Choice (0 means not chosen)						
4		1	2	3	4	5	6	7	8	9	10	MAX	3	4	5	6	7	8	9	10	Correct?
5	1	3412	200	5459	3183	1277	8054	9659	4531	8494	3049	9359	0	0	0	8054	0	0	0	0	0
6	2	4124	6123	3998	2760	3624	2528	8022	8226	6552	9730	9730	0	0	0	0	8022	0	0	0	0
7	3	2849	8013	464	6544	9420	8877	323	3739	1672	5042	9420	0	0	9420	0	0	0	0	0	1
8	4	8196	5511	1705	6920	2675	5843	925	7250	8584	2809	8584	0	0	0	0	0	0	8584	0	1
9	5	1915	8771	8516	907	9238	7146	7493	409	2579	3841	9238	0	0	9238	0	0	0	0	0	1
10	6	5119	2325	9735	1797	3219	430	3422	1416	2325	6608	9735	0	0	0	0	0	0	0	6608	0
11	7	6939	3560	9619	1067	7974	3037	486	7692	8951	8377	9619	0	0	0	0	0	0	0	8377	0
12	8	1581	2953	2390	7824	6085	3320	6610	41	7192	7135	7824	0	7824	0	0	0	0	0	0	1
13	9	8646	9235	7264	9565	9110	7375	2431	2715	1913	2879	9565	0	9565	0	0	0	0	0	0	1
14	10	892	8448	4739	6172	645	3036	5973	7689	6819	7073	8448	0	0	0	0	0	0	0	7073	0
15	11	3654	464	5071	7280	7742	7563	8042	3610	8801	6592	8801	0	7280	0	0	0	0	0	0	0
16	12	133	3110	8117	3032	7210	9264	4882	9863	7410	1421	9863	0	0	0	9264	0	0	0	0	0

Figure 5.17 Sample worksheet with 377 counts of success in 1000 trials

Framework Component	"Who do we hire?"

4. HOW to **solve** the problem/model?	• For $n \geq 5$, we can set up an *Excel* simulation:
	  • fix n to be for example 10 and consider strategy 4,
	  • for each simulation trial, generate random scores for all 10 candidates and obtain the maximum score,
	  • determine if the score of the jth candidate ($4 \leq j \leq 9$) is higher than the previous candidates, provided that no candidate has been chosen yet. If yes, we choose the candidate and record the score,
	  • if none of candidates 1 to 9 has been chosen, choose candidate 10 and record the score,
	  • check if the score of chosen candidate is the maximum score among all candidates. If yes, it means the best secretary was chosen,
	  • obtain the success rate over the 100 trials,
	  • repeat the simulations and average the results,
	  • design similar simulations for different strategies and choose the best strategy among them.

5. WHY is this experience a **success**?	In this lesson, students learn about: • coming up with various strategies to hire a secretary, • determining and comparing outcomes of different strategies used, • experimental probabilities, • constructing simulations using *Excel*.

Possible discussion points

Some students may find it rather challenging to understand the secretary problem, develop a way to think of possible strategies and then to construct a simulation to model the process, especially without suitable guidance. The following questions and points of discussions are suggested for teachers to explore with their students:

- Do the assumptions given make sense to you? Give reasons for your answer.
- What are the ways to choose a secretary under the given assumptions?
- Should we just always choose the first or the last candidate? Why, or why not?
- How can we determine the number of candidates we should reject before we consider hiring the next best one?
- How can we simulate the outcomes of hiring a secretary under a given strategy if there are more candidates? For example, what random values do we need to generate? How can we determine which candidate to choose?
- From your simulation, what is the likely probability of choosing the best secretary under your chosen strategy?
- How can we maximize the probability of choosing the best secretary using *Excel*?
- What is the highest probability that you obtained?

The Secretary Problem first appeared in Martin Gardner's *Mathematical Games* column in the February issue of *Scientific American* in 1960, albeit in a slightly different form known as the Marriage Problem. In practice, one may argue that the idea of rejecting a fixed proportion of candidates in such a selection process may not be very sound. However, one counter-argument would be that the rejection is not simply a blind rejection, but the interviewers are examining and assessing the candidates that they "intend" to reject so that a comparison can be made later. Nevertheless, the problem is mathematically rich, arises from a real-life situation, and has practical implications. It is therefore an excellent candidate for a mathematical modelling task.

Bibliography

Dougherty, E.R. (1990). *Probability and Statistics for the Engineering, Computing and Physical Sciences*. New Jersey: Prentice Hall.

Dworsky, L.N. (2008). *Probably Not: Future Prediction using Probability and Statistical Inference*. Hoboken: John Wiley and Sons, Inc.

Ferguson, T.S. (1989). Who solved the secretary problem? *Statistical Science*, 4(3), 282–96.

Jones, J. (n.d.). *Stay or switch*. Retrieved from www.stayorswitch.com.

Mark Lehman. (2013, February). *Monty Hall problem explained with tree diagram* [Video file]. Retrieved from www.youtube.com/watch?v=cphYs1bCeDs&feature=youtu.be.

Newcombe, J. [niansenx]. (2007, January 21). *The Monty Hall problem* [Video file]. Retrieved from www.youtube.com/watch?v=mhlc7peGlGg&feature=youtu.be.

Office for Mathematics, Science, and Technology Education, University of Illinois. (n.d.). *Buffon's needle*. Retrieved from https://mste.illinois.edu/activity/buffon.

Triangle inequality theorem proof. (n.d.). Retrieved from www.basic-mathematics.com/triangle-inequality-theorem-proof.html.

Wolfram Alpha LLC (2017, November 6). *Buffon's needle problem*. Retrieved from http://mathworld.wolfram.com/BuffonsNeedleProblem.html.

6 Mathematical modelling projects

Introduction

The mathematical modelling activities discussed in previous chapters are meant to be carried out in the classroom over a relatively short period of instructional time. This could range from a typical one-period mathematics class to two or three lessons over a couple of days. These are useful learning experiences aimed at developing specific skills or modelling competencies. However, as students mature in their abilities to handle modelling tasks, they can be further challenged to tackle more complete modelling projects. In some sense, modelling projects are designed so that they provide students with opportunities to demonstrate their abilities in mathematical modelling in a more holistic manner. In this chapter, four such projects are described, each requiring a certain level and field of mathematical ability, and suggestions on how the problems in the projects may be solved are presented.

A model for queues

Problem situation: Queueing is part of our everyday life. We queue for banking services, at checkout counters in supermarkets, to buy food at fast-food restaurants, and so on. A queue forms whenever demand for the product or service exceeds the existing capacity to provide that service or product. Consider a single queue and a single server. Depending on the frequency of customer arrivals, the type of service required and the efficiency of the server in providing the service, the waiting times and service times of customers will vary. Knowledge of the average waiting time and average service time, among other quantities, will be useful to both businesses and customers.

The task: Construct a model that can simulate a single queue with a single server.

Teacher notes

There are three components involved in a simple queueing system, namely, the *arrival process*, the *service process* and the *queue structure*. Within the arrival process, there are three important aspects to consider, and these are (a) how customers arrive (for example, single arrivals or in groups), (b) how arrivals are distributed in time (for example, the distribution of times between arrivals or the **inter-arrival times**), and (c) whether there is finite or infinite number of customers.

A service process typically has characteristics such as the length of service time (that is, the **service time distribution**), the number of servers available, and whether there is a

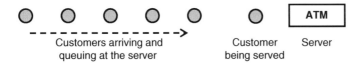

Figure 6.1 A single-server queue at an ATM

separate queue for each server. A queue structure determines how a person is chosen to be served; for instance, a "first-in first-out" or "last-in first-out" paradigm, or a random selection of any person in the queue. There are also considerations of whether there is balking (people do not join a queue if it is too long), reneging (people leave a queue after a long wait) or jockeying (people switching between queues). It may also be important to consider if the queue is of finite or infinite capacity.

To introduce the modelling of queues to students, we can consider a single queue at a single server, such as a queue at an Automatic Teller Machine (ATM), for simplicity. Figure 6.1 shows a schematic of a typical queue at an ATM with a corresponding schematic to represent the three distinct components, namely, the server, the customer being served and the customers waiting to be served. Customers arrive randomly at the ATM, wait for their turns in a single line, and then spend a certain amount of time at the machine before leaving. In other words, this queue clearly conforms to a "first-in first-out" queue structure.

To simulate a queueing system, two important variables are the **arrival rate** and the **service rate**. Suppose we let a represent the number of customers arriving per unit time, and b be the number of customers served per unit time. These values can be estimated and calculated from relevant data and information collected from a typical queue at an ATM. It is common to assume both the customer arrivals and service to be Poisson processes, and this means that the inter-arrival times and service times are assumed to be governed by an exponential distribution. This assumption is reasonable, and is used because the exponential distribution is the only continuous distribution that possesses the unique *memoryless* property. That is, the chance of waiting one more time unit for the next customer arrival does not depend on the time that has passed since the previous arrival, and the probability of a service being completed within the next given time period does not depend on how long the person has been served already. These assumptions lead to the well-known M/M/1 queueing model.

The term "M/M/1" needs some explanation. The "M" stands for Markov process, which is essentially a random process in which the future is independent of the past, given the present. In other words, a Markov process is stochastic analogue of the deterministic process described by differential equations, and is ideal to represent the memoryless process that we wish to model. Here, the first "M" indicates that the arrival process is Markov, and so is the service process, represented by the second "M". The "1" simply means that there is one server. The reader may refer to Bunday (1996) for more details.

To simulate a M/M/1 queue at an ATM, it is necessary to generate a list of arrival times of customers to the ATM, and another list of service times each individual customer spends at the machine. To generate a list of random arrival times, it is sufficient to generate the random inter-arrival times, denoted by Δt. This may be done using the "Inverse Transform

112 *Mathematical modelling projects*

Method" in the following manner. First, we find a random number, r generated from a uniform distribution over the interval $[0,1]$. Then, we let $r = 1 - e^{-at}$ (the cumulative distribution function of an exponential distribution), which leads to the formula, $t = -\frac{1}{a}\log(1-r)$. Since $r \sim U(0,1)$, it follows that $(1-r) \sim U(0,1)$. Hence, for convenience and to make things simple, we let $t = -\frac{1}{a}\log(r)$. In other words, we may now generate a list of inter-arrival times, or Δt, using $\Delta t = -\frac{1}{a}\log(r)$, for some value of the parameter a.

In a similar fashion, by similar argument, a list of random service times, denoted by st, may be obtained by the formula, $st = -\frac{1}{b}\log(r')$, where r' is also a random number generated from the uniform distribution over $[0,1]$ and b is the parameter that needs to be estimated. Once these random times are generated, the other variables such as arrival times, finish times, and waiting times of customers, and so on may be calculated.

Though the theory of queues is, in general, not an easy concept for Pre-University students to grasp, queues are a phenomenon often experienced in real life. Using simulation models, it is possible to demonstrate how mathematics can be used to study such a complex process. Until students are ready, they may not need to understand the Poisson process or exponential distribution. In the meantime, students can be guided in this modelling task involving an everyday life experience through the use of appropriate technological tools to help them understand the process and appreciate the mathematics.

A suggested approach

Although it is possible to use the formulae to generate some simulated values of Δt and st, there are two important parameters, namely the arrival rate a and the service rate b in the model that need to be addressed. These can be estimated from appropriate data collected at an ATM queue. For example, students can use a stopwatch to record the arrival times of customers on site and the time taken for them to finish what they need to do at the ATM, or video-record a queue and study the video later to gather this information. They can then proceed to compute the inter-arrival times, service times, wait times and total times (wait time and service time) using an electronic spreadsheet. Figure 6.2 shows a screenshot of such a worksheet on *Excel*, obtained from Soon and Ang (2015). In that work, an ATM queue was observed for approximately an hour at a university campus around late lunchtime. For simplicity, only the data of customers who finished their services were used.

The actual arrival times of customers were recorded in Column C, and the time at which each customer left the ATM was recorded in Column E. From the values in Column C, the inter-arrival times were obtained and recorded correspondingly in Column B. For instance, for Customer 2, the value in Cell B7 is obtained using the formulat "=C7-C6". The service times recorded in Column D were computed using the values in Columns C and E. For example, for Customer 2, the formula "=E7-MAX(E6,C7)" was used to find out how long the ATM took to serve the customer and recorded in Cell D7. The total times in Column F were obtained by taking the differences between the finish times in Column E and arrival times in Column C, while the wait times in Column G were the differences between total times (in Column F) and service times (in Column D).

	A	B	C	D	E	F	G
1							
2		Ave arrival rate	Ave service rate			Ave total time	Ave wait time
3		a = 1.087/min	b = 1.239/min			0:03:25	0:02:37
4							
5	cust no.	Inter-arrival time	arrival time	service time	finish time	Total time	Wait time
6	1	0:00:00	13:05:52	0:01:31	13:07:23	0:01:31	0:00:00
7	2	0:00:10	13:06:02	0:00:53	13:08:16	0:02:14	0:01:21
8	3	0:00:42	13:06:44	0:01:03	13:09:19	0:02:35	0:01:32
9	4	0:00:09	13:06:53	0:00:43	13:10:02	0:03:09	0:02:26
10	5	0:00:05	13:06:58	0:00:38	13:10:40	0:03:42	0:03:04
11	6	0:00:15	13:07:13	0:00:27	13:11:07	0:03:54	0:03:27
12	7	0:00:04	13:07:17	0:00:35	13:11:42	0:04:25	0:03:50
13	8	0:00:49	13:08:06	0:00:32	13:12:14	0:04:08	0:03:36

Figure 6.2 Screenshot of *Excel* worksheet with data from an ATM queue

	A	B	C	D	E	F	G	H	I
1			Ave arrival rate			Ave service rate			
2			a = 1.087			b = 1.239			
3									
4	n	IAT	AT	ST	FT	Total time	Wait time	Ave total time	Ave wait time
5	1	1.40	1.40	0.09	1.50	0.09	0.00	1.82	1.14
6	2	3.16	4.57	0.62	5.18	0.62	0.00		
7	3	0.37	4.94	0.02	5.21	0.27	0.25		
8	4	0.68	5.62	2.42	8.04	2.42	0.00		
9	5	0.73	6.35	0.47	8.51	2.16	1.69		
10	6	0.06	6.40	0.11	8.62	2.21	2.10		
11	7	0.04	6.45	0.02	8.63	2.18	2.17		
12	8	0.76	7.21	0.81	9.45	2.23	1.42		
13	9	0.18	7.39	0.71	10.15	2.76	2.05		
14	10	0.05	7.45	0.09	10.24	2.80	2.71		

Figure 6.3 Screenshot of a queue simulation in an *Excel* worksheet

Since $a = \dfrac{\text{no. of customers}}{\text{sum (inter-arrival times)}}$ and $b = \dfrac{\text{no. of customers}}{\text{sum (service times)}}$, the values of a, b, average total and average wait times were then calculated accordingly, and entered in Cells B3, C3, F3 and G3 as shown in Figure 6.2.

After the students learn how to use real-life data collected to obtain the arrival rate and service rate (as shown in the sample above), they can move on to experiment with the mechanism of queues and to learn more about generating randomness through a simple simulation, again on an *Excel* worksheet. Figure 6.3 shows a screenshot of a simulation run involving 100 customers using estimated values of the arrival and service rates, $a = 1.087$ and $b = 1.239$ respectively, as found in the sample above.

114 Mathematical modelling projects

This simulation is executed as follows

1) The first column lists the set of customers, that is, $n = 1,\ldots,100$, if we have 100 customers
2) In Column B, random inter-arrival times (indicated as "IAT" in Figure 6.3) are obtained using $t = -\frac{1}{a}\log(r)$ as discussed earlier. The formula "=(-1/\$D\$2)*LN(RAND())" is entered in Cell B5 and copied down to B104. The expression in the formula "\$D\$2" ensures that the value of the parameter, a, is used throughout
3) Assuming that time starts from 0, we set the arrival time ("AT") of Customer 1 (in Cell C5) to be the first inter-arrival time generated randomly (in Cell B5). The arrival times of Customers 2 to 100, recorded in Column C, are obtained by adding the arrival times of the previous customers to the corresponding inter-arrival times. For example, "=C5+B6" is entered in Cell C6 for Customer 2
4) Similarly, the formula "=(-1/\$G\$2)*LN(RAND())" is used in Column D to generate random service times ("ST")
5) The finish time ("FT") of Customer 1, recorded in Cell E5, is obtained using the formula, "=C5+D5". The remaining values in Column E are obtained by taking the larger of the sum of the previous FT and the corresponding ST, and the sum of the corresponding AT and ST. For example, the formula "= MAX(E5+D6, C6+D6)" is used in Cell E6
6) Column F records the total times spent by the customers, obtained by taking the differences between the customers' FT and AT. For example, "= E5−C5" is entered in Cell F5
7) In Column G, the wait time for each customer is the difference between the customer's total time spent and ST (for example, in Cell G5, the formula "= F5 − D5" is entered)
8) Finally, the average total time and average wait time are calculated by entering the formulae "=AVERAGE(F5:F104)" and "=AVERAGE(G5:G104)" in Cells H5 and I5 respectively.

In the sample worksheet shown in Figure 6.3, based on the given values of a and b, the results of this particular simulation run shows that the average total time taken by a customer is about 1.82 minutes and the expected waiting time is about 1.14 minutes. This simulation can be repeated, with different number of customers if necessary, to obtain averages of the "average total time" and "average wait time". In addition, the model may be studied and examined further by varying the values of a and b and observing if the changes in average total time and average wait time are reasonable.

For example, if the arrival rate a is increased, one would expect both the average total time and average wait time to increase. If the service rate b is increased, both the average total time and average wait time would be expected to decrease. By making suitable changes to these two parameter values and observing the results, one could conclude if the simulation models would yield reasonable outcomes. This model can be extended to a single-queue-multiple-server structure, but it would require further analysis and the model will be considerably more complicated. For example, different random service times will need to be generated for the multiple servers, and it may be necessary to identify idle servers and decide which ones among them should serve the succeeding customers.

This modelling project can be introduced to students from the upper secondary level onwards, who are familiar with topics in probability and statistics, and who possess the required skills in using the spreadsheet. Teachers can use the following framework as a guide in planning this activity.

Using the framework

Framework Component	"A model for queues"
1. WHICH **level** of learning experience?	Level 3.
2. WHAT is the **skill/Competency**?	• Understanding the problem. • Making assumptions to simplify the problem. • Collecting data carefully. • Data manipulation using *Excel*. • Designing and carrying out a simulation.
3. WHERE is the **mathematics**?	• Probability. • Statistics (in particular, the exponential distribution). • Random numbers and the use of a random number generator.

4. HOW to **solve** the problem/model?	• Collect data at an ATM queue on the arrival and finish times of customers.
	• Use *Excel* to obtain the inter-arrival times, service times, total times and wait times of all customers. Then compute the average arrival rate a and average service rate b.
	• Set up a simulation on *Excel*:
	  • generate random inter-arrival times and service times for 100 customers using a and b,
	  • compute the arrival times, finish times, total times and wait times for all customers,
	  • obtain the average total time and average wait time.
	• Repeat the simulation and average the results to use as estimates of average total and wait time.
	• Validate the model by changing a and b to see if the corresponding changes in average total and wait time are reasonable.

5. WHY is this experience a **success**?	In this lesson, students learn about: basics of queues that occur in everyday life, deeper understanding of random processes, generating random numbers, use of *Excel* to construct a simulation, validation of simulation models.

Possible discussion points

This modelling project can be a challenging task for many students, especially when they are not familiar with some of the concepts in queueing theory and applied probability. It will take some time for students, presented with such a problem, to be able to arrive at a plausible solution or approach, without the benefit of such conceptual understanding. Nonetheless, this project can still be managed by students or a group of students if they are guided by the teacher. To help students with this modelling task, the following questions could serve to guide their thinking:

116   *Mathematical modelling projects*

- When does a queue form at an ATM?
- What may affect the length of a queue?
- What are the corresponding variables to consider in studying queues?
- What kind of data or information do we need and what computations do we need to do so as to obtain the average arrival rate and average service rate of customers in a queue?
- What simplifying assumptions can we make?
- How can we simulate the queue based on the average arrival rate and average service rate obtained earlier? What are the outcomes that would be useful to obtain?
- How will the average total time and average wait time change if the arrival rate or service rate changes?
- Suggest ways to reduce the wait time for customers.

Having to queue up for something is a very common experience. However, to actually model the phenomenon or the process requires a fairly sophisticated level of mathematical knowledge. Yet, it is possible, through the use of simulation and some basic spreadsheet skills, to carry out a simple study of queues, and to verify some of the theory involved. Therefore, teachers who are looking for a modelling project for students based on a familiar setting and with the possibility of stretching their abilities could consider this project.

The SARS epidemic

Problem situation: In 2003, the world saw the emergence of a deadly, contagious disease known as the Severe Acute Respiratory Syndrome, or SARS. This disease is a severe form of pneumonia and is highly contagious, and it was believed that it all started in Asia. More than 8000 cases were reported globally and around 774 deaths was recorded worldwide. The island state of Singapore was not spared from this episode. During the outbreak in Singapore that lasted around 70 days, 33 lives were lost ("Sars in Singapore", 2013). This was indeed a major event in the history of the country, and it certainly would be useful if the spread of the disease could be studied and investigated in some way.

The task: Construct a mathematical model to describe the outbreak of the SARS epidemic.

Teacher notes

As SARS had a great impact on the lives of people, for instance the residents in Singapore in 2003, it provides a relevant context for students to experience the process of mathematical modelling. One way to study it is through the use of a deterministic model. Students can undertake this modelling project in groups. Depending on their abilities, they can either be required to consider some well-known epidemic models, or develop a differential equation that models the outbreak. For a start, students can be tasked to read up on SARS, and on how disease epidemics in general, in order to have a better understanding of the problem. They can study the factors or variables that are involved in the spread of a disease, and examine some existing models for the transmission of diseases. Students can also be provided with the recorded data for the SARS outbreak in Singapore to have an idea of the extent of the outbreak.

The factors involved in typical disease transmissions include environmental conditions (for example, sanitation facilities, water supply and climate), population patterns (where people live and how they interact with one another), population densities (number of people in a defined area), infection status of infected individuals, immunity status of uninfected individuals, and whether the community is open or closed. A closed community is one where the individuals in the community do not leave and no new individual joins the community during the period of interest. The important variables involved in an outbreak of a disease include the number of infected individuals, healthy (uninfected) individuals, healthy (recovered) individuals, and time. Given this knowledge, students can proceed to study the various ways in which the spread of an epidemic may be modelled, and consider the use of empirical data to test the chosen model or to estimate relevant parameters.

A suggested approach

As there are many factors and variables to consider, one could consider making some assumptions to simplify the situation. In the present case, for example, we could assume a homogeneous population in a closed community of constant size N throughout the period under consideration. In addition, all infected individuals are equally infectious and none is immune to the disease. With these assumptions, a common model in which the population is compartmentalised into two groups, as depicted schematically in Figure 6.4, can be considered.

In this model, one part of the population consists of the "healthy and susceptible" individuals, who, upon some form of contact with the other part, consisting of the "infected and infectious" individuals, become infected. In other words, individuals in the susceptibles ("S") compartment may move to "infected" ("I") compartment. For this reason, this model is known as the *S-I model*, a well-known model and the simplest of disease models. The S-I model is typically used to represent the spread of a contagious disease in a closed community over a short period of time, and in the case of the SARS, this could be a suitable model to consider.

Students may be prompted to think about the independent and dependent variables involved in the S-I model. In this case, the independent variable is clearly time, denoted by t, and the dependent variable here would be the number of infected individuals. Students can be tasked to discuss the factors on which the change in number of infected individuals should depend. It is not surprising that with more susceptible or infected individuals, the increase in number of infected individuals should also be higher. This is because the transmission of this disease is dependent on interaction between or amongst the individuals, and with more individuals interacting, chances of spreading would naturally increase.

Using these ideas, and letting $x(t)$ and $y(t)$ be the number of infected and susceptible individuals at time t respectively, a possible simple deterministic model constructed using a single, first-order ordinary differential equation is

$$\frac{dx}{dt} = \beta xy,$$

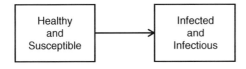

Figure 6.4 The S-I model for the spread of diseases

where β is some positive constant of proportionality. The right-hand side, consisting of a product of the two population variables, is essentially an application of the "mass-action interaction" principle in population dynamics.

To simplify the equation, since the community is closed and the total population is assumed to be of constant size N, it follows that $y = N - x$. Upon substitution, we obtain

$$\frac{dx}{dt} = \beta x (N - x) = kx \left(1 - \frac{x}{N}\right), \quad \text{where} \quad k = \beta N.$$

This is the well-known logistic equation and students who have been introduced to differential equations may be familiar with it. Using separation of variables and partial fractions, we can obtain

$$\int \left(\frac{1}{x} + \frac{1}{N-x}\right) dx = \int k \, dt$$

which works out to

$$\ln x - \ln(N - x) = kt + C,$$

where C is some arbitrary constant. Rearranging, the following is obtained.

$$\Rightarrow \frac{x}{N - x} = e^{kt+C}.$$

Suppose that initially, there is x_0 number of infected individuals; that is, $x(0) = x_0$. Then it follows that $\frac{x_0}{N - x_0} = e^C$ and so $\frac{x}{N - x} = \frac{x_0}{N - x_0} e^{kt}$. Simplifying and rearranging the expression, the solution to the logistic equation may be written as

$$x(t) = \frac{N}{1 + \left(\frac{N}{x_0} - 1\right)e^{-kt}}.$$

With this solution, students can proceed to test the model using the case of the SARS epidemic in Singapore. The relevant set of data shown in Table 6.1 is obtained from Ang (2004).

As can be seen from the table, $x_0 = 1$ and $N = 206$. Substituting these known values, we obtain $x(t) = \frac{206}{1 + 205e^{-kt}}$. The unknown constant k can be estimated from the data set. This is done by finding a value of k that would best fit the model to the data set. One way to do this is to use the method of least squares and the Solver tool in *Excel*, as mentioned in Chapter 1 and described in detail in Appendix A.

As reported in Ang (2004), the value of k in this case is found to be 0.16858. In addition, the "average error" E obtained is 1.9145, where $E = \frac{\sqrt{\sum_{i=1}^{n} (x_i - \bar{x}_i)^2}}{n}$, x_i and $\bar{x}_i$ are

Table 6.1 Cumulative number of individuals infected with SARS in Singapore from 24 February to 7 May 2003

Day	Number	Day	Number	Day	Number
0	1	24	84	48	184
1	2	25	89	49	187
2	2	26	90	50	188
3	2	27	92	51	193
4	3	28	97	52	193
5	3	29	101	53	193
6	3	30	103	54	195
7	3	31	105	55	197
8	5	32	105	56	199
9	6	33	110	57	202
10	7	34	111	58	203
11	10	35	116	59	204
12	13	36	118	60	204
13	19	37	124	61	204
14	23	38	130	62	205
15	25	39	138	63	205
16	26	40	150	64	205
17	26	41	153	65	205
18	32	42	157	66	205
19	44	43	163	67	205
20	59	44	168	68	205
21	69	45	170	69	205
22	74	46	175	70	206
23	82	47	179		

the model and data values respectively, and n is the number of data points. A graph of SARS data points and the logistic curve fitted to the data is shown in Figure 6.5.

While the S-I model and the resulting solution to the logistic equation seems to represent the general evolution of the SARS outbreak fairly well, it can be observed from Figure 6.5 that the model seems to deviate from the actual data between $t = 10$ and $t = 60$ quite significantly. One can ask if there is a reason for this, or if there is any way to improve the model.

One possible way is to consider a general form of the logistic equation. That is,

$$\frac{dx}{dt} = kx\left(1 - \left(\frac{x}{N}\right)^p\right),$$

where p is a positive constant. In the usual logistic model (where $p = 1$), it is assumed that the proportional growth rate or fractional rate of change in the number infected, that is, $\frac{dx}{dt} / x$, varies linearly with the number of individuals infected. However, this may not be so, and a more general treatment is possible. Using the last equation, we can vary p to obtain a *modified* logistic model that could possibly fit the data better. To solve it, we let $u = \left(\frac{x}{N}\right)^p$ and perform a change of variables to yield

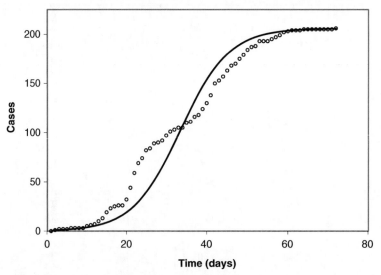

Figure 6.5 SARS outbreak data (○) and the simple logistics model with $k = 0.16858$

$$\int \frac{1}{u(1-u)} du = \int pk\, dt.$$

The solution may be obtained in a similar fashion as before (using separation of variables, and integrating), and in this case, we obtain

$$x(t) = \frac{N}{\left(1 + Ae^{-pkt}\right)^{\frac{1}{p}}},$$

where A is some arbitrary constant. Applying the initial condition $x(0) = x_0$ yields the solution,

$$x(t) = \frac{N}{\left(1 + \left(\left(\frac{N}{x_0}\right)^p - 1\right)e^{-pkt}\right)^{1/p}}.$$

Although this solution may appear more complex than the previous, the Solver tool in *Excel* may be used in a similar way to find estimates for the unknown parameters. In this case, there are two parameter values, k and p, to be found but the process is the same. The values of k and p that minimise the average error E are found to be 0.43337 and 0.19882 respectively for the same data set. This model provides a much better approximation to the data, and the error is $E = 0.9644$. As reported by Ang (2004), the graph of SARS data points and the modified logistic curve fitted to the data is given in Figure 6.6.

Mathematical modelling projects 121

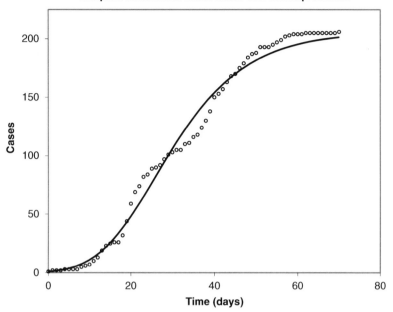

Figure 6.6 SARS outbreak data (∘) and the modified logistics model with $k = 0.16858$ and $p = 0.19882$

The following framework can serve as a guide for teachers in planning this modelling activity. Note that as the concepts in differential equations and skills required for this task are non-trivial, this activity may be more relevant to students from the post-secondary level onwards.

Using the framework

Framework Component	"The SARS epidemic"
1. WHICH **level** of learning experience?	Level 3.
2. WHAT is the **skill/Competency**?	Understanding the problem. Identifying factors and variables involved in the problem. Making assumptions to simplify the problem. Constructing differential equation models. Use of the Solver tool in *Excel*.
3. WHERE is the **mathematics**?	• Functions and Graphs. • Differential equations, for example, the general form of the logistic equation: $$\frac{dx}{dt} = kx\left(1 - \left(\frac{x}{N}\right)^p\right),$$ • with the solution of the form $x(t) = \dfrac{N}{\left(1 + Ae^{-pkt}\right)^{\frac{1}{p}}}.$

122 Mathematical modelling projects

Framework Component	"The SARS epidemic"
4. HOW to **solve** the problem/model?	• Make reasonable simplifying assumptions and construct the logistic equation model (with $p = 1$ above) based on the assumptions. • Solve the logistic equation to obtain the solution $x(t)$, using the initial number of infected individuals and size of the population obtained from the SARS data set. • Estimate the parameter k that gives a good fit to the data set using the Solver tool in *Excel*. • Improve on the model by varying p and k to find a logistic curve that provides a better fit to the given data (using *Excel*).
5. WHY is this experience a **success**?	In this lesson, students learn about: • diseases and how they spread, • different epidemic models that describe the transmission of diseases, • real-life applications of differential equations, • techniques of solving differential equations, • use of *Excel* in finding parameters that generate curves of best fit to data points, • interpretation of parameters involved in differential equations.

Possible discussion points

This modelling project is likely to be a challenge to many students, due to the level of mathematics required or involved. Teachers may want to guide their students engaged in this project by asking the following questions and using them as points of discussion.

- What is SARS and how did the disease spread in Singapore in 2003?
- What factors should be considered when studying the spread of diseases?
- What are the variables involved?
- What are some existing mathematical models that describe the transmission of diseases?
- What assumptions can we make on some of the factors to simplify the problem?
- How is the increase in the number of infected individuals affected by the number of healthy or infected individuals present in the population?
- How can we use the data set to test our model?
- Do the parameters present in the differential equation have any physical meaning?

This modelling project serves as an excellent introduction to the study of epidemics and population dynamics. Students may not be familiar with these topics, or have not come across them previously, but they can always start with some reading or do some research on their own. There are several important parameters and terms that are related to epidemics, such as the disease transmission rate, k and the carrying capacity, N in the logistic equation. Such terms need to be discussed with students as they progress in the project so that the exercise will not be just one that is merely focussed on curve-fitting or solving a differential equations. These parameters have real physical meanings, and it is critical that students are aware of them as they develop their understanding of these models.

Mathematical modelling projects 123

The approach to the problem discussed above is part of what has been reported by Ang (2004). For details, the reader may wish to read the original article, in which another model known as the double logistic model is also presented.

A checksum algorithm

Problem situation: The use of barcodes as a means of identification is very common. However, its use in the form of a transhipment license for pets may not be as well known. Pets are often transhipped via certain cities and ports, as they travel between countries. They typically transit in these cities for short period, typically less than 24 hours. A transhipment license is required for each pet in such a situation, and there is a need to check the authenticity of the transhipment licenses using a robust and reliable algorithm. Such checks are necessary in order to detect errors in the license numbers, as well as to deter smuggling of expensive pets, such as the prized dog, "Big Splash". Big Splash is a red Tibetan mastiff that became the most expensive dog in the world after being sold for 10 million Chinese yuan or 1.5 million US dollars ("Big Splash", 2017). A transhipment license number consists of a 6-digit number followed by a check number or letter (called the checksum).

The task: Design a checksum algorithm to authenticate the transhipment license numbers of pets.

Teacher notes

There are many uses of checksum algorithms, for example, in authenticating identification numbers or codes of people, food products and pets, and for detecting errors in data that surfaced during its transmission or storage of these identification numbers. The most famous use of a checksum is perhaps in barcodes, such as those used in supermarkets to keep track of their products, as shown in Figure 6.7 below.

Barcodes were first developed for the purpose of automating checkouts in supermarkets. Now they are used on almost all manufactured goods, and ensure that the goods are recognised internationally. On each barcode, the checksum is the number located at the end of the sequence, on the right. Its purpose is to make sure that the barcode is composed or constructed correctly. The barcode reader's decoder calculates the checksum using the digits that precede the check number, and compares the result with the check number. If the two numbers match, the reader usually emits a signal that indicates that the scan has been successful.

Students can first be given an assignment to find out what a checksum is and why we use it. Teachers may then choose to ask students to construct a checksum algorithm based on their understanding of what a checksum is and how it is used. Typically, modular arithmetic is used to calculate a checksum as it is easy to understand and use. In addition, the largest value of the check number is known and hence space required to hold the number may be suitably allocated. Teachers can also guide students in listing out the factors that should be considered when designing a checksum algorithm, and the variables involved in an algorithm.

One factor is the type or types of errors that the algorithm should be able to detect. For example, single-digit transcription errors, or transposition error of a pair of digits are common errors. To illustrate this, suppose that the correct license number of a pet is 1524585. A possible single-digit error could result in the number 1324585, and a possible transposition error could result in the number 5124585. Other factors include the choice

124 *Mathematical modelling projects*

Figure 6.7 An example of a barcode used in a supermarket product

of a number or letter as the checksum, the amount of space needed to hold the checksum, the accuracy and speed of the algorithm. The variables involved are the number of digits in a transhipment license number preceding the checksum and the check number or letter. When students have sufficient understanding of a checksum, they can proceed to design their algorithms based on simplifying assumptions made on the factors.

A suggested approach

For simplicity, it may be assumed that a number should be used as the checksum and the speed of the algorithm is not important. The focus of the exercise therefore, will be on designing algorithms that can accurately detect as many types of errors as possible, with as few digits needed for the check number as possible. Suppose we wish to design a checksum algorithm for a license with six digits preceding the checksum. Let $d_1, d_2, \ldots, d_6$ represent the six digits and N represent the checksum that is generated by any algorithm.

Consider first the detection of single-digit errors. A simple way to accurately detect single-digit errors with as few digits used as possible for the checksum is to set $N = \left(\sum_{i=1}^{6} d_i\right)$ modulo 10 (or mod 10). For example, if the six preceding digits are 142894, then the checksum is

$$N = (1+4+2+8+9+4) \bmod 10 = 28 \bmod 10 = 8.$$

In this case, the maximum value of the checksum is 9 in all cases. However, it is easy to see that transposition errors will not be detected by this algorithm.

An improvement on the above algorithm is to use a suitable weighted sum of the six digits before taking the modulus. For example, let $N = (3d_1 + d_2 + 3d_3 + d_4 + 3d_5 + d_6)$

mod 10. Then any change in a single digit, say from d_i to $(d_i + m)$ mod 10 (where $m = 1,\ldots,9$), will lead to a change in k or $3k$ in the weighted sum for some integer k. Since k and $3k$ cannot be divisible by 10 for any such k (as 1 and 3 are co-prime with 10), single-digit errors can be detected by this algorithm. Now suppose that there is a transposition error of two consecutive digits, say d_1 and d_2. Then the difference between the new weighted sum and the original weighted sum will be $|2(d_2 - d_1)|$. Now, if $|d_2 - d_1| = 5$, then the transposition error will go undetected. This is because the weights 1 and 3 differ by 2 (which is not co-prime with 10). In addition, if there is a transposition error in any pair of odd or even positioned digits, for example, d_1 and d_3 or d_2 and d_4, then this algorithm will not be able to detect the error since the corresponding weights are the same.

From the above discussion, it can be deduced that in order to detect single-digit errors and all transposition errors, all the chosen weights must be different, be co-prime with 10 and each pair of weights can only differ by numbers co-prime with 10. However, it is not possible to choose weights that can satisfy all these criteria. This means that modulo 10 should not be used. One solution is then to use modulo 11 since it is a prime number and we can use the weights, $2, 3, \ldots, 7$. All these six numbers are different, are co-prime with 11, and each pair of these weights differ by a number that is co-prime with 11. That is, we set

$$N = (2d_1 + 3d_2 + 4d_3 + 5d_4 + 6d_5 + 7d_6) \bmod 11.$$

A spreadsheet such as *Excel* may be used to create examples by randomly selecting digits so that one could experiment with different algorithms, instead of doing the calculations by hand. Figure 6.8 shows an implementation on such a spreadsheet with examples to demonstrate the difference in error detection between the two algorithms discussed above. The formulae used in the spreadsheet are straightforward, involving just addition and the modulo function. For example, Cell H4 contains the formula, "=B4*B3+C4*C3+D4*D3+E4*E3+F4*F3+G4*G3", and in Cell I4, the formula "=MOD(H4,10)" is entered. The entries and results shown in Figure 6.8 are self-explanatory, and the reader may verify them or generate new examples to test both algorithms.

This modelling activity should be of some interest to students as checksums are used in many applications. For instance, barcodes and transmission of identification codes, are very common in the modern world and our everyday lives. In addition, the use of QR (or Quick

	(3,1) weights, mod 10								(2,3,4,5,6,7) weights, mod 11							
---	d1	d2	d3	d4	d5	d6	Sum	Sum mod 10	d1	d2	d3	d4	d5	d6	Sum	Sum mod 11
weights	3	1	3	1	3	1			2	3	4	5	6	7		
Test case 1	1	2	3	4	5	6	39	9	1	2	3	4	5	6	112	2
Single Digit Error	1	5	3	4	5	6	42	2	1	5	3	4	5	6	121	0
Two Digit Error	1	3	6	4	5	6	49	9	1	3	6	4	5	6	127	6
Tranposition Error 1	2	1	3	4	5	6	41	1	2	1	3	4	5	6	111	1
Tranposition Error 2	1	2	5	4	3	6	39	9	1	2	5	4	3	6	108	9
Test case 2	1	6	2	3	4	5	35	5	1	6	2	3	4	5	102	3
Tranposition Error 1	6	1	2	3	4	5	45	5	6	1	2	3	4	5	97	9

Figure 6.8 A screenshot of the *Excel* spreadsheet with examples showing the difference between the two checksum algorithms (boxed cells indicate cases of failure in error detection)

126 *Mathematical modelling projects*

Response) codes is also becoming very common. QR codes are actually two-dimensional barcodes that also use checksums as a means of checking authenticity and accuracy. It may be suitable to post this modelling task to students from the upper secondary level onwards, as they need to have sufficient arithmetic background. Teachers can use the following framework as a guide when designing the activity.

Using the framework

Framework Component	"A checksum algorithm"
1. WHICH **level** of learning experience?	Level 3.
2. WHAT is the **skill/competency**?	• Understanding the problem. • Identifying factors that affect the problem. • Making assumptions to simplify the problem. • Validation and refinement of models.
3. WHERE is the **mathematics**?	• Arithmetic (for example, modular arithmetic).
4. HOW to **solve** the problem/model?	• Start with a simple algorithm that detects single-entry errors in the digits $d_1, d_2, \ldots, d_6$. An example of a checksum is $N = \left(\sum_{i=1}^{6} d_i \right)$ modulo 10. Identify the shortfall of the algorithm and improve on the model. • Design an algorithm that can detect transposition errors as well. For example, set $N = (3d_1 + d_2 + 3d_3 + d_4 + 3d_5 + d_6) \bmod 10$. • Analyse the merits and shortfalls of this algorithm and come up with a criteria that can lead to a better model. • One possible algorithm to detect the various types of errors is to use the checksum $N = (2d_1 + 3d_2 + 4d_3 + 5d_4 + 6d_5 + 7d_6) \bmod 11$.
5. WHY is this experience a **success**?	In this lesson, students learn about: • interesting real-life application of arithmetic, • how to design a checking algorithm, • analysing advantages and disadvantages of a model, • setting up suitable criteria for a valid model.

Possible discussion points

This modelling project does not actually require very sophisticated mathematical knowledge or skills. However, it may not be easy for students to think of a suitable solution or a method to address the problem. The following questions could possibly be helpful to prompt students and point them to the appropriate direction:

- What is a checksum and why is it used?
- How is it used in a barcode?
- What sort of errors may occur in the transshipment license numbers of pets?
- What should be considered in designing a suitable algorithm?
- Why is modular arithmetic commonly used in calculating a checksum?
- What are some simplifying assumptions that we can make?

- What type or types of errors can your proposed model detect?
- What are the merits and pitfalls of your model?
- Can you validate or improve on your model?

To some, this project on checksum algorithm may not look like a mathematical modelling problem or task. Most of the modelling tasks described earlier have involved using equations to model a situation, or represent some data, or generating some form of simulation. However, mathematical modelling in the wider context would include developing a method, through the use of appropriate mathematics, to solve a real-life problem. Here, the problem is in checking a certain code and detecting errors when the code is transmitted or transcribed. The solution suggested here is an algorithm, not an equation or formula, and is a mathematical construct that serves as the model to address the problem. Of course, other algorithms or solutions are possible, and this only goes to show the mathematical richness in this modelling project.

Testing Torricelli

Problem situation: Suppose that we fill up a tank with water and then let the water drain out through an outlet, as shown in Figure 6.9. How quickly will the water level in the tank decrease over time? Will the water drain out at a constant rate? We wish to describe this process using a mathematical model.

The task: Investigate how the water level in a tank changes with time as water is being drained out.

Teacher notes

Students can first be asked to identify the important variables that are involved in the investigation. These could include the height of the water level in the tank, as a dependent variable, and time as one independent variable. Teachers can then discuss with students about the factors that should be considered when investigating the process of water draining out of a tank. These factors could include the shape and size of the tank, the shape and size of outlet of the container, the viscosity of the liquid that is flowing out (if it is not water), and fluid drag force (that is, the friction between the fluid or water and the tank). For a start, we could consider a cylindrical tank with a cylindrical outlet or round hole near the bottom,

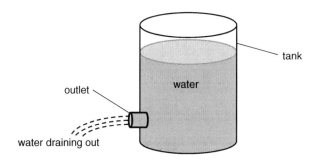

Figure 6.9 Draining of water tank

as shown in Figure 6.9. To approach this problem, some conceptual understanding of fluid flow and related theory may be required, and these are described below.

The change in water level in a tank over time can be explained using *Torricelli's law* for fluid flow. Torricelli's law states that the water in a tank will drain out through a hole with the velocity it would have if it fell freely from the water level to the hole. This law, however, is based on several assumptions made to simplify the situation. For example, the cross-sectional area of the hole or outlet must be very small as compared to the cross-sectional area of the tank that contains the water. In addition, the fluid drag force is assumed to be negligible and water is taken to be a non-viscous fluid.

To use Torricelli's law, we first find the velocity of water when it lands after falling freely from a certain height. Let $h(t)$ be the height of water at time t (in seconds), and g be the gravitational acceleration. Now the second-order differential equation for acceleration due to gravitational force is given by $\dfrac{d^2 h}{dt^2} = -g$. As the initial velocity of the water is zero since it falls from rest, it follows that

$$\frac{dh}{dt} = -gt \text{ which yields } h(t) = -\frac{gt^2}{2} + h_0,$$

where $h_0 = h(0)$.

Let v denote the velocity of the water at the terminal point and T be the time taken to reach there. Then,

$$v = -gT \text{ and } 0 = -\frac{gT^2}{2} + h_0.$$

Thus

$$0 = -\frac{g}{2}\left(-\frac{v}{g}\right)^2 + h_0 \Rightarrow v = -\sqrt{2gh_0}.$$

By Torricelli's law, the velocity of water emerging from a hole in a tank is $v = -\sqrt{2gh(t)}$, where $h(t)$ is the height of the water in the tank at any time t. Let A be the cross-sectional area of the cylindrical tank and a be the area of the hole. Then the volume of the water in the tank at time t, denoted by $V(t)$, is $V(t) = Ah(t)$, and the volume of water leaving the outlet per second is $av = a\sqrt{2gh(t)}$.

Thus the rate of change of volume of water in the tank is

$$\frac{dV}{dt} = A\frac{dh}{dt} = -a\sqrt{2gh},$$

which implies that

$$\frac{dh}{dt} = -\frac{a}{A}\sqrt{2gh}.$$

We can solve this differential equation using separation of variables as follows:

$$\frac{dh}{\sqrt{h}} = -\frac{a\sqrt{2g}}{A}dt \Rightarrow \int_{h_0}^{h(t)} \frac{1}{\sqrt{h}}dh = \int_0^t -\frac{a\sqrt{2g}}{A}dt$$

$$\Rightarrow 2\left(\sqrt{h(t)} - \sqrt{h_0}\right) = -\frac{a\sqrt{2g}}{A}t \tag{6.1}$$

Hence, it follows that

$$h(t) = \left(\sqrt{h_0} - \frac{a\sqrt{g}}{\sqrt{2}A}t\right)^2.$$

Alternatively, from Equation 6.1, we may derive the expression for the time needed for the water to fall from height h_1 to h_2 ($h_1 > h_2$) in the container, given by

$$\Delta t = \frac{2A}{a\sqrt{2g}}\left(\sqrt{h_1} - \sqrt{h_2}\right). \tag{6.2}$$

In other words, Torricelli's law can be used to predict how long it would take for the water tank to drain completely, by substituting $h_1 = h_0$ and $h_2 = 0$ in Equation 6.2.

A suggested approach

For students who are not yet able to handle the mathematics to deal with Torricelli's law, one possible way to approach this project is the empirical modelling approach. Experiments can be carried out to investigate and examine the relationship between the height of the water in a tank, denoted by, say, h, and time, t. A typical set up for such an experiment is as shown in Figure 6.10.

Firstly, a cylindrical container that is used for this experiment should have a small hole punctured near the bottom as shown in Figure 6.10 (a). Special care should be taken when creating this small circular hole and the edge of the hole should be as smooth as possible. To keep track of the water level, a paper ruler can be taped on the outside as shown, taking care to align the zero mark with the level of the outlet hole. A video-recording can be made to record the water level over time, as shown in (b) in Figure 6.10. For better accuracy, only data collected when the water is in the part of the container with constant cross-sectional area are used.

The experiment can be performed several times to ensure that data collected are correct and consistent. Sample results from experiments conducted with the set up depicted in Figure 6.10 are summarised and shown in Figure 6.11 in a graph plotted using the electronic spreadsheet, *Excel*.

From the graph shown in the figure, it can be observed that the water level (or the height of water) decreases at a slightly decreasing rate over time. The "Add Trendline" function in *Excel* may be used to find a possible curve that fits the data. In this case, a quadratic function, or polynomial of degree two, can be used to fit the data to some extent, as shown in Figure 6.11. Therefore, it is fair to say that a possible

130 *Mathematical modelling projects*

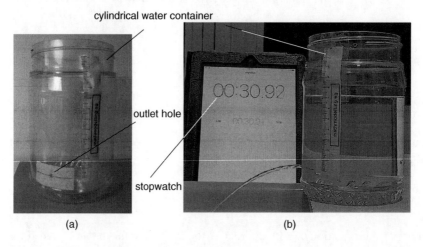

Figure 6.10 Experiment to study the relationship between water level and time as water drains out from a cylinder

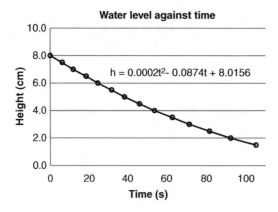

Figure 6.11 Graph of data and a polynomial approximation

mathematical model representing the relationship between the height of water in the tank and time is $h(t) = 0.0002t^2 - 0.0874t + 8.0156$.

If students were to carry out this experiment, and if Torricelli's law is introduced to them, they can examine how well their experimental results compare with the law using the equations discussed earlier. For instance, the relationship derived from Torricelli's law, namely, $h(t) = \left(\sqrt{h_0} - \dfrac{a\sqrt{g}}{\sqrt{2A}}t\right)^2$, could be validated or verified using the data collected.

The values of A and a, which relate to some physical dimensions on the cylindrical container, should be measured carefully and as accurately as possible. That is, the circumference of the container (at the points where the cross-sectional area is constant) and the diameter of the outlet should be measured very accurately. In the case of the experiment described here, the radius of the container is found to be $R = 5.46$ cm, the radius of the outlet is $r = 0.15$ cm and $h_0 = 8$ cm. This gives the following.

$$A = \pi(5.46)^2 \text{ cm}^2, \text{ and } a = \pi(0.15)^2 \text{ cm}^2,$$

and we will assume that the acceleration due to gravity, $g = 980 \text{ cm}/\text{s}^2$.

Based on Torricelli's law, substituting these values, it follows that $h(t) \cong (2.828 - 0.01671t)^2$. A graph of the data points, together with the curve representing the model obtained derived from Torricelli's law, is shown in Figure 6.12.

From Figure 6.12, it is observed that the model obtained from Torricelli's law approximates the experimental data quite well near the beginning of the experiment, but appears not to agree with the data as time increases. There are various possible reasons for the deviation or discrepancy. This would provide scope and opportunity for discussion among students engaged in the project.

Some possible reasons for the difference could include the following:

- The outlet may not be perfectly circular and therefore, the value of a may not have been obtained very accurately. This lack of accuracy in the value of a becomes more pronounced as the water level gets closer to the outlet.
- The outlet could have been created with a very rough tool, resulting in rough edges. This can cause resistance to the water leaving the tank and decreases the rate of water flow.
- The assumption of negligible fluid drag force may not be reasonable.
- The cross-sectional area of the container used in the experiment may not be constant throughout.

The modelling project is fairly substantial in the sense that both a deterministic and an empirical model can be considered, and experiments can be carried out to validate the model. Moreover, it may be neccessery to do a bit of reading before embarking on the project. Yet, it is still possible to further extend the study. For instance, different types of containers can be used and analysed. One could consider a conical tank shown in Figure 6.13 below, where water drains through a small, round hole at the bottom of the tank.

Let $A(h)$ be the cross-sectional area of the water in the tank at height h and a be the area of the drain hole (as shown in Figure 6.13). Applying Torricelli's law, an expression for the

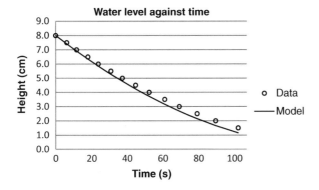

Figure 6.12 Graph of data and the model based on Torricelli's law

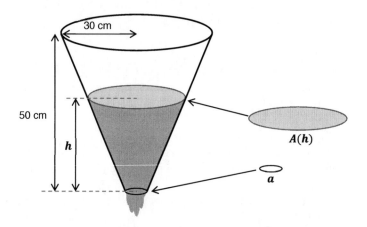

Figure 6.13 Water draining from a conical tank

rate of change of h, that is, $\dfrac{dh}{dt}$ may be derived. Assuming the measurements shown in the figure and a diameter of, say, 1 cm for the hole at the bottom, the differential equation can be solved to obtain a relationship between h and t. The solution will allow one to predict the time it would take for the tank to drain completely. As a project, students can make a conical tank with the same dimensions and perform experiments to find out the time required to drain the tank completely. They can then see how well or how badly the formula derived from Torricelli's law compares with their experimental results.

Depending on the mathematical ability of students, this modelling project can be adjusted accordingly by making certain requirements explicit. For instance, empirical modelling could be the focus without the need to verify with theoretical formulae. Alternatively, if students are able to solve differential equations, they could be required to derive the required relationship after reading up on Torricelli's law. The following framework can serve as a guide for teachers when they design this modelling project for their students.

Using the framework

Framework Component	"Testing Torricelli"
1. WHICH **level** of learning experience?	Level 3.
2. WHAT is the **skill/competency**?	• Understanding the problem.
	• Listing the dependent and independent variables.
	• Identifying the factors that can affect the problem.
	• Careful data collection.
	• Use of a graphing tool or *Excel*.
	• Validation of model.
3. WHERE is the **mathematics**?	• Polynomial functions and their graphs, for example, quadratic functions.
	• Geometry, in particular, cross-sections, area and volume.
	• Differential equations and solving differential equations.

Framework Component	"Testing Torricelli"
4. HOW to **solve** the problem/model?	• Collect data by video-recording the height of water in a cylindrical container with a small outlet near the bottom over time. • Plot the water level vs time using *Excel*. • Use "Add Trendline" function in *Excel* to find a curve that approximately fits the data. • If Torricelli's law for fluid flow is to be introduced to students, then they must construct a model based on the law and compare it with the experiment result.
5. WHY is this experience a **success**?	In this lesson, students learn about: • a real-life application of differential equations, • conducting a physical experiment, • use of *Excel* tools or functions, • comparison of experimental and theoretical results, • interpretation and analysis of results.

Possible discussion points

As a mathematical modelling project, this activity is intended to be slightly more challenging than those described in earlier chapters. There may be a need for students to read up on their own, or to consult their teachers on the ideas behind Torricelli's law for fluid flow. The difficulty level of this project can vary, depending on what is expected and how much assistance students receive from teachers. Nevertheless, it would help if teachers provide some guidance to students embarking on this project with the following questions:

- What are the important variables involved in the problem? Identify the dependent variable(s) and the independent variable(s) in the problem.
- Which shape of water tank do you wish to consider?
- Would an experiment help in addressing the problem? If so, what kind of data would you collect from the experiment?
- What do you hope to gather from the data?
- How can we construct a mathematical model?
- How would you validate or evaluate the model?
- How would you extend the project?

Although the study of water flow, or fluid flow, is often seen as a topic in applied mathematics that is suitable for students of higher mathematics, the actual principle governing the relationship between water level in a tank and the speed at which water drains out from a hole in the tank is not a difficult concept. In fact, this principle is used in various real-life applications, including the construction of a clepsydra, or water clock, which measures or keeps track of time by the flow of water. In principle, the amount of water escaping gives an indication of the duration of time passed. This project, therefore, is not only mathematically rich, it also has practical, engineering implications.

Bibliography

Ang, K.C. (2004). A simple model for a SARS epidemic. *Teaching Mathematics and its Applications*, 23(4), 181–8.

Big Splash has become the world's most expensive dog. (2017, January 4). *New Tang Dynasty Television*. Retrieved from www.ntd.tv/2017/01/04/big-splash-become-worlds-expensive-dog.

Bunday, B.D. (1996). *An Introduction to Queuing Theory*. London: Arnold.

Sars in Singapore: Timeline. (2013, March 16). *The Straits Times*. Retrieved from www.straitstimes.com/singapore/sars-in-singapore-timeline.

Soon, W.M. and Ang, K.C. (2015). Introducing queuing theory through simulations. *Research Journal of Mathematics and Technology*, 4(2), 33–47.

7 Assessing mathematical modelling

Introduction

Assessment plays an important role in multiple ways in many aspects of education. In mathematics education, as far as assessment is concerned, there have been debates, arguments and discussions among mathematics educators on what is proper or appropriate assessment in mathematics.

In recent years, assessment in mathematics has taken on an international stage. For instance, the *Trends in International Mathematics and Science Study* (TIMSS) is a series of assessments established by the International Association for the Evaluation of Educational Achievement (IEA) and it attempts to assess the mathematics and science knowledge of students around the world. Another such international assessment is the Organisation for Economic Co-operation and Development, or OECD's Programme for International Student Assessments (PISA), which includes a mathematics performance component. It is no exaggeration to suggest that in some countries, educational policies and curricula have been influenced to some extent, as a consequence of these assessments.

In schools, many mathematics teachers would agree that they assess students so that they are able to determine what students know, have learnt or are able to do. More specifically, in the mathematics classroom, teachers want to know if students have learnt the mathematical terms and definitions, and if they are able to carry out certain procedures or use certain techniques to solve a mathematical problem. In fact, a more pertinent question is whether students understand the mathematical concepts taught or discussed in lessons, and whether they are able to apply these concepts appropriately, or demonstrate the mathematical problem solving skills related to these concepts. School leaders and policymakers are interested in using such information to award grades, or make decisions about the students and their academic progression, or perhaps the curriculum.

Whether the assessment is within the mathematics classroom or carried out as a large scale, international exercise, what is clear is that there should always be a purpose for the assessment. In other words, one needs to know why there is a need or reason to assess, and what the outcomes of the assessment will be used for. While the traditional modes of assessment often focus on assessment *of* learning, many mathematics educators now subscribe to the notion of assessment *for* learning as well. Assessment of learning is usually summative, done at the end of a teaching unit or teaching semester, for the purpose of providing feedback on or evidence of achievement. On the other hand, assessment for learning tends to be more formative in nature and happens during the learning, for the purpose of providing feedback to students to help them improve their learning.

136 *Assessing mathematical modelling*

Typical summative assessments in mathematics carried out in schools would involve assessing students' learning in areas such as mathematical content knowledge, skills in applying certain techniques or procedures in solving mathematical problems and ability in extending conceptual understanding to tackle unseen or non-routine problems. In order to know what needs to be assessed, it seems reasonable to first examine the goals and objectives of mathematics learning in the most general sense.

In many school mathematics curricula, one large piece of mathematics assessment would be the focus on the student's ability to recall mathematical facts, concepts, methods or techniques of solving standard mathematical problems. For instance, test items or worksheet questions that require students to recall and perhaps apply mathematical theorems, or to employ a certain method of solution to find answers to a given problem, or to perform a procedure to solve a problem are typical kinds of items that assess mathematical content knowledge. These are often regarded as items that students should be able to learn and master through drill and practice. Though many teachers would agree that it is essential to ensure that students have acquired such basic knowledge and skills, it should not form the entire assessment because mathematics should be more than just facts and techniques.

Another aspect of mathematics learning involves constructing mathematical arguments in a logical and systematic fashion. Very often, in order to craft such arguments, one would also need to organise and interpret relevant mathematical information. This is an important part of mathematics learning which may be far more valuable than simply performing calculations or solving problems using standard techniques or methods. The ability to use logical, mathematical arguments to arrive at a conclusion is an attribute often seen in research mathematicians. For instance, when constructing a conjecture or developing a proof for a theorem, logical arguments derived from relevant mathematical information are critical.

Many mathematics educators now feel that it is not enough just to be able to perform computations, apply methods or techniques of solution in a problem, or develop logical arguments to arrive at convincing conclusions. The mathematics student should be able to read and comprehend basic mathematics, think mathematically and communicate mathematical ideas. Communication, both verbal and written, is an essential because it requires and encourages one to analyse and think critically, and then synthesise these thoughts into coherent pieces. There is no doubt this is difficult, if not impossible to test or assess in the usual summative, pen-and-paper assessments, or in standardised international assessments. However, alternative forms of assessments have been suggested that may serve to provide teachers with the opportunities and means to gauge students' abilities to demonstrate these attributes.

Figure 7.1 summarises the broad aspects of mathematics learning which are considered to be worthwhile, and learners should be assessed in these areas.

Assessing the process

As can be seen from the examples of modelling tasks described in preceding chapters, learning experiences in mathematical modelling can often be quite different from the traditional mathematics lessons. Many teachers who first introduce mathematical modelling in the classroom have the tendency to *do* the modelling, rather than guide or facilitate students into completing the tasks themselves. It can then be difficult to tell whether students have actually engaged in the process, or merely completing a worksheet that the teacher has designed. Nevertheless, if the goal of teaching mathematical modelling is to provide

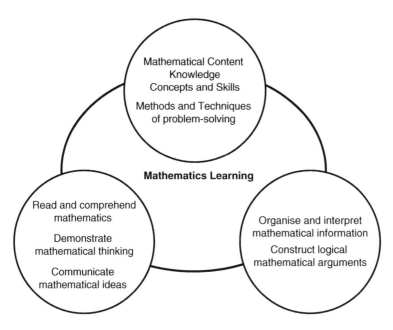

Figure 7.1 Some important aspects of mathematics learning worth assessing

students with the opportunity to truly engage in a meaningful journey of using mathematics to tackle or solve a real-life problem, and acquire or sharpen some related and important skills and competencies in the process, then there ought to be some means of determining if this goal has been achieved.

Assessing students while they are going through the process of mathematical modelling is as important as, if not more important, than assessing the product that students may come up with at the end of the learning experience. It is essential to see mathematical modelling as a process during which students try to make connections between the world and mathematics in an attempt to address, examine, investigate or solve a problem. The modelling process may involve stages or phases, and as the student moves from one stage to another, and sometimes back and forth, one hopes that there is some progress and some learning. It is this progress through the stages and the learning that takes place through those stages, which can and should be assessed.

As described in Chapter 1, mathematical modelling is a process that begins with a real-life problem, goes through several stages and should eventually end with a real-life "solution" (or at least some plausible solution) to the real-life problem (see Figure 1.1). In addition, the process of mathematical modelling requires students to use some skills and demonstrate some modelling competencies.

Some mathematical skills and competencies related and useful to mathematical modelling have been presented and discussed (see Chapter 1). In addition, a specific tool is also introduced to show how some Information Technology (IT) skills can be very useful in mathematical modelling. To be able to engage in mathematical modelling, one has to learn some of these skills and develop some modelling competencies. Therefore, it may be of interest to the teacher to assess if students have acquired or develop these skills and

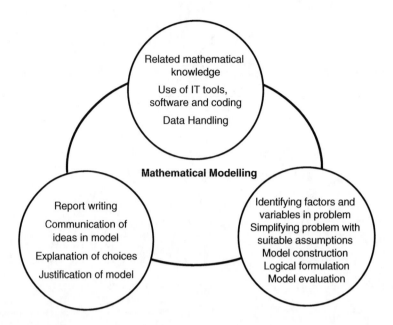

Figure 7.2 Some important aspects of mathematical modelling worth assessing

competencies while going through, or after having gone through the modelling exercise. Several of these skills may be related to mathematics content, while others could be related to IT tools, such as data loggers or the use of computer software. Coding and computer programming could also be an essential skill in some cases.

In a mathematical modelling learning experience, it is common to require students to present their model orally, or write a report, or both. This provides opportunities for students to communicate their ideas, share their experience in the modelling process, explain or justify their choice of model, and convince the audience or the reader of the report that the model is an appropriate or suitable one. In a typical mathematics lesson, such reports or presentations may not be common, and even if practised, are usually short with limited room for extensive discussion. Provided the mathematical modelling task is rich and well designed, opportunities for meaningful discussion and discourse on the use of mathematics to solve real-life problems are plentiful and should be capitalised as much as possible.

Figure 7.2 shows some of the elements and aspects of mathematical modelling learning experiences that are valuable and that we hope students will develop. These are also possible areas to focus on in assessing mathematical modelling, apart from the final product, which is the model itself.

It can be seen from Figures 7.1 and 7.2 that there is a strong parallel between what is valued in learning mathematical modelling and in general mathematics learning. In general, these are concepts and skills, logical argument and communication of mathematical ideas.

Assessing modelling competencies

Now that there is some clarity about what we want students to learn, acquire and develop through the practice of mathematical modelling in the classroom, it is a little easier to write down the aspects of the learning that can or should be assessed. However, these aspects are closely linked to the kind of pedagogical principles or approaches used in teaching mathematical modelling. The framework for teaching mathematical modelling introduced in Chapter 2 suggests that a similar line of thought could follow in terms of assessing mathematical modelling.

In the last two decades, many researchers and educators have written about and debated on the assessment of mathematical modelling. For instance, while acknowledging the complexity of assessment endeavours in mathematics education, Niss (1993) had hoped to find answers to some of the relevant questions in relation to assessment of mathematical modelling. These include concerns about the reasons for assessing modelling, what should be assessed using what kind of tasks, who should be assessed and how they should be assessed, and by whom. While these are important questions, there are no easy answers. In fact, answers that suit one country, educational system, state or community, may not be applicable to another.

Mathematical modelling competencies

In an attempt to address these questions and to describe what it means to master mathematics, Niss and his colleagues embarked on project, supported by the Danish Ministry of Education, called the *KOM project* (KOM is an abbreviation of Kompetencer og matematiklæring, which in Danish means "competencies and the learning of mathematics"). Under the KOM project, a definition for mathematical competence was introduced, and eight mathematical competencies were identified. To Niss and his colleagues, mathematical competency refers to the ability to understand, judge, do and use mathematics both within and outside of mathematical contexts and situations where mathematics can play a role (Niss, 2003). In other words, they believe that competencies are not just knowledge, abilities or skills, but it includes the willingness to act on a problem using these skills and abilities.

The eight competencies identified in the KOM project are thinking mathematically, posing and solving mathematical problems, representation, handling symbols and formalism, communication, making use of aids and tools, reasoning and, finally, modelling. It is claimed that a set of mathematical competencies can potentially be the core of mathematics education, and guide teachers to what may be more important to teach, develop and assess.

The Danes, however, were not the only ones who had adopted a competency-approach towards mathematics education or assessment. In the United States, the Common Core State Standards initiative had also identified a set of "standards for mathematical practice" that may be applied to all school levels (CCSSM, 2010). These are:

- Make sense of problems and persevere in solving them.
- Reason abstractly and quantitatively.
- Construct viable arguments and critique the reasoning of others.
- Model with mathematics.
- Use appropriate tools strategically.
- Attend to precision.
- Look for and make use of structure.
- Look for and express regularity in repeated reasoning.

Blum, working with his German colleagues, decided that having these broad categories of competencies is not sufficient, and defined the term "modelling competencies" by specifying a list of sub-competencies that related to the modelling process (Maaß, 2006). These include competencies to: make assumptions to simplify the situation; to construct relations between variables; to choose appropriate mathematical notations and to represent situations graphically; to use problem-solving heuristics; to interpret mathematical results outside of the mathematical contexts; to check and reflect on found solutions; and so on.

The research project Co^{2}CA (Conditions and Consequences of Classroom Assessment) carried out by professors in Germany attempts to investigate the impact of competence-oriented assessment on teaching and learning in different disciplines, including mathematics.[1] The project was carried out in several phases. In the initial phase, tasks, including modelling tasks, focussing on competencies were constructed. This was followed by gathering feedback to student responses to the tasks in the second phase. The impact of the feedback, used as a form of formative assessment, on students' cognitive and motivational development was investigated. The final phases involved intervention studies in which items as well as the feedback were implemented in a 13-lesson teaching unit across some 39 Year 9 classes of German middle track schools. It appears that despite such a large scale research project, the question of whether students given oral and written feedback outperform their counterparts in terms of modelling competencies remains difficult to answer (Besser, Blum and Klimczak, 2013).

The preceding discussion is certainly only a small sample of what has been done among researchers who have tried to define the term "mathematical modelling competency" and make a list of such competencies or sub-competencies, and does not in any way represent the state of affairs in mathematical modelling assessment. For a more complete and critical review of literature discussing and investigating assessment of mathematical modelling, the reader may refer to the paper by Frejd (see reference at the end of the chapter). Nonetheless, the discussion presented here is enough to show that educators do value and focus on the development of modelling competencies in learners of mathematical modelling. Moreover, these modelling competencies are closely linked and aligned to the modelling process, which is not unexpected.

Based on the modelling process presented in Figure 1.1, it is quite clear that while there are different activities expected in the process, mathematical modelling generally should involve three main stages: model formulation, model solution, and model interpretation and evaluation. In each of these stages, there are certain skills and competencies that could help a student be successful in the process, or that a student may learn. One aspect of assessing modelling while a student goes through the process would be to see if these competencies are demonstrated, and to what extent or degree they are demonstrated.

It would be useful then, to write down some of these important competencies as they appear in the different stages. Table 7.1 provides the modelling competencies and sub-competencies in the three broad stages of the modelling process that a teacher might hope to develop in students.

Validity and reliability

In any assessment, *validity* and *reliability* are two important considerations that ensure quality in the assessment instrument or method. Validity in assessment refers to how well or accurately an assessment item tests what it is intended to test. In other words, an assessment item that is designed to assess a particular skill or piece of knowledge, say, the ability to use the Solver tool in *Excel*, actually assesses the student's ability in that skill and not something else. Reliability in assessment refers to the consistency or reproducibility in the measurement.

Table 7.1 Mathematical Modelling Competencies

Modelling Stage	Competencies and sub-competencies
Model Formulation	• Make sense of the real-life problem • Identify factors/variables in the problem • Simplify situation by making appropriate and suitable assumptions • Identify possible mathematical constructs to represent the real situation • Choose or decide on a suitable mathematical construct for the problem • Find relationships between variables of the problem • Write down the mathematical problem
Model Solution	• Choose or decide on a method of solving the mathematical problem • Use or collect data if necessary • Use appropriate tools (for example, computer software, or programming tools) if required • Use relevant and appropriate mathematical knowledge to solve the problem
Model Interpretation and Evaluation	• Interpret mathematical results in the real-life context • Check and validate results quantitatively or qualitatively • Communicate the results in some manner • Generalise results if possible • Justify, review and refine model if necessary

A reliable assessment instrument would give the same result every time, of course, under the same or similar conditions as specified.

Recall that in the framework for teaching mathematical modelling introduced in Chapter 2, the framework component 2 asks the "What" question – "What is the skill/competency?" Of course, there may be more than one skill or competency expected in the task, but the main point of asking that question is to remind the teacher to write down the skills or competencies that are expected of the student performing this modelling task. This is, of course, in relation to the problem to be solved, which the teacher would need to clearly state in the plan, as well as the framework component 1, the level of the learning experience.

Stating the competencies expected and the level of the learning experience will help guide the teacher in ensuring validity when designing assessment instruments for the modelling task. The teacher may refer to the framework written out and be reminded of the specific skills or competencies that the task is aiming to develop in the students. For instance, if the task requires or expects students to identify variables in the real situation, and then simplify the problem by making suitable assumptions, then the teacher should be looking for the presence of these competencies, or the extent or degree to which these competencies are demonstrated. An assessment item could then be design to specifically look for evidence of competencies in this particular area.

Referring to the framework again, components 3 and 4, which ask the questions "Where is the mathematics" and "How to solve the problem/model" respectively, provides further guidance to the teacher. Here, the teacher will be mindful of the possible pieces of mathematics that may be used or applied, and the method of solution that could be employed in the task. While these may vary from case to case, and in some instances, students may come up with something totally unexpected, these framework components draws attention to the mathematical competencies that should be considered in the assessment.

Worksheets for modelling classes

Very often, in the classroom, teachers use worksheets as a means of formative assessment to see if students are able to perform a task or carry out an activity successfully. As a brief set of guiding principles, competency-oriented assessment items that are contained in worksheets for mathematical modelling tasks should bear the characteristics listed below.

Assessment items in such modelling worksheets should

1) be valid – they should test what it is intended or designed to test
   As mentioned above, being aware and mindful of the competencies expected or required in any one particular task, and the level to which the competencies are to be demonstrated, can help in designing valid assessment items.
2) have clear and definite instructions given to students
   Students engaging in modelling activities should know what they need to do, even if the task is meant to be open.
3) be presented clearly, using suitable language
   The language used in the instructions or task requirements should be carefully chosen to ensure clarity. For instance, it would not make sense to require students to "run a simulation" if they are not expected to understand what a "simulation" actually means.
4) specify the conditions under which it is used
   Conditions such as whether the item in the worksheet is to be completed individually or in a group, as in-class work or homework, and so on, may influence the assessment. This has to be specified so that judgement of achievement or levels of achievement can be more relevant.
5) contain clear criteria for assessors to make judgements
   A marking scheme, or a set of rubrics, should accompany the worksheet if marks or grades are required. These should provide details to the assessor (or teacher) on the competencies as well as the outcome expected.
6) provide opportunities for students to demonstrate the breadth and depth of their competencies
   Typical worksheets provide white space for students to write down their answers or responses to the items. For mathematical modelling tasks, it may be useful to allow or remind students to attach additional material to their worksheets.

The two examples described below serve to illustrate some of these principles.

Example 1: Level 1 modelling task

Consider the Level 1 task on "Mountain climbing" and the framework for implementing this task as discussed and described in Chapter 2 (see Page 31).

In this task, as can be seen from the framework, students are to learn or practise the skill of using the Solver tool in *Excel* to find a most suitable estimate for a parameter after deciding a function that best describes the set of data given. There are a number of skills, knowledge and competencies required to complete this task. These include the ability to:

- Use a software (such as a spreadsheet) to construct a scatter plot.
- Observe and identify an appropriate function that could fit the data.

Assessing mathematical modelling 143

Name: _____ Class: _____ Date: _____

Atmospheric Pressure and Altitude

Mountain climbers often experience thinning of air as they climb higher. This thinning of air can lead to a lack of oxygen, and sometimes cause mountain climbers to experience headaches or other physical discomfort.

The table on the right contains data obtained from the National Aeronautics and Space Administration (NASA), and shows how the atmospheric pressure changes with altitude.

What is the relationship between air pressure (atmospheric pressure) and altitude?

Altitude (km)	Pressure (mb)
0	1013
1	899
2	795
3	701
4	616
5	540
6	472
7	411
8	356
9	307
10	264
11	226

Instructions to students:
You are to use Microsoft *Word* to type out your answers, and print out the document for submission at the end of the lesson.
(a) Plot a graph of atmospheric pressure against altitude. What do you observe?
(b) Write down the general form of a function that can possibly fit the data. Explain why you think this general form is suitable.
(c) Use a tool (such as *Excel*) to obtain estimates for any parameters that may appear in your model.
(d) What are some limitations of this model?

Figure 7.3 Worksheet for the Level 1 Modelling Task, "Mountain climbing"

- Apply the Solver tool or Trendline tool in *Excel* (for instance) to find an estimate for any parameter.
- Explain any limitations of the model.

Now, if the four items above are what students are required to achieve, then it would not be difficult to design a worksheet in the usual way to see if students are able to demonstrate these skills and competencies. Figure 7.3 shows a possible way to design such a worksheet.

Note that in the main task instruction, there is no mention of "model" – students are merely asked to find a relationship between the atmospheric pressure and altitude. However, the word "model" appears in the sub-parts (c) and (d). This may be intentional, in the sense that the teacher may want students to realise that an equation showing the relationship between important quantities in a problem is the mathematical model that we are looking for, without being too explicit. Alternatively, the teacher may wish to be more explicit and explain that the task is to develop or find a mathematical model that describes the relationship between atmospheric pressure and altitude. This piece of instruction has to be clearly stated so that we may assess to see if students will eventually produce a "model".

One of the competencies that the teacher may wish to assess through this task is the ability to choose an appropriate function to represent the relationship, and to find the actual equation. As this is a Level 1 learning experience, there is a lot of guidance provided for the student. First, the student is asked to produce a scatter plot, and make some observations in sub-part (a). This is a useful skill which students will need in many empirical modelling situations, and achieving such a competency is something that can be directly assessed using this item.

Next, from the observation, the student is to decide on a suitable formula or function that can best fit the set of data points that have been plotted in sub-part (b). An explanation is expected. In this case, we expect students to say a decreasing exponential function of the form "$y = Ae^{-kx}$" is suitable. This is also an important competency that can be directly assessed. The model solution process requires the student to use an IT tool, namely *Excel*, to find the best estimate for the parameter. The last sub-part is fairly open, and this is where provision is made for students to think a little wider, beyond the computations and calculations.

We note that in this case, a competency like "identify variables" may not be applicable since the task does not really require the student to do so. Being a Level 1 task, it is deliberately targetted at developing a specific skill or competency. The assessment instrument, therefore, should also be focussed to measure the achievement of the specific skill or competency.

Example 2: Level 2 modelling task

Consider the following Level 2 task on the warming of water discussed in Page 31 of Chapter 2. In this case, based on the framework entries, students attempting this task are expected to demonstrate a number of modelling competencies. These include:

- Identifying and listing variables of the problem.
- Simplifying the situation through making suitable assumptions.
- Using a data-logger (and associated software) to collect data.
- Observing the data, and finding a suitable equation to represent the data set.
- Using suitable mathematics to solve the problem.
- Using suitable IT tools to find parameters, if any.

Before embarking on the data collection phase, students may be given the situation and asked to list the factors that could influence the temperature of the ice-water as it warms up in the room. Now, one could expect various responses, including factors as the material of the cup holding the water, the presence of wind in the air, the temperature of the surrounding, the temperature of the water itself, and so on. It is clear that some of these factors may be more important than others, and some assumptions (such as constant ambient temperature) can be made. Therefore, in designing an assessment, the level at which students are able to achieve this competency can be included.

Since this is a Level 2 task, we assume that students undertaking this task may already have had some previous experience with mathematical modelling activities. For instance, they may already know how to use a suitable tool to produce a scatter plot, and to find the best estimate for the parameter (related to rate of warming). If this is the case, and if students are able to perform the task of finding the parameter using a suitable tool without any prompting or hint from the teacher or the worksheet (if there is one), then it would be fair to say that they have achieved a certain satisfactory level insofar as this particular competency is concerned.

Whether the assessment requires students to complete a worksheet or to write a report is a choice that the teacher has to make. It all depends on how much work on the part of the student is required, what the teacher wishes to assess, and how able are the students. What is important is to specify in the assessment instrument the competencies expected, as well as the expected level of competency.

Assessing modelling projects

The two examples described in the preceding section are learning experiences or activities that can be carried out in the classroom in a typical one- or two-period lesson. Assessments for these activities can be formative in nature, competency-oriented, and focussed on the specific skills or knowledge that the activity is aimed towards developing. As discussed, worksheets with items specifying the requirements and allowing for possible exploration and expansion can be designed quite easily. Even if a set of rubrics is required for consistency in assessment, a trained mathematics teacher should be able to design a suitable one.

A more complex modelling task that requires a wider range of modelling competencies or deeper knowledge, mathematical and outside of mathematics, or requires more time to complete, could possibly require a more detailed set of rubrics for assessment. A typical Level 3 task, for instance, may require students to search for relevant material on the Internet, or gather information in a subject from another discipline, or to work as a team to complete. Apart from individual "modelling competencies", in such instances, other extra-mathematical attributes, including the ability to work as a team and to collaborate, may be included in the assessment rubrics.

Whether these modelling projects are carried out individually or as a group, undertaken as part of a curricular activity or in a competition, they are usually assessed or judged based on the products (in the form of a report or oral presentation, or sometimes both). The tendency is to focus on the model, the outcome. That is, the product.

However, mathematical modelling is a process, and one should not undermine the importance of students going through the whole process of formulating the mathematical problem, making assumptions, finding suitable mathematical representations and methods of solving the mathematical problem, interpreting the results and refining the model, and so on. Therefore, however difficult and complex it may be, the assessment and judging of mathematical modelling projects should take into account both the process and the product.

If the modelling process is what we are interested in assessing, then it makes sense to develop a set of scoring rubrics based on or by taking reference from the modelling cycle. In this case, the assessment becomes more process-oriented; this does not mean, however, that competencies are no longer important. In fact, one could even argue that in this case, the modelling competencies of the students participating in the project are driving and directing the modelling process.

Modelling reports and presentations

There are several reasons why reports or presentations are often considered an essential and even necessary part of the mathematical modelling experience. The report or the oral presentation serves as a product for the modelling process. To some extent, it marks the end of the process (at least until a refinement or extension is made) and provides a form of closure.

Moreover, in the course of preparing the report or presentation, there is a need to be very clear about the problem, the assumptions, solution process and other essential components of the model and process of modelling. The exercise will help and encourage students to reflect on the model and examine it critically.

In addition, as pointed out earlier, communication is an important part of learning mathematics and in many classrooms across the world, this is seldom emphasised. A student may know how to solve a mathematical problem, but being able to explain the solution and implications not just in mathematical terms but also in practical (or sometimes layman) terms can be very challenging. Doing so adds a dimension to learning mathematics. In real life, conclusions from mathematical models need to be communicated to the people who asked for the model to be constructed. These could be employers, an organization or authority, clients or customers. These people may not be mathematicians or know enough mathematics to understand the details of the model. Being able to use a mathematical model to present conclusions convincingly is an important skill for the modeller.

Finally, if mathematical modelling is used as part of a mathematics curriculum, then writing a report or giving an oral presentation can serve as a mode of assessment.

Project reports

A written report represents a slightly more tangible product of the mathematical modelling project. Very often, students are required to submit a report at the end of a modelling activity and the instructor, teacher or judge is supposed to assess the students based on the report. A set of scoring rubrics is suggested here to guide teachers in assessing such reports.

The set of scoring rubrics shown in Table 7.2 is based on the competencies listed in Table 7.1, albeit with a few adjustments. Instead of the three broad stages of modelling as described earlier, in this case, the last stage is divided into model interpretation and model evaluation. For assessment purposes, it may be good to distinguish between the process of interpreting and presenting the results of the model, and justifying and refining the model. The latter is of a higher order as it involves evaluating the model that one has developed, while the former involves consolidating and communicating outcomes.

In this scoring rubrics or scoring sheet, a five-point rating system is used, with the points 0 to 4 assigned for standards representing "Not Evident", "Some Evidence", "Acceptable", "Proficient" and "Excellent". These standards refer to the modelling competencies demonstrated, and the descriptors for these are as shown in Table 7.2.

As there may be different emphases on the different stages or parts of the modelling process, some form of weighting system may be useful. For instance, in this case, we use weights 1, 2 and 3, to indicate the relative importance of the competencies in this set of rubrics. The score for each category of competencies, then, is the product of the rating and the weight. For instance, if a particular team has shown "proficient" level of competency in identifying variables, they will be given a rating of 3, and when multiplied by the weight of 2, the team will obtain a score of 6 for this category. In this set of scoring rubrics, the weights add up to 25, and with a top rating of 4 points for each competency category, the maximum score possible is 100.

Of course, this is the not the only way to set up scoring rubrics. Depending on which category of competencies is considered important (or essential or valuable) for the particular

Table 7.2 Scoring Rubrics for a Mathematical Modelling Project Report

Stage of Modelling Process	Points	Weight	Score
Model Formulation		1	
• Show understanding of the given situation		2	
• Identify factors/variables in the problem		2	
• Simplify situation by making suitable assumptions		1	
• Identify mathematical constructs for the real situation		1	
• Find relationships between variables of the problem		3	
• Write down the mathematical problem			
Model Solution		1	
• Choose a suitable method of solution		2	
• Use or collect data if necessary		2	
• Use appropriate tools		3	
• Use relevant and correct mathematics to solve the model			
Model Interpretation and Validation		3	
• Interpret mathematical results in the real context		1	
• Validate results quantitatively or qualitatively		1	
• Communicate results			
Model Evaluation and Refinement		1	
• Generalise results		1	
• Justify and refine model			

Note: Score is obtained by multiplying Points by Weight.

Competency Standards and Descriptors

Points	Standard	Descriptor
0	Not Evident	Fails to show any evidence of attempt of any kind
1	Some Evidence	Demonstrates attempts that are useful to the modelling process
2	Acceptable	Demonstrates competency useful to the success of the modelling process
3	Proficient	Demonstrates in-depth level of competency to address the problem
4	Excellent	Achieves broad, in-depth level of competency evident in high quality work

task in that particular situation, the weights may be adjusted accordingly. In addition, there may be additional or specific competencies that can be added to the set suggested, if so desired. The ratings and standards suggested may also be modified if necessary. Generally, the standards expected should range from absence of any attempt to a demonstration of proficiency in that particular skill.

A word of caution here. Many researchers and educators have proposed similar kinds of rubrics for assessing mathematical modelling, suggesting that the instrument assesses the *process* of modelling. The scoring rubrics suggested here is no different. In reality, however, unless the assessor or teacher is with the student or group of students while they work on the problem, what is being assessed is really the written report and, maybe, the oral presentation. Therefore, if it is the report – which, to some, is the "product" of the modelling exercise – that is being assessed using such rubrics, then the assessor needs to be aware that in some areas of the assessment, one can only infer rather than conclude that there is evidence of achievement.

Nonetheless, the set of scoring rubrics presented here is developed for a competency-driven, process-based form of assessment of mathematical modelling, even though in practice, it is administered on possibly a written report only.

While rubrics are useful for awarding marks, points or grades for a mathematical modelling exercise or project, it remains important that we are able to recognise a "good" mathematical model when we see one. So, what do we look for in a good mathematical model?

Firstly, a good mathematical model must be based on sound mathematics that lead to a mathematical construct. In other words, the model may be an equation, a formula, graph, table, computer program, decision tree, simulation, an algorithm, and so on. When applied to the real context, the mathematical construct should help make sense of the physical problem, the real world, a system or phenomenon, a social situation, and so on. In other words, it can be translated to the real world readily to address the problem originally posed.

Secondly, a good mathematical model should be simple but not simplistic. It should be simple enough to be feasible and applicable in the situation that it addresses, but should not be overly simplistic to render it unusable in the practical world.

Next, a good mathematical model should result from some form of iteration or improvement process. The model should have stated assumptions, and perhaps revisited and revised assumptions. Assumptions in a model can often restrict its practicality and usability, and a good mathematical model should have gone through rounds of refinement in addressing assumptions.

Finally, a good mathematical model should convince users or consumers that it has addressed the problem at hand. This may be done either through reports on validation, testing with simulation, or comparison with data and so on. In other words, it should be able to answer the question, "how do we know it works?"

Oral presentations

While going through the process of mathematical modelling is an important part of the experience, communicating the outcomes, results and conclusions is just as important and necessary. Besides a written report, communicating the conclusions of a mathematical modelling problem or project may also take the form of an oral presentation.

Table 7.3 Scoring Sheet for a Mathematical Modelling Project Presentation

The team …	Strongly Disagree	Disagree	Agree	Strongly Agree
Presented an accurate and correct interpretation of the problem	1	2	3	4
Stated suitable and justified assumptions	1	2	3	4
Identified and stated suitable variables in the problem	1	2	3	4
Used appropriate mathematics in their approach	1	2	3	4
Explained the model and method of solution clearly	1	2	3	4
Addressed the model's strengths and weaknesses	1	2	3	4
Presented the final solution clearly	1	2	3	4
Used good visual aids in their presentation	1	2	3	4
Was able to engage the audience during the presentation	1	2	3	4
Demonstrated good teamwork	1	2	3	4

Whether carried out as a group or individually, very often there is a need for results of a mathematical modelling project to be presented orally. It is also quite common for the audience of such a presentation to be not entirely well versed in all areas of mathematics.

A good oral presentation on a mathematical modelling project requires good planning and preparation. When planning and preparing, the following questions and pointers may serve as useful guidelines:

- How much time is given to the entire presentation?
- If presentation is to be shared amongst group members, how much time does each member have?
- What will be the most essential material to be included, and how should these be sequenced?
- What presentation tools are available and which ones should or will be used?
- What is the best way to present the problem, solution and results to the audience?
- Are there questions that the members of the audience are likely to ask?

The score sheet presented in Table 7.3 serves as a general set of rubrics for assessing a team's performance at an oral presentation of the results or outcome of their mathematical modelling project. It can also be used by other teams as an instrument for peer assessment.

Note

1 www.dipf.de/en/research/projects-archive/use-and-impact-of-competence-measurement-in-mathematical-learning-and-teaching-processes

Bibliography

Besser, M., Blum, W. and Klimczak, M. (2013). Formative assessment in everyday teaching of mathematical modelling: Implementation of written and oral feedback to competency-oriented tasks. In G. Stillman, G. Kaiser, W. Blum and J. Brown (Eds.), *Teaching Mathematical Modelling: Connecting to Research and Practice* (pp. 469–78). Dordrecht: Springer.

Blum, W. (1993). Mathematical modelling in mathematics education and instruction. In T. Breiteig, I. Huntley and G. Kaiser-Messmer (Eds.), *Teaching and Learning Mathematics in Context* (pp. 3–14). Chichester: Ellis Horwood.

Consortium for Mathematics and Its Applications (COMAP) and Society for Industrial and Applied Mathematics (SIAM). (2016). *Guidelines for Assessment and Instruction in Mathematical Modelling Education*. Retrieved from www.siam.org/reports/gaimme-for_print.pdf.

Frejd, P. (2013). Modes of modelling assessment: A literature review. *Educational Studies in Mathematics*, 84(3), 413–38.

Højgaard, T. (2007). Assessing mathematical modelling competency. In C. Haines, P. Galbraith, W. Blum and S. Khan (Eds.), *Mathematical Modelling: Education, Engineering and Economics* (pp. 141–8). Chichester: Horwood Publishing.

Houston, K. (2007). Assessing the "phases" of mathematical modelling. In W. Blum, P. Galbraith, H-W. Henn and M. Niss (Eds.), *Modelling and Applications in Mathematics Education* (pp. 249–56). New York: Springer.

Leong, R.K.E. (2012). Assessment of mathematical modelling. *Journal of Mathematical Education at Teachers College*, 3(1), 61–5.

Maaß, K. (2006). What are modelling competencies? *ZDM– International Journal on Mathematics Education*, 38(2), 113–42.

Niss, M. (1993). Assessment in mathematics education and its effects: An introduction. In M. Niss (Ed.). *Investigations into Assessment in Mathematics Education: An ICMI Study* (pp. 1–30). Dordrecht: Kluwer Academic Publishers.

Niss, M. (2003). Mathematical competencies and the learning of mathematics: The Danish KOM project. In A. Gagatsis and S. Papastavridis (Eds.), *Proceedings of the 3rd Mediterranean Conference on Mathematical Education,* Athens, Greece (pp. 115–24). Athens: The Hellenic Mathematical Society.

8 Conclusion

Introduction

In the past two decades, there has been an increase of interest in mathematical modelling among teachers, mathematics educators and researchers. Some see it as a new "topic" in the mathematics curriculum, while others view it as an approach to teaching and learning mathematics. Increasingly, we see mathematical modelling appearing in school mathematics curricula. Along with this new found interest in mathematical modelling comes demand for more resources. While there are books and journal articles written on the subject, these may not always be accessible to the teacher or educator, especially those in institutions that have financial constraints.

In the interest of promoting mathematical modelling among students and in schools, several organisations have set up resources in the form of websites and internet resources. Some of these are affiliated to schools or universities, or mathematical societies, while others are private, non-profit enterprises. Some of these websites are good starting points for the novice teacher to look for ideas, and for the more experienced teachers to adopt and adapt the ideas.

In this chapter, websites related to mathematical modelling are briefly introduced and described. We note that just like any other Internet content, these websites may not be available forever. However, those described here have been around for many years, and should continue to grow and be available for a while longer.

The future of mathematical modelling as a worthwhile endeavour in the mathematics classrooms of schools depends on the teacher. In concluding this book, some final thoughts on the teaching of mathematical modelling are offered to the teacher.

Resources on the Web

The following are some Internet websites that contain useful resources and ideas that may be useful to a teacher wishing to get started on teaching mathematical modelling in the classroom.

1) MATHmodels (URL: www.mathmodels.org)
    This site contains a range of contemporary modelling problems that may interest students and teachers. The site is managed by COMAP (Consortium for Mathematics and Its Applications) that has given access and permission to its registered teacher-users to use their problems as modelling assignments for their students. The intention is to serve as a resource to the mathematics community.

The site hopes that teachers can use the problems in their database to conduct their own modelling lessons, as well as to prepare students for modelling competitions. An example of a modelling problem is given below.

Problem: City crime and safety[1]

What can we make of the massive amount of crime statistics collected in major cities? Beyond just reporting numbers, how can we use these data to determine the safeness of a city?

Assume that you and your modelling team live in My City, a large international hub of commerce, technology, finance and travel, with a current population of 2.8 million people impacted by a metropolitan area of an approximately additional 6 million people.

The data set provided shows two weeks from police reports in My City and includes crimes listed by case number, date of occurrence, primary and secondary crime descriptions, crime location, whether an arrest was made, whether or not this was domestic crime, and the beat number of the police route.

---

2) Plus Magazine (URL: https://plus.maths.org)

This is an internet magazine whose aim is to "introduce readers to the beauty and the practical applications of mathematics". It's objective is to help change the mindset that mathematics is "boring", and it hopes to do so through its plethora of articles, podcasts, reviews and puzzles posted on the site. This effort was started in 1997 as a project for interactive courseware at the Universities Cambridge and Keele, United Kingdom.

One useful section in this magazine is called *Teacher Package: Mathematical Modelling*. It contains several useful ideas for mathematical modelling activities, including the following activity on exploring basic epidemiological models for disease spread.

Activity: Build your own disease[2]

Here is a classroom activity exploring basic epidemiological models. It uses basic probability, and can be used to discuss exponential growth and geometric progressions.

A new and potentially dangerous infectious disease has broken out in the UK. You're an epidemiologist and the government has asked you to forecast how widely the disease will spread.

The authorities have been carefully monitoring those people already infected and their friends and families. Their data show that an infected person typically goes on to infect either one or two others.

Details on how to proceed with the activity are available on the Plus Magazine website.

3) IMMC (URL: www.immchallenge.org)

The International Mathematical Modelling Challenge (IMMC) serves to "promote the teaching of mathematical modelling and applications at all educational levels for all students". The inaugural IMMC was run in 2015, and since then, it has grown in terms of the number of participating teams from all over the world. Although this site mainly contains information about the IMMC, past problems and solutions are also posted.

The 2015 Challenge problem reads as follows.

Challenge problem: Movie scheduling[3]

A great deal of preparation must take place before a movie can be filmed. Important sets and scenes need to be identified, resource needs must be calculated, and schedules must be arranged. The issue of the schedule is the focus of modeling activities. A large studio has contacted your firm, and they wish to have a model to allow for scheduling a movie. You are asked to answer the questions below. You should provide examples and test cases to convince the movie executives that your model is effective and robust.

Question 1: Develop a model that will produce a filming schedule given the following constraints:

- The availability dates of the stars of the film.
- The time required to film at a list of specific sites.
- The time required to construct and film on a list of sets.
- The availability dates for specific resources. For example, a war movie might require helicopters which are available only at specific times.
- Some scenes cannot be shot until after certain computer generated content is defined and other physical items are constructed. Your schedule must include extra time to allow for redoing some shots if they turn out to be inadequate after editing and review.

Question 2: Develop a model that will take the information and schedule generated from the first question and can adjust them in the event that some delay in one aspect or the availability of some asset changes. For example, if one of the stars has an accident and cannot film for a certain period of time, you should be able to adjust the schedule.

Question 3: Use the model developed in the first question to develop a way to determine the most important constraints. That is, identify the constraints that will cause the longest delays if a problem occurs.

Sample solutions of the above problem are available on the IMMC website.

4) ACER IMMC (URL: www.immchallenge.org.au)

This is a similar website for IMMC, hosted by the Australian Council for Educational Research (ACER) for Australian schools and teachers. Although it mirrors the IMMC, it does contain various support features and resources for the community. In particular, it has a section called *Supporting Resources*, which includes *Example Problems* ranging from simple modelling tasks such as the "Adapting a recipe" problem, to harder ones like the "Temporary traffic lights" problem. These problems are available as files that can be downloaded for free by anyone.

154   *Conclusion*

5) mm@sg (URL: www.mathmodelling.sg)

This is a fairly new website and is a virtual resource centre for teachers, set up in 2017. The main feature of this website is the abundance of short video clips that provide help and guidance for teachers who plan to introduce mathematical modelling in their mathematics classes. It contains three main sections, namely *Learn*, *Practise* and *Share*. In *Learn*, users learn about mathematical modelling through video clips of talks and slideshows, and demonstrations of how certain skills can be learnt. Under *Practise*, users will see how some of the modelling tasks introduced can be enacted in the classroom. The *Share* section provides a platform for teachers from all over the world to share their experiences, post articles or ask questions. The virtual centre hopes to progress from a virtual resource centre to a virtual professional learning community.

Advice for teachers

While mathematical modelling may seem like an exciting adventure for some of us, many teachers who either need to or want to introduce it to their students have found it a daunting, uphill task. This is because many teachers have not had the experience of doing any mathematical modelling themselves when they were learning mathematics. Even if they have done it before, many not have seen how mathematical modelling is taught in the school classroom. It is with the hope of providing teachers with useful resources that this book is written. In addition, the following pieces of advice may serve as useful reminders to teachers who wish to embark on this journey:

1) "Get your hands dirty"

It is always assumed that in order to be able to teach something, one must be able to do that thing to some satisfactory level of standard. Similarly, in order to teach mathematical modelling, one should be able to complete some mathematical modelling tasks up to a certain acceptable level of competency. Therefore, teachers are encouraged to work on the problems they have come across, or have set up for their students – from the beginning of the process to the end, including having to formulate the model, solve the model and then interpret the solutions. In other words, teachers should get their hands dirty and solve the problem that they have set up before even planning a lesson on it. Very often, through the experience of going through the problem and solving it, or making attempts to solve it, teachers will learn so much more about the difficulties that students may face in the task. They may then be in a better position to provide scaffolding, or even to re-design the task.

2) "Facilitate, not just teach"

One important reason for teaching mathematical modelling is that we hope students will learn and develop some of the competencies for modelling. These competencies are deemed to be not only useful but also essential for students to be able to apply the mathematics that they learn in school to real-life situations and problems in future. But by now, one should realise that these competencies are *developed* and usually, over a period of time. It is easy to just *tell* students that they need to, say, for instance, make assumptions to simplify the problem. But it is quite another thing for them to internalise it to the extent that it becomes a habit of mind. Teachers, therefore, should remember that in the classroom, it might be more useful for them to facilitate the process of modelling, and allow students the time and space to explore, make mistakes, ask questions and then develop the competencies bit by bit over time. Facilitating the modelling process would also mean to refrain from just presenting the model, but asking questions, probing and encouraging discussion.

3) "Focus on the process"

Very often, the aim of a modelling task is to find a mathematical model to address or solve the problem. While that may be an objective that a teacher presents to the students in a modelling lesson or activity, the teacher should also focus on the important objective of letting and seeing students go through the process of mathematical modelling. Ultimately, the problem is either too unrealistic (that is, it is a made-up problem set in a real-world context), or too complex and huge for students in schools to solve. So, the model that students obtain is not really going to solve any real problem, and the whole activity ends up as an academic exercise. One may then ask, "So, what's the point?" The answer is simply that through the process, students learn – they learn about the problem, they learn about using mathematics to tackle the problem, they learn about methods of attacking a mathematical problem, they learn about teamwork (if working in groups), they learn about communicating ideas, arguing and defending their ideas, and so on. Students will learn all these, even if the model is not applicable or usable in any practical sense, because they have gone through the process. Teachers, therefore, should focus on the process, and if students do come up with an excellent product, that would be bonus.

4) "Read extra-mathematical material"

Mathematical modelling tends to be inter- and cross-disciplinary in nature. It would help if teachers have a mindset that one should be prepared to read material and source for information outside of mathematics. For instance, in order to understand the modelling of the avascular growth of tumours, it may be necessary to read up on the biology of cancers, and learn about how a cell could mutate and divide uncontrollably, and the factors that either influence or inhibit the growth and so on. It may not be necessary to know as much about the subject as the expert in the field, but it would be good to know some basics. This is so that when presenting or discussing the problem, the teacher is able to at least use the correct technical jargon and be knowledgeable to carry out a proper discourse on the topic. Of course, some problems may not require such specialised knowledge, but it is necessary to at least be conversant about the topic in question.

5) "Learn coding and start programming"

One useful skill that is gaining importance and relevance is the ability to code and program. There are many resources, in the form of open courseware or videos on free video sharing sites, from which teachers can pick up some basics of programming and learn to code. In many applied problems of the world, some form of computer tool is required. This could range from very simple applications of a spreadsheet or graphing tool, to sophisticated special-purpose software for solving computational fluid dynamic problems. In the United Kingdom, a nationwide initiative encourages schools to get kids to learn coding. In his State of the Union address in 2016, the United States then president, President Obama, urged students from kindergarten to high school to learn computer science. In Singapore, the country's Smart Nation push sees more kids learning programming. In mathematical modelling, as can be seen from the many examples discussed in this book, coding, programming and the use of computer tools will come in useful in many situations. Therefore, it will definitely be advantageous for a mathematics teacher to learn coding and start programming, especially if the aim is to do, learn and teach mathematical modelling.

6) "Start small, think big"

At first it may be intimidating and overwhelming, especially when one is new to mathematical modelling. There are too many unknowns, and the lesson can be unstructured. This may be how a mathematics teacher can feel about teaching mathematical modelling the first time. One way to overcome this, therefore, is to start with a small, simple, Level 1 activity, while planning for a more advanced and complex task for the future. In other words, start small but think big. For instance, the task aimed for could be a simulation model with several variables, but one could start with just a simple simulation of a coin toss, or a football game between teams with given probabilities of winning, and so on. This way, while the students learn about mathematical modelling, the teacher is learning about teaching it, each at a pace determined by the teacher.

Final remarks

Mathematical modelling is both an art and a science. The science of it is obvious – the fact that it uses mathematics. But mathematical modelling can also be seen as the art of applying mathematics to real-life situations. Just as not every artist would paint a scene or a portrait in the same way, not every mathematician or mathematics student would model the same situation mathematically in the same way. There are many positive outcomes to gain from learning and teaching mathematical modelling, and mathematics educators from all over the world are beginning to see its value. Global educational systems are also in support. The remaining piece in the puzzle, and probably the hardest piece to find a fit, is support for the teachers who need to teach it in the schools.

The framework for teaching mathematical modelling, examples of how it may be applied and used in various modelling tasks and activities, and suggestions on assessment of mathematical modelling that are presented in this book are an attempt to fill this gap. It is hoped that the material, resources and ideas contained in this book continue to serve as a contribution to the international community of teachers of mathematical modelling and applications.

Notes

1 See www.mathmodels.org/Problems/2015/HIMCM-B/index.html (dataset available at this website).
2 See https://plus.maths.org/content/build-your-own-disease-0.
3 See www.immchallenge.org/Contests/2015/Problem.html.

Bibliography

Galbraith, P. (2012). Models of modelling: genres, purposes or perspectives. *Journal of Mathematical Modelling and Application*, *1*(5), 3–16.

Tan, L.S. and Ang, K.C. (2013). Pre-service secondary school teachers' knowledge in mathematical modelling: A case study. In Kaiser, G. and Stillman, G. (Eds.), *International Perspectives on the Teaching and Learning of Mathematical Modelling* (pp. 373–84), New York: Springer.

Appendix A: The Solver tool

Microsoft *Excel* provides a tool known as Solver, which is an add-in function designed to solve optimisation problems numerically. In most cases, when set up properly, it is able to help find an optimal (maximum or minimum) value for a formula in one cell (called the "target cell") by modifying values of other cells (called the "variable cells") subject to some constraints.

The Solver tool is an add-in; this means that it may need to be added to or loaded into the *Excel*'s default suite of functions and menu bar. To add Solver to your *Excel*, depending on the version of *Excel*, click the appropriate button to go launch the *Excel* Options window (See Figure A.1). Look for the "Add-Ins" option, and if "Solver Add-In" is in the list of Add-Ins, then choose "Excel Add-In" at the bottom of the window under the "Manage" field, and click "Go" to install it. In the Add-Ins dialogue box, check the Solve Add-in box, and click "OK".

This procedure may be slightly different for different versions, but the idea is the same – go to Options to add the Solver tool. Once the Solver tool is successfully added, it should appear as a menu button under the "Data" tab.

Although the Solver tool may be used for many optimisation problems, here, the focus here is in using it to find the best values for parameters in a model by minimising the error between the model and data. Suppose we have a set of n data values $\bar{x}_i$ at some points t_i, and the model values at these points are given by x_i. We define the "average error" as

$$E = \frac{\sqrt{\sum_{i=1}^{n}(\bar{x}_i - x_i)^2}}{n}.$$

The data values ($\bar{x}_i$) will not change, but the model values, x_i can be different for different sets of values of parameters that may appear in the model equation. The key is to minimise this error by finding the best set of the parameters values, so that the model will be as close to the data points as possible. To do so analytically and algebraically can be very challenging, especially when there are more parameter values. *Excel*'s Solver provides a way to find this best set of parameter values, using certain numerical methods.

Therefore, all we need to do is to set up the Excel worksheet so that we can find the "average error" E, and then use Solver to minimise it.

Consider the set of data values in Table 1.1 (see Chapter 1) for the total area of leaves at various times. Suppose we wish to find the parameters, b and c in the model, $f(t) = at^2 + bt + c$. Figure A.2 shows a typical Excel worksheet set up for this purpose.

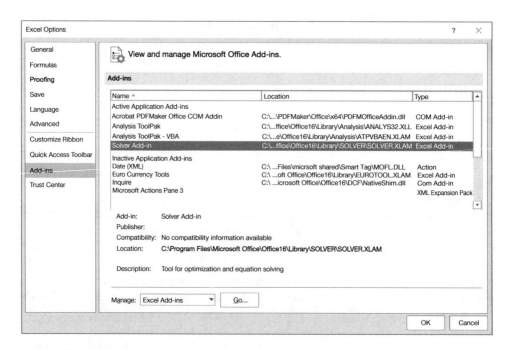

Figure A.1 *Excel* Options window

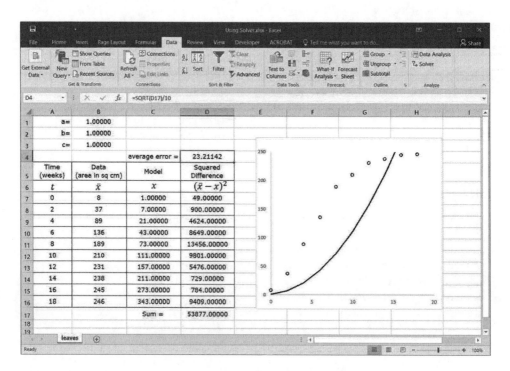

Figure A.2 Excel worksheet set up to find parameter values using the Solver tool

Appendix A   159

In Column C, from Row 7 onwards, the formula for the model is keyed in as usual, with the values of, b and c as shown in Cells B1, B2 and B3. These values are arbitrarily chosen and will probably be incorrect or unsuitable. Cell D17 is the sum of all the squared differences, and Cell D4 contains the formula for the average error. The key is to minimise the value in Cell D4, by changing the values in Cells B1, B2 and B3. That is, find the best set of values in B1, B2 and B3, so that the error value in Cell D4 is the smallest.

By clicking Solver button on the Data tab of *Excel*, the Solver tool is launched. Figure A.3 shows the Solver window. The objective is set as shown, and the variable cells are also chosen accordingly. In this case, we do not have any additional constraints. In addition, the "Make Unconstrained Variables Non-Negative" box should be unchecked because in this case, the unconstrained variables (a, b and c) can take negative values and there is no reason to constrain them. Select the "GRG Nonlinear" method, and click "Solve".

The Solver tool will work to minimise the target cell, and when a solution is found, a window pops up to ask if the user would want to accept the solution. Figure A.4 shows the solution found by Solver in this particular example.

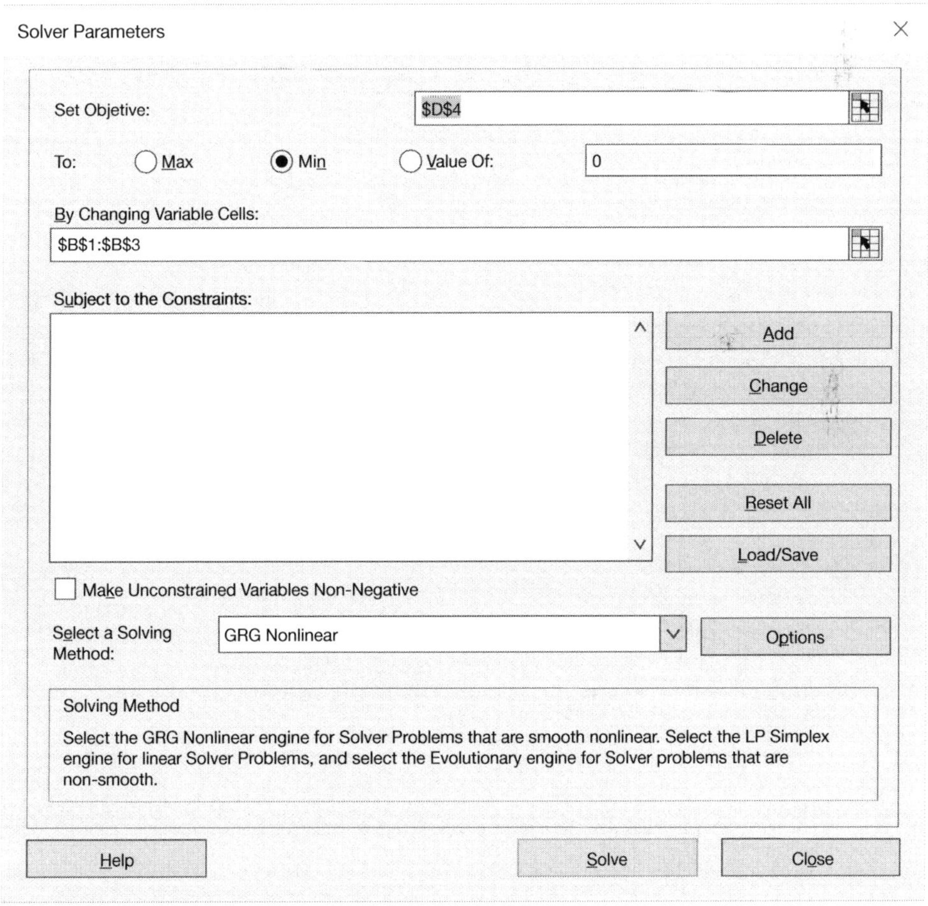

Figure A.3 The Solver window

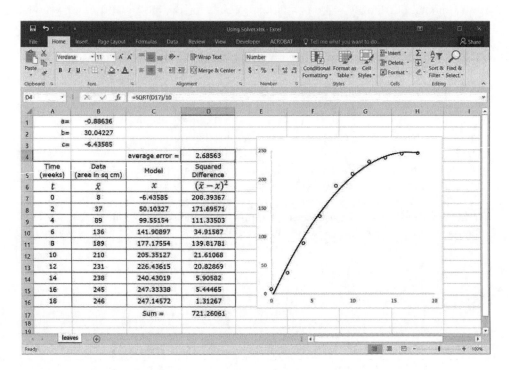

Figure A.4 The Solution – set of values found to minimise the average error

Appendix B: Sample lesson plan and handouts

The lesson plan

Lesson	*Mathematical Modelling – Warming of iced water (Newton's law of warming/cooling)*
Level	Grade 11 or JC 1 (17 year-old, pre-University students) **Duration** 100 minutes (about two periods of 50 minutes each)
Lesson Objectives	At the end of the lesson, students will 1) be able to list the important variables needed in modelling a water-warming process; 2) be able to develop a first-order differential equation to model warming of iced water; 3) be able to use an appropriate tool to find the best curve that fits a set of collected data; and 4) have experienced the process of modelling in a specific situation.
Pre-requisite Knowledge	• Knowledge of first-order differential equations and their methods of solutions. • Ability to use a data-logger and temperature probe to collect data. • Skills in using a technological tool (e.g. trendline, Solver, etc.) to find the best fit curve for a set of data.
Materials	1) Handout 2 2) Iced-water in a thermos flask 3) Sufficient sets of data-logger with temperature probes 4) Sufficient number of paper cups 5) Computer (or Laptop) with LoggerPro software (or other graphing or data capture software), *Excel*, etc.

Time	Activity	Remarks / Teacher Notes
10 mins	**Induction** 1) Teacher begins lesson asking the question: If I take a can of coke out from the fridge, how long will it take for the drink to warm up to, say, 20 degrees? 2) Teacher continues with the question: How does the temperature of the drink vary with time? 3) Teacher introduces the day's lesson: We will make an attempt to use mathematics to understand the warming process better by constructing a **mathematical model** using differential equations to represent the warming of iced water.	Students may give very wild guesses, but teacher can allow it at this stage. Link students' responses to previous knowledge on the rates of change and differential equations, and their use in representing physical phenomena.

Appendix B

20 mins	<u>Development</u> 1) **Organize** the class appropriately (e.g. into pairs or groups of threes depending on availability of materials and resources). Distribute **handout 2**. All students should have one handout each. 2) **Explain** the task for the day. **Emphasize** that the objective is to obtain **a model (in the form of a first-order differential equation)** that can model the warming of iced water. 3) **Facilitate** student group work: discuss the factors that influence and affect the temperature of water that has just been removed from the fridge, and complete <u>Item 1</u> of handout. Some of these should include: • Initial temperature of water • Room temperature (or ambient temperature or temperature of surrounding) • Some physical property (e.g. specific heat capacity) of water that determines rate of change of temperature • Time (as an independent variable) *Other answers such as size of cup, amount of water, etc. may be given, but these are not important factors to consider in the mathematical model at this stage.* 4) Students will then be **instructed** to narrow their list down to **three most important** factors to include in their model. This process will help them answer <u>Item 2</u>, which requires them to list assumptions. Three most important factors are: • Rate of warming of water (k) • Initial temperature of water (θ_0) • Surrounding temperature (S) The assumptions are: • k is constant • S is constant	Note that students may not be able to provide technical or scientific terms. At this point, teacher should check with each group to make sure that they are all agreeable on these three important factors.
20 mins	5) <u>Data collection</u> Either **facilitate** data collection, or **demonstrate** data collection process. Students will collect data in their groups. Each group is given a data-logger with temperature probe, a cup of water with ice.	In the event that there is only one set of equipment, or that students are not familiar with the use of the data-logger, teacher may carry out the data collection as a demonstration, and display the values on the screen for all to see.

Although it is more correct to leave the probe in the cup and measure the temperature of the water, it will take a long time to see the effects. To speed things up, one may dip the probe in the iced water at the start, and remove it from the water and let it warm up. Technically, this is warming up of the probe, not the water, but in view of the constraint of time, we shall assume that the two processes (warming of probe and warming of water) are similar.

Students complete <u>Item 3</u> of the handout individually.

10 mins 6) Students are now **instructed** to complete <u>Item 4</u> individually. They are to write down what they observe from the data points.

May need to prompt and provide hints along the way.

Teacher **consolidates** by asking students for their descriptions. Important points include:
- Temperature rises very quickly at the beginning of the warming process
- Temperature continues to rise, but the rise is not as rapid after a certain time
- Near the end of the process, temperature rise is slow

Students may be guided by the graph

20 mins 7) In their groups, students are **guided** in their attempt to complete <u>Items 5 and 6</u>.
Hints or scaffolds with questions:
(1) What happens to θ as it $\to \infty$?
(2) Is the difference between S and θ an important factor in determining the rate?
(3) Can we write down a relationship between $\dfrac{d\theta}{dt}$ and, θ, k and S?

Teacher may **lead students** to arrive at a differential equation of the form

$$\frac{d\theta}{dt} = k(S - \theta)$$

Note: if students are not able to determine this differential equation, teacher may wish to provide students with a list of possible first-order differential equations involving the variables. Students then decide which is the most appropriate or suitable.

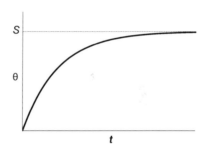

to realize that as θ approaches S, the rate of change (slope) decreases. So, we may guess that

$$\frac{d\theta}{dt} \propto (S - \theta)$$

It is assumed that students are familiar with the use of these tools, as such skills are a pre-requisite to this lesson.

10 mins	8) Once the differential equation is decided, teacher **instructs** students to work on <u>Item 7</u>.	
	This will require students to solve the differential equation first, and then use a tool – which may be the solver tool or trendline in Excel – to find an appropriate value of k in the model.	Teacher may mention that Newton discovered the law of cooling/warming around 1700. This law is used by forensic pathologists in determining the time of death in homicide or murder cases.
	Students complete their model and plot the graph of the model alongside the data points.	
5 mins	9) Teacher **summarizes** lesson by writing down the final form (based on students' answers) of the model on the board. If there are more than one (i.e. students may have other data sets or other function forms), teacher should, as far as possible, write them all down.	
	Teacher **challenges** students with the question: "Is this an appropriate model?" or, if there are more than one model, "Which is the most appropriate model?"	
	Students are encouraged to think about the above questions as homework.	
5 mins	Closure	Teacher should emphasize Point 1, and may leave Point 2 for students to think about in their own time.
	Point 1:	
	Close the lesson by showing students the diagram on the modelling process, and describing how they have navigated the cycle in the lesson. This forms a summary of the entire lesson.	
	Point 2:	
	Challenge students mathematically by asking the question:	If time does not permit, teacher may choose to do either Point 1 or Point 2 depending on class profile and student abilities.
	"What if we now have a cup of hot coffee placed in a cool room, and left to cool down … what would be an appropriate model?"	

Teacher reflections:

References:
(1) www.ugrad.math.ubc.ca/coursedoc/math100/notes/diffeqs/cool.html
(2) www.biology.arizona.edu/biomath/tutorials/applications/Cooling.html

Handout for students

Warming of Iced-Water

Task A cup of iced-water is removed from the fridge and left in a room to warm up. **Construct a mathematical model that describes the rise in temperature of the iced-water as time passes.**

1. Write down factors that would influence or affect the temperature of the water as it warms up.

2. What assumptions may be made to simplify the situation?

3. Collect data using a data-logger with temperature probe. Take measurements at 5-second intervals, for about 5 minutes, and plot the points on the graph paper below.

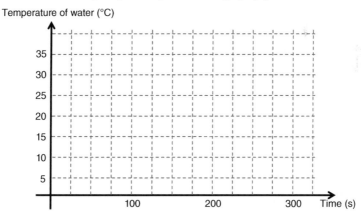

4. Describe the pattern of the data points plotted, paying particular attention to the difference between the points near the beginning and near the end of the data collection process.

Warming of Iced-Water

5. How does the rate of change of temperature vary (with time, and with the temperature of water)?

6. Write down a possible differential equation that may be used to describe the rate of change of temperature of the water with time.

7. Use the available data to find any parameters that may appear in the differential equation.

Teachers' guide to student handout

Warming of Iced-Water

Task   A cup of iced-water is removed from the fridge and left in a room to warm up.
Construct a mathematical model that describes the rise in temperature of the iced-water as time passes.

1. Write down factors that would influence or affect the temperature of the water as it warms up.
   - Initial temperature of water
   - Surrounding temperature or room temperature
   - Material of cup (heat gained through conduction and radiation)
   - Time (how long it has been out from the fridge)
   - Heat capacity of water
   - Rate at which water absorbs heat from surrounding

Warming of Iced-Water

2. What assumptions may be made to simplify the situation?
    - Assume surrounding temperature is constant
    - Assume material of cup has little or no effect on warming

So, the important variables are:
    - temperature of water when it is first removed from the fridge (T_0)
    - rate at which water warms (k)
    - room temperature (S)
    - time (t)

3. Collect data using a data-logger with temperature probe. Take measurements at 5-second intervals, for about 5 minutes, and plot the points on the graph paper below.

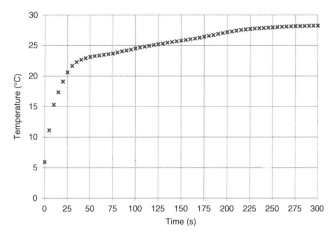

4. Describe the pattern of the data points plotted, paying particular attention to the difference between the points near the beginning and near the end of the data collection process.
    - Temperature (θ) increases with time (t)
    - Rate of change in θ is large at the beginning (first 25–30 seconds)
    - After about 30 seconds, θ continues to increase but at a slower rate
    - At around the 250 second mark, θ increases only very slowly, if at all

5. How does the rate of change of temperature vary (with time, and with the temperature of water)?

The rate of change of θ (with respect to time, t) is always positive but the rate seems to change as time passes. Initially, the rate is high, but as time passes, it decreases but remains positive. In other words, $\dfrac{d\theta}{dt}$ decreases and tends to zero.

Intuitively, we know that the temperature θ will rise from its initial temperature of θ_0 and will get closer and closer to the room temperature of S. Common sense tells us that θ will not exceed S (even if we are unfamiliar with the laws of thermodynamics).

Therefore, we deduce that as time passes, the difference $(S - \theta)$ decreases and tends to zero.

6. Write down a possible differential equation that may be used to describe the rate of change of temperature of the water with time.

From the discussion in (5), we may conjecture that the rate of change of θ is related to the difference $(S - \theta)$. Physically, we could imagine that when the difference is large, θ changes more rapidly (warms faster), and as the difference becomes smaller, θ changes more gradually (warms slower).

The simplest relationship to assume would be a linear relationship. We propose $\dfrac{d\theta}{dt} \propto (S - \theta)$ or,

$$\dfrac{d\theta}{dt} = k(S - \theta)$$

for some constant, k.

Appendix B

Warming of Iced-Water

7. Use the available data to find any parameters that may appear in the differential equation.
We first solve the differential equation. Using separation of variables and by applying the initial condition $\theta(t) = \theta_0$ at $t = 0$, we obtain the solution (or model):

$\theta = S + (\theta_0 - S)e^{-kt}$.

With $S = 28$, and $\theta_0 = 5.9$, and the average error defined as

$$E = \frac{\sqrt{\sum_{n=1}^{N}(\theta_n - \overline{\theta_n})^2}}{N}$$

where θ_n and $\overline{\theta_n}$ are the model and data values respectively, and N is the total number of data points, we use *Excel*'s Solver tool to find the best value of k that minimizes E.
We obtain $k \approx 0.03047$.

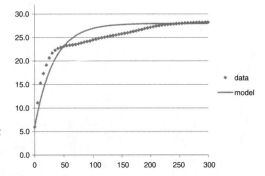

Index

abstraction 77
advice for teachers 154–6
altitude 31, 32
angle of strike 73, 75
animals: dispersal and population redistribution 92
area: circle 20–3
argument: logical 136, 138
arrival process 110
arrival rate 111, 112, 113, 114, 116
arrival times 56, 57, 111, 112, 114
assessment: for learning 135–6; of learning 135–6; mathematical modelling process 136–8; in mathematics 135–6, 137; modelling competencies 138–45; modelling projects 145–9
assumptions: making 10–11
atmospheric pressure 31, 32
Australia: mathematical modelling in 25–6, 27
Australian Council for Educational Research (ACER) 153
Automatic Teller Machine (ATM) 111–16
average error 19, 157

balking 111
ball-dropping game 82
barcodes 123–7
beansprouts growth 51
Big Splash 123
braking distance 56
bread mould *see* growing mould
Broken Spaghetti Problem 83–8; discussion points 88; suggested approach 85–6; teacher notes 84–5; using framework 87–8
Brownian motion 92
Buffon's Needle experiment 97–102; discussion points 101–2; online simulation tools 99; suggested approach 99–100; teacher notes 97–9; using framework 101

car parks 65–9; discussion points 68–9; suggested approach 66–7; teacher notes 65–6; using framework 68
carnivals 77, 78, 82; *see also* dart board games
carrying capacity 49, 122
Causeway 43
CCSSM 24–5
central limit theorem 89
chaos game 6–7
check marks 52, 53, 54
checksum algorithm 123–7; discussion points 126–7; suggested approach 124–6; teacher notes 123–4; using framework 126
circle: area 20–3
city crime and safety problem 152
clepsydra 133
closed communities 117
Co^2CA 140
coding: learning 155–6
coffee cooling 10
coin tossing 89, 90, 91
COMAP 1, 151
Common Core State Standards 139
communication 136, 137, 146, 148
competencies: modelling 28, 30
computer simulation 83; *see also* simulation models
correction tapes 11, 60–4; discussion points 64; identifying factors 61; suggested approach 61–3; teacher notes 60–1; using framework 64
covered walkways 73–7; cross-sectional shapes 74, 75–6, 77; discussion points 77; suggested approach 75–6; teacher notes 73–4; using framework 76
curve fitting 28

dart board games 77–82; discussion points 81–2; standard dart board 77, 78; suggested approach 79–81; teacher notes 77–9; using framework 81
data-loggers 31, 33, 144, 162, 165, 167

decision-making models 60, 97
deep water *see* water sustainability
Denmark: mathematical competencies approach 139; mathematical modelling in 25
desalinated water 44–5, 47
deterministic models 7–9, 60–82, 116, 117, 131; *see also* car parks; correction tapes; covered walkways; dart board games; drainage systems
difference equations 8
dimensions 11
discharge capacities 69–70
disease spread 8; classroom activity 152; factors 116–17
downsweep method 52
drainage systems 69–73; cross-sectional shapes 69, 70–1, 72; discussion points 72–3; suggested approach 70–1; teacher notes 69–70; using framework 72
drug concentration 17–20
dynamic geometry software 76

empirical models 3–5, 39–58, 129–32; disadvantages 5; examples of problems *see* growing mould; pedestrian crossings; playing detective; relay race; water sustainability
epidemic models 116; *see also* SARS epidemic
epidemics 8, 11–12, 122
equations: as mathematical models 60, 64
errors: average 19, 157; single-digit transcription 123, 124–5; transposition 123, 125
Excel 12–17; in Broken Spaghetti Problem 86–7; in Buffon's Needle experiment 99–100, 101; in checksum algorithm 125; features 83; in Monty Hall problem 93; in mountain climbing task 142–3, 144; in one-dimensional random walk 90; in queuing system 112–14; random number generator 35; re-calculating cell values 87; in SARS epidemic 118, 120, 122; in Secretary Problem 104–6, 108; in water tank draining 129; *see also* Solver tool
exchange zone 52, 54
exponential distribution 111, 112
extra-mathematical material 155

facilitation 154–5
factors: identifying 10
flash floods 69
flood management *see* drainage systems
fluid drag force 127, 128, 131
footprints 39–42

framework for mathematical modelling 29–37; and competencies assessment 141; components 30; hierarchical nature 36; purposes 36–7; using 31–6

gambler's ruin 92
Geogebra 76
Geometer's Sketchpad 76
Germany: competencies approach 139–40; mathematical modelling in 25
giant shoes problem 42–3
gravitational acceleration 128
growing mould 47–51; discussion points 50–1; suggested approach 48–50; teacher notes 47–8; using framework 50

handout for students: sample 165–8
heat dissipation/diffusion 92
heights: and shoe lengths 39–43
hiring problem *see* Secretary Problem
horizontal span of cover 73
hydraulic radius 70

influenza epidemic 8–9, 11–12
Information Technology skills 137–8
inter-arrival times 110, 111–12, 114
International Mathematical Modelling Challenge (IMMC) 1, 152–3
Inverse Transform Method 111–12
IT skills 137–8

Japan: mathematical modelling in 26
jockeying 111
Johor 43

KOM project 139

Land Transport Authority (LTA) 65
law of large numbers 88
Leaf Area Index (LAI) 3
learning experience: Level 1 28, 30, 31; Level 2 28, 30, 31–4; Level 3 28–9, 30, 34–6
leaves: area of 3–5, 157–60
lesson plan: sample 161–4
"Let's Make a Deal" 92
Linggui Reservoir 43, 44
LoggerPro 31, 33
logical argument 136, 138
logistic equation 49, 118, 119, 122
logistic growth function 5
logistic growth models 49; double 123; modified 119–21

M/M/1 queuing model 111
Malaysia: and Singapore 43–7
Manning's equation 70, 71, 72, 73

Index

Manning's roughness coefficient 70, 71
Marriage Problem 109
Mass Rapid Transit (MRT) accident 34–6
mass-action interaction 118
mathematical modelling approaches 2–9
mathematical modelling assessment *see* assessment
mathematical modelling definitions 1–2, 24
mathematical modelling projects 110–33; assessment 145–9; *see also* checksum algorithm; queuing system; SARS epidemic; water tank draining
mathematical modelling stages 140, 141, 146, 147
MATHmodels 151–2
memoryless property 111
method of least squares 4
micro-organisms: dispersal and population redistribution 92
mm@sg 154
model evaluation 140, 141, 146, 147
model formulation 140, 141, 147
model interpretation 140, 141, 146, 147
model solution 140, 141, 147
modelling cycle 2, 25
modelling project reports 145–8
Monte Carlo methods 88
Monte Carlo simulation models 20–3
Monty Hall problem 92–7; discussion points 96–7; online versions 93; suggested approach 94–6; teacher notes 92–4; using framework 96
mould: growing *see* growing mould
mountain climbing 31, 142–3
movie scheduling probability 153

National Darts Association 77
neck sizes: and waist sizes 43
needle: dropping *see* Buffon's Needle experiment
"nested IF" statement 105
Netherlands: mathematical modelling in 25
NEWater 44, 45
Newton's law of cooling/warming 32, 161
Newton's laws of motion 7, 60

one-dimensional random walk 88–92; discussion points 91–2; suggested approach 90–1; teacher notes 88–90; using framework 91
oral presentations 145–6, 148–9

parking lots 65–9; *see also* car parks
passing of baton *see* relay race
peak runoffs 69, 70
pedestrian crossings 55–8; discussion points 58; suggested approach 56–7; teacher notes 55–6; using framework 57–8

pet transhipment licenses 123–7
π: estimating 97, 99–100, 101–2
playing detective 39–43; discussion points 42; similar problems 42–3; suggested approach 41–2; teacher notes 39–40; using framework 42
Plus Magazine 152
Poisson processes 111, 112
population dynamics 7–8, 24, 49, 51, 118, 122; micro-organisms 49
presentations: oral 145–6, 148–9
probability distribution functions 90, 92
probability trees 93
process: focussing on 155
Programme for International Student Assessments (PISA) 135
programming: starting 155–6
project reports 145–8
Public Utilities Board (PUB) 69, 70
push pass method 52

QR codes 125–6
queue structure 110, 111
queuing system 110–16; discussion points 115–16; suggested approach 112–13; teacher notes 110–12; using framework 115

random numbers: generating 15–17
random walks 34–6; applications 92; *see also* one-dimensional random walk
Rational Formula 69
reaction time 56
relationships: behaviour of 12
relay race 51–5; baton passing methods 52; discussion points 54–5; suggested approach 52–3; teacher notes 51–2; using framework 53–4
reliability 140–1
reneging 111
reports: project 145–8
running profiles 52–3, 54
runoffs 69–70

S-I model 8, 117, 119
safe distance 56
SARS epidemic 116–23; discussion points 122–3; suggested approach 117–21; teacher notes 116–17; using framework 121–2
scatter plots 13, 14, 17, 22–3, 41, 144
scoring rubrics 142, 145–8, 149
Secretary Problem 102–9; discussion points 108–9; strategy k 102; suggested approach 103–6; teacher notes 102–3; using framework 106–7
service process 110–11

service rate 111, 112, 113, 114, 116
service times 110, 111, 112, 114
Severe Acute Respiratory Syndrome *see* SARS epidemic
shoe lengths: and heights 39–43
shoeprints 39–42
Sierpinski gasket 7
simulation models 5–7, 83–109; continuous 6; discrete 6; Monte Carlo 20–3; *see also* Broken Spaghetti Problem; Buffon's Needle experiment; Monty Hall problem; one-dimensional random walk; Secretary Problem
Singapore: car parking 65–6; covered walkways 73, 74; flood management 69; learning programming 155; and Malaysia 43–7; mathematical modelling in 26; SARS outbreak 116, 118–22; *see also* water sustainability
Singapore International Mathematics Challenge (SIMC) 26
single-digit transcription errors 123, 124–5
skills: in modelling 10–12
Smart Nation 155
Solver tool 157–60; adding to *Excel* 157; in empirical modelling 4; in mathematical modelling projects 118, 120, 122; in mountain climbing task 142–3
spaghetti sticks *see* Broken Spaghetti Problem
spreadsheets 12–15; in mathematical modelling projects 116, 125; in simulation models 86, 100, 102; *see also Excel*
student safety 58
supermarkets 123
Sweden: mathematical modelling in 25

tables: as mathematical models 60, 64
target cell 157, 159
teachers: advice for 154–6
teaching of mathematical modelling 24–38; Level 1 learning experience 28, 30, 31; Level 2 learning experience 28, 30, 31–4; Level 3 learning experience 28–9, 30, 34–6; teacher readiness 26–7; *see also* framework for mathematical modelling
terms: relative impact 11
toothpicks: throwing 99

Torricelli's law 128, 129, 130–2, 133
transmission rates 9, 12, 122
transposition errors 123, 125
trapezoids: isosceles 71
trend lines: adding 13–15, 17–18
Trends in International Mathematics and Science Study (TIMSS) 135
triangle inequality theorem 84, 85, 88
trigonometry 68, 76

uniform distribution 112
United Kingdom: learning coding 155
United States: learning computer science 155; mathematical modelling in 24–5; standards for mathematical practice 139
units 11
upsweep method 52

validation 2
validity 140–1, 142
variable cells 157
variables: identifying 10
video clips resource 154
Visual Basic Applications (VBA) 83

waist sizes: and neck sizes 43
wait times 112, 114, 116
walk in the park *see* one-dimensional random walk
water clock 133
water sustainability 43–7; discussion points 47; suggested approach 45–6; teacher notes 43–5; using framework 46
water tank draining 127–33; discussion points 133; suggested approach 129–32; teacher notes 127–9; using framework 132–3
water warming 31–4, 37, 144–5, 161–8; lesson plan 161–4; student handout 165–6; teachers' guide to student handout 166–8
Web resources 151–4
wetted perimeter 70, 71
worksheets for modelling classes 142–5; assessment items in 142; Level 1 task example 142–4; Level 2 task example 144–5

zone of proximal development (ZPD) 29